W. D. (William Douw) Lighthall

Songs of the Great Dominion: voices from the forests and waters, the settlements and cities of Canada

W. D. (William Douw) Lighthall

Songs of the Great Dominion: voices from the forests and waters, the settlements and cities of Canada

ISBN/EAN: 9783742865052

Manufactured in Europe, USA, Canada, Australia, Japa

Cover: Foto ©Thomas Meinert / pixelio.de

Manufactured and distributed by brebook publishing software (www.brebook.com)

W. D. (William Douw) Lighthall

Songs of the Great Dominion: voices from the forests and waters, the settlements and cities of Canada

SONGS OF THE GREAT DOMINION:

VOICES FROM THE FORESTS AND WATERS, THE SETTLEMENTS AND CITIES OF CANADA.

SELECTED AND EDITED BY

WILLIAM DOUW LIGHTHALL, M.A.,

of Montreal.

> "All the future lies before us
> Glorious in that sunset land."
> —FREDERICK G. SCOTT.

LONDON:
WALTER SCOTT,
24 WARWICK LANE, PATERNOSTER ROW.

1889.

> When men unto their noblest rise,
> Alike for ever see their eyes;
> Trust us, grand England, we are true,
> And, in your noblest, one with you.

TO

THAT SUBLIME CAUSE,

The Union of Mankind,

WHICH

THE BRITISH PEOPLES,

IF THEY ARE TRUE TO THEMSELVES AND COURAGEOUS IN THE

FUTURE AS THEY HAVE BEEN IN THE PAST,

WILL TAKE TO BE

THE REASON OF EXISTENCE OF THEIR EMPIRE;

AND

TO THE GLORY OF THOSE PEOPLES IN THE

SERVICE OF MAN;

THIS BOOK IS

Dedicated.

CONTENTS.

	PAGE
INTRODUCTION	xxi
ENTRY OF THE MINSTRELS "*The Masque of Minstrels*"	xxxix
ARTHUR J. LOCKHART.	

I.—THE IMPERIAL SPIRIT.

HASTINGS	"*Merlin, and Other Poems*"	3
	JOHN READE.	
ADVANCE OF THE EMPIRE . . . *Jubilee Poem*		5
	MARY BARRY SMITH.	
CANADA TO ENGLAND		7
	ANONYMOUS.	
EMPIRE FIRST		10
	JOHN TALON-LESPÉRANCE—"LACLÈDE."	
THE CANADIANS ON THE NILE . . .	"*Poems*"	11
	WILLIAM WYE SMITH.	

II.—THE NEW NATIONALITY.

DOMINION DAY . . .		15
	"FIDELIS."	
CANADA	"*In Divers Tones*"	18
	CHARLES G. D. ROBERTS.	

CONTENTS.

		PAGE
THE CONFUSED DAWN . "*Thoughts, Moods, and Ideals*"		21
WILLIAM DOUW LIGHTHALL.		
NATIONAL HYMN . "*Thoughts, Moods, and Ideals*"		22
WILLIAM DOUW LIGHTHALL.		
FROM "'85"		24
BARRY STRATON.		
SONG FOR CANADA		25
CHARLES SANGSTER.		
HERE'S TO THE LAND . . . . "*Poems*"		27
WILLIAM WYE SMITH.		
CANADA NOT LAST . "*Thoughts, Moods, and Ideals*"		28
WILLIAM DOUW LIGHTHALL.		
AN ODE FOR THE CANADIAN CONFEDERACY "*In Divers Tones*"		30
CHARLES G. D. ROBERTS.		
COLLECT FOR DOMINION DAY . . "*In Divers Tones*"		32
CHARLES G. D. ROBERTS.		

III.—THE INDIAN.

	PAGE
A BLOOD-RED RING HUNG ROUND THE MOON .	35
JOHN E. LOGAN—"BARRY DANE."	
THE DEPARTING OF CLOTE SCARP . "*In Divers Tones*"	36
CHARLES G. D. ROBERTS.	
CHANGE ON THE OTTAWA . . "*Marguerite*"	38
GEORGE MARTIN.	
FROM "TECUMSEH."—ACT I., SCENE 2	42
CHARLES MAIR.	
THE ARCTIC INDIAN'S FAITH . . . "*Poems*"	44
THOMAS D'ARCY M'GEE.	

CONTENTS.

		PAGE
TAAPOOKAA: A HURON LEGEND . "*Hesperus*"		45
CHARLES SANGSTER.		
THE CAUGHNAWAGA BEADWORK-SELLER .		49
WILLIAM DOUW LIGHTHALL.		
THE INDIAN'S GRAVE		51
BISHOP GEORGE JEHOSAPHAT MOUNTAIN.		
WAHONOMIN.—INDIAN HYMN TO THE QUEEN "*Soul's Quest*"		52
FREDERICK GEORGE SCOTT.		
WABANAKI SONG		59
Tr. CHARLES G. LELAND.		
WABANAKI SONG		60
Tr. CHARLES G. LELAND.		
CAUGHNAWAGA SONG		62
Tr. JOHN WANIENTE JOCKS.		

IV.—THE VOYAGEUR AND HABITANT.

THE OLD RÉGIME . . . "*Song of Welcome*"	67
MRS J. F. W. HARRISON—"SERANUS."	
MALBROUCK . . . . . *Old Chanson*	71
Tr. WILLIAM M'LENNAN.	
À LA CLAIRE FONTAINE . . . *Old Chanson*	74
Tr. WILLIAM DOUW LIGHTHALL.	
EN ROULANT MA BOULÉ . . . *Old Chanson*	76
Tr. WILLIAM M'LENNAN.	
GAI LE ROSIER . . . . *Old Chanson*	78
Tr. WILLIAM M'LENNAN.	
ENTRE PARIS ET SAINT-DENIS . . *Old Chanson*	80
Tr. WILLIAM M'LENNAN.	

CONTENTS.

		PAGE
MARIANSON . . . . . *Old Chanson*		83
Tr. WILLIAM M'LENNAN.		
THE RE-SETTLEMENT OF ACADIA . . .		87
ARTHUR WENTWORTH EATON.		
AT THE CEDARS		91
DUNCAN CAMPBELL SCOTT.		
ROSE LATULIPPE . . *A French Canadian Legend*		94
MRS J. F. W. HARRISON—"SERANUS."		
ADIEU TO FRANCE . . . . "*De Roberval*"		104
JOHN HUNTER-DUVAR.		

V.—SETTLEMENT LIFE.

SONG OF THE AXE . . . "*Old Spooks's Pass*"		107
ISABELLA VALANCEY CRAWFORD.		
FIRE IN THE WOODS; OR, THE OLD SETTLER'S STORY		109
ALEXANDER M'LACHLAN.		
BURNT LANDS		114
CHARLES G. D. ROBERTS.		
ACRES OF YOUR OWN . . . "*Poems and Songs*"		115
ALEXANDER M'LACHLAN.		
FROM "MALCOLM'S KATIE" . . "*Old Spooks's Pass*"		117
ISABELLA VALANCEY CRAWFORD.		
FROM "MALCOLM'S KATIE" . . "*Old Spooks's Pass*"		119
ISABELLA VALANCEY CRAWFORD.		
THE SECOND CONCESSION OF DEER . . "*Poems*"		125
WILLIAM WYE SMITH.		
THE SCOT ABROAD . . . "*Spring Flowers*"		127
SIR DANIEL WILSON.		

CONTENTS.

		PAGE
THE FARMER'S DAUGHTER CHERRY . *"Old Spooks's Pass"*		129
ISABELLA VALANCEY CRAWFORD.		
A CANADIAN FOLK-SONG . . .		133
WILLIAM WILFRED CAMPBELL.		
THE PIONEERS . . . . . *A Ballad*		134
WILLIAM DOUW LIGHTHALL.		
"ROUGH BEN" . . *North-West Rebellion Incident*		136
KATE B. SIMPSON.		
"THE INJUN" . . *Incident of Minnesota Massacre*		142
JOHN E. LOGAN—"BARRY DANE."		
SHAKESPEER AT DEAD-HOS' CRICK *A North-West Romance*		148
JOHN E. LOGAN—"BARRY DANE."		

VI.—SPORTS AND FREE LIFE.

THE WRAITH OF THE RED SWAN .		157
BLISS CARMAN.		
BIRCH AND PADDLE . . . *"In Divers Tones"*		163
CHARLES G. D. ROBERTS.		
THE NOR'-WEST COURIER		166
JOHN E. LOGAN—"BARRY DANE."		
THE HALL OF SHADOWS . . *"Poems and Songs"*		168
ALEXANDER M'LACHLAN.		
CANADIAN HUNTER'S SONG		172
MRS SUSANNA (STRICKLAND) MOODIE.		
CANADIAN CAMPING SONG . .		173
JAMES D. EDGAR.		
THE FISHERMAN'S LIGHT . *A Song of the Backwoods*		174
MRS SUSANNA (STRICKLAND) MOODIE.		

CONTENTS.

		PAGE
THE KINGFISHER		175
CHARLES LEE BARNES.		
THE CANOE	"*Old Spooks's Pass*"	177
ISABELLA VALANCEY CRAWFORD.		
CANOE SONG	"*Old Spooks's Pass*"	180
ISABELLA VALANCEY CRAWFORD.		
THE WALKER OF THE SNOW . . .		181
CHARLES DAWSON SHANLY.		
IN THE SHADOWS		184
E. PAULINE JOHNSON.		
ON THE CREEK	"*In Divers Tones*"	187
CHARLES G. D. ROBERTS.		
THE RAPID	(*St Lawrence*)	190
CHARLES SANGSTER.		
THE WINTER SPIRIT . .	(*Origin of the Ice Palace*)	192
HELEN FAIRBAIRN.		
SNOWSHOEING SONG . . .		195
ARTHUR WEIR.		
SKATING		197
JOHN LOWRY STUART.		
THE WINTER CARNIVAL . .		199
JOHN READE.		
THE SPIRIT OF THE CARNIVAL .		203
"FLEURANGE."		
THE FOOTBALL MATCH . . .		209
ANONYMOUS.		

VII.—THE SPIRIT OF CANADIAN HISTORY.

JACQUES CARTIER . . . . "*Poems*"	213
HON. THOMAS D'ARCY M'GEE.	
L'ISLE STE. CROIX	216
ARTHUR WENTWORTH EATON.	
THE CAPTURED FLAG . . . "*Fleurs de Lys*"	219
ARTHUR WEIR.	
HOW CANADA WAS SAVED . .	222
GEORGE MURRAY.	
MADELEINE DE VERCHÈRES . .	228
JOHN READE.	
THE BATTLE OF LA PRAIRIE . . . *A Ballad*	233
WILLIAM DOUW LIGHTHALL.	
THE BATTLE OF GRAND PRÉ . . .	236
M. J. KATZMANN LAWSON.	
SPINA CHRISTI . . . . "*Canadian Idylls*"	240
WILLIAM KIRBY.	
THE LOYALISTS . . . . "*Laura Secord*"	253
SARAH ANNE CURZON.	
BROCK . . . "*Hesperus*"	254
CHARLES SANGSTER.	
CAPTURE OF FORT DETROIT, 1812 . .	256
CHARLES EDWIN JAKEWAY.	
TECUMSEH'S DEATH . . . "*Tecumseh*"	260
MAJOR RICHARDSON.	
A BALLAD FOR BRAVE WOMEN .	262
CHARLES MAIR.	

xiv   CONTENTS.
                                                                    PAGE
IN THE NORTH-WEST   267
            WILLIAM WILFRED CAMPBELL.

THE VETERAN   269
                J. A. FRASER.

IN HOSPITAL   270
                ANNIE ROTHWELL.

IN MEMORIAM   .   .   .   . "*The Soul's Quest*" 275
            FREDERICK GEORGE SCOTT.

———

VIII.—PLACES.

THE TANTRAMAR REVISITED   .   . "*In Divers Tones*" 279
            CHARLES G. D. ROBERTS.

LOW TIDE ON GRAND-PRÉ   .   .   283
                BLISS CARMAN.

THE INDIAN NAMES OF ACADIA   .   .   285
                Attributed to DE MILLE.

ON LEAVING THE COAST OF NOVA SCOTIA   .   287
            GEORGE FREDERICK CAMERON.

THE FAIRIES IN PRINCE EDWARD ISLAND   .   288
                JOHN HUNTER-DUVAR.

THE VALE OF THE GASPEREAU   . "*Masque of Minstrels*" 290
            ARTHUR JOHN LOCKHART.

IN THE AFTERNOON   .   .   . "*In Divers Tones*" 291
            CHARLES G. D. ROBERTS.

A DREAM FULFILLED   .   .   .   294
                BARRY STRATON.

THE ISLE OF DEMONS   .   .   . "*Marguerite*" 297
                GEORGE MARTIN.

CONTENTS.   xv

		PAGE
THE SECRET OF THE SAGUENAY	"*Fleurs-de-Lys*"	303
ARTHUR WEIR.		
SAGUENAY	L. H. Fréchette	306
Tr. J. D. EDGAR.		
QUEBEC	"*St Lawrence and Saguenay*"	307
CHARLES SANGSTER.		
MONTREAL.		308
WILLIAM M'LENNAN.		
MONTREAL		309
WILLIAM DOUW LIGHTHALL.		
THE ST LAWRENCE		310
K. L. JONES.		
NIGHT IN THE THOUSAND ISLES	"*St Lawrence and Saguenay*"	312
CHARLES SANGSTER.		
OTTAWA		314
DUNCAN CAMPBELL SCOTT.		
AT THE FERRY		315
E. PAULINE JOHNSON.		
NIAGARA		317
WILLIAM KIRBY.		
LAKE COUCHICHING		320
W. A. SHERWOOD.		
THE HEART OF THE LAKES	"*Lake Lyrics*"	321
WILLIAM WILFRED CAMPBELL.		
VAPOUR AND BLUE	"*Lake Lyrics*"	322
WILLIAM WILFRED CAMPBELL.		
MEDWAYOSH	"*Lake Lyrics*"	323
WILLIAM WILFRED CAMPBELL.		

CONTENTS.

		PAGE
MANITOU . . . . . "*Lake Lyrics*"		324
WILLIAM WILFRED CAMPBELL.		
TO THE LAKES . . . . . "*Lake Lyrics*"		326
WILLIAM WILFRED CAMPBELL.		
THE LEGEND OF RESTLESS RIVER . "*Lake Lyrics*"		327
WILLIAM WILFRED CAMPBELL.		
MORNING ON THE BEACH . . "*Lake Lyrics*"		330
WILLIAM WILFRED CAMPBELL.		
DAWN IN THE ISLAND CAMP . . "*Lake Lyrics*"		331
WILLIAM WILFRED CAMPBELL.		
LAKE HURON . . . . "*Lake Lyrics*"		332
WILLIAM WILFRED CAMPBELL.		
INDIAN SUMMER . . . . "*Lake Lyrics*"		333
WILLIAM WILFRED CAMPBELL.		
SAULT STE. MARIE . "*Poems of the Heart and Home*"		334
PAMELIA VINING YULE.		
LE LAC DES MORTS . . "*Songs of the Wilderness*"		337
BISHOP GEORGE J. MOUNTAIN.		
THE BUFFALO PLAINS . "*Tecumseh*," Act IV., Scene 7		339
CHARLES MAIR.		
THE LAST BISON . . .		342
CHARLES MAIR.		
A PRAIRIE YEAR . . "*Eos: A Prairie Dream*"		349
NICHOLAS FLOOD DAVIN.		
THE LAURENTIDES . . . "*Western Life*"		352
H. R. A. POCOCK.		
THE LEGEND OF THUNDER . . "*Western Life*"		357
H. R. A. POCOCK.		

IX.—SEASONS.

HEAT . . . *"In the Millet"*	369	
ARCHIBALD LAMPMAN.		
TO A HUMMING-BIRD IN A GARDEN .	371	
GEORGE MURRAY.		
IN THE GOLDEN BIRCH . . .	374	
ELIZABETH GOSTWYCKE ROBERTS.		
THE FIR WOODS	376	
CHARLES G. D. ROBERTS.		
CLOUDS . . . . *"In the Millet"*	377	
ARCHIBALD LAMPMAN.		
FROGS	378	
CHARLES G. D. ROBERTS.		
TWILIGHT . . *"Jephthah's Daughter"*	379	
CHARLES HEAVYSEGE.		
THE WHIP-POOR-WILL . . .	380	
"FIDELIS."		
A CANADIAN SUMMER EVENING . *"Poems"*	382	
MRS LEPROHON.		
EVENING ON THE MARSHES . .	383	
BARRY STRATON.		
THE FIRE-FLIES . . . *"Dreamland"*	385	
CHARLES MAIR.		
MIDSUMMER NIGHT . . *"In the Millet"*	387	
ARCHIBALD LAMPMAN.		
THE AUTUMN TREE . *"Jephthah's Daughter"*	388	
CHARLES HEAVYSEGE.		

xviii   CONTENTS.

		PAGE
IN APPLE TIME		389
BLISS CARMAN.		
THE AURORA BOREALIS		390
JOHN E. LOGAN—"BARRY DANE."		
THE MAPLE	"*Orion*"	391
CHARLES G. D. ROBERTS.		
OCTOBER . . .	"*Poems and Songs*"	392
ALEXANDER M'LACHLAN.		
FIRST SNOW		394
JOHN TALON-LESPÉRANCE—"LACLÈDE."		
INDIAN SUMMER		396
MRS SUSANNA (STRICKLAND) MOODIE.		
INDIAN SUMMER . . "*Voices from the Hearth*"		397
ISIDORE G. ASCHER.		
AN INDIAN SUMMER CAROL . .		399
"FIDELIS."		
TO WINTER	"*Orion*"	401
CHARLES G. D. ROBERTS.		
A MID-WINTER NIGHT'S DREAM "*Snowflakes and Sunbeams*"		404
WILLIAM WILFRED CAMPBELL.		
WINTER NIGHT . . "*Jephthah's Daughter*"		405
CHARLES HEAVYSEGE.		
CARNATIONS IN WINTER . .		406
BLISS CARMAN.		
ICICLE DROPS		407
ARTHUR JOHN LOCKHART.		
THE SILVER FROST . . .		409
BARRY STRATON.		

CONTENTS.

		PAGE
THE JEWELLED TREES		411
GEORGE MARTIN.		
MARCH	"*Old Spooks's Pass*"	413
ISABELLA VALANCEY CRAWFORD.		
THE WINDS		417
JOHN E. LOGAN—"BARRY DANE."		
APRIL	"*In the Millet*"	421
ARCHIBALD LAMPMAN.		
IN LYRIC SEASON . . .		424
BLISS CARMAN.		
AN OLD LESSON FROM THE FIELDS .	"*In the Millet*"	425
ARCHIBALD LAMPMAN.		
THE FROGS . . .	"*In the Millet*"	426
ARCHIBALD LAMPMAN.		
BOBOLINK . . .	"*Poems and Songs*"	429
ALEXANDER M'LACHLAN.		
THE CANADIAN SONG-SPARROW . .		431
J. D. EDGAR.		
IN JUNE		432
E. W. THOMSON.		

APPENDIX.

I. The Old Chansons of the French Province . . .	437
II. Leading Modern French-Canadian Poets .	440
Notes Biographical and Bibliographical .	449
Note of Thanks . .	464

INTRODUCTION.

THE poets whose songs fill this book are voices cheerful with the consciousness of young might, public wealth, and heroism. Through them, taken all together, you may catch something of great Niagara falling, of brown rivers rushing with foam, of the crack of the rifle in the haunts of the moose and caribou, the lament of vanishing races singing their death-song as they are swept on to the cataract of oblivion, the rural sounds of Arcadias just rescued from surrounding wildernesses by the axe, shrill war-whoops of Iroquois battle, proud traditions of contests with the French and the Americans, stern and sorrowful cries of valour rising to curb rebellion. The tone of them is *courage;*—for to hunt, to fight, to hew out a farm, one must be a man! Through their new hopes, doubts, exultations, questionings, the virility of fighting races is the undertone. Canadians are, for the most part, the descendants of armies, officers and men, and every generation of them has stood up to battle.

The delight of a clear atmosphere runs through it too, and the rejoicings of that Winter Carnival which is only possible in the most athletic country in the world; with the glint of that heavenly Palace of illumined pearl, which is the February pilgrimage of North America.

Canada, Eldest Daughter of the Empire, is the Empire's completest type! She is the full-grown of the family,—the one first come of age and gone out into life as a nation; and she has in her young hands the solution of all those questions which must so interest every true Briton, proud and careful of the acquisitions of British discovery and conquest. She is Imperial in herself, we sons of her think, as the number, the extent, and the lavish natural wealth of her Provinces, each not less than some empire of Europe, rises in our minds; as we picture her coasts and gulfs and kingdoms and islands, on the Atlantic on one side, and the Pacific on the other; her four-thousand-mile panorama of noble rivers, wild forests, ocean-like prairies; her towering snow-capped Rockies waking to the tints of sunrise in the West; in the East her hoary Laurentians, oldest of hills. She has by far the richest extent of fisheries, forests, wheat lands, and fur regions in the world; some of the greatest public works; some of the loftiest mountain-ranges, the vastest rivers, the healthiest and most beautifully varied seasons. She has the best ten-elevenths of Niagara Falls, and the best half of the Inland Seas. She stands fifth among the nations in the tonnage of her commercial marine. Her population is about five million souls. Her Valley of the Saskatchewan alone, it has been scientifically computed, will support eight hundred millions. In losing the United States, Britain lost the *smaller* half of her American possessions:—the Colony of the Maple Leaf is about as large as Europe.

But what would material resources be without a corresponding greatness in man? Canada is also Imperial in her traditions. Her French race are still conscious that they are the remnants of a power which once ruled North America from Hudson's Bay to the Gulf of Mexico. Existing English Canada is the result of simply the noblest epic migration the world has ever seen:—more loftily epic than the retirement of Pius Æneas from Ilion,—the withdrawal, namely, out of the rebel Colonies, of the thirty-five thousand United Empire Loyalists after the War of the Revolution. "Why did you come here?" was asked of one of the first settlers of St John, New Brunswick, a man whose life was without a stain;—"Why did you come here, when you and your associates were almost certain to endure the sufferings and absolute want of shelter and food which you have narrated?" "*Why did we come here?*" replied he, with emotion which brought tears:—"*For our loyalty.*"

Canada has, of historic right, a voice also in the Empire of to-day, and busies herself not a little in studying its problems. For example, the question whether that Empire will last is being asked. Her history has a reply to that :—IT WILL, IF IT SETS CLEARLY BEFORE IT A DEFINITE IDEAL THAT MEN WILL SUFFER AND DIE FOR; and such an Ideal—worthy of long and patient endeavour—may be found in broad-minded advance towards the voluntary Federation of Mankind. She has a special history, too, which even under the overshadowing greatness of that of the Empire—in which she also owns her part—is one of interest. First explored in 1535, by Jacques-Cartier, of St Malo, by command of Francis I., and its settlement established in 1608 through the foundation of Quebec by the devoted and energetic Maker of French Canada, Samuel de Champlain, its story down to the Conquest in 1759-63 is full of romance,—Jesuit missionaries, explorers, chevaliers, painted Indian war-parties, the rich fur trade, and finally the great struggle under Montcalm, closing with his expiry and Wolfe's at the hour of the fall of Quebec, passing like a panorama. Then came the entry of the Loyalists, and from that to the present there has been a steady unfolding to power and culture, broken only by the brave war of 1812, and a French, and two half-breed, rebellions. She is, to-day, next to the United States, the strongest factor in American affairs.

The Literature of this daughter-nation in the West, as distilled by its poets, ought to be interesting to Englishmen. That other Colonial poetic literature, presented in the Australian volume of this series, has shown that there can be a signal attractiveness in such a picture of a fresh world. On the part of Canada the semi-tropical Australian surroundings are matched in beauty by a Northern atmosphere of objects which make vivid contrasts with them; her native races were the noblest of savage tribes; while the Imperial and National feelings, developing in two such different hemispheres, are instructive in their divergences and similarities. The romantic life of each Colony also has a special flavour,—Australian rhyme is a poetry of the *horse;* Canadian, of the *canoe.*

Now, who are those who are drinking these inspirations and

breathing them into song? In communing with them, we shall try to transport you to the Canadian clime itself. You shall come out with us as a guest of its skies and air, paddling over bright lakes and down savage rivers; singing French *chansons* to the swing of our paddles, till we come into the settlements; and shall be swept along on great rafts of timber by the majestic St Lawrence, to moor at historic cities whose streets and harbours are thronged with the commerce of all Europe and the world. You shall hear there the chants of a new nationality, weaving in with songs of the Empire, of its heroes, of its Queen.

A word first about the personnel of our conductors. The foremost name in Canadian song at the present day is that of Charles George Douglas Roberts, poet, canoeist, and Professor of Literature, who has struck the supreme note of Canadian nationality in his "Canada" and "Ode for the Canadian Confederacy." His claim to supremacy lies, for the rest, chiefly in the quality of the two volumes, "Orion and other Poems," which he published in 1880 at the age of twenty-one, and "In Divers Tones," which appeared in 1887. The style and taste of Roberts at its best—and he is frequently very good—are characterised by two different elements—a striking predilection for the pictorial ideals and nature-poetry of classical Greece; and a noble passion, whose fire and music resemble and approach Tennyson's. "Orion," "Actæon," "Off Pelorus," and "The Pipes of Pan" are purely Greek, drawn direct from "ancient founts of inspiration." On the other hand, his "O Child of Nations, giant-limbed!" which stirs every true Canadian like a trumpet, is, though of different subject and metre, of the stamp and calibre of "Locksley Hall." His pure Hellenic poems must be dismissed from consideration here, but an account of the man himself makes it proper to say of them that they have obtained for him a growing recognition in the ranks of general English literature; and that his feeling for beauty of colour and form is so really artistically correct as well as rich, that he deserves a permanent place in the Gallery of *Word-painters*.

Roberts loves his country fervently, as is apparent in all his Canadian themes. His heart dwells with fondness on the scenes of his Maritime Provinces, "the long dikes of Tantramar," and the ebb-tide sighing out, "reluctant for the reed-beds"; and he was one of the first to sing Confederation. His sympathy is also Britain's:

> "Let a great wrong cry to heaven,
> Let a giant necessity come;
> And now as of old she can strike,
> She will strike, and strike home!"

The personal quality in his poetry is distinguished, next to richness of colour and artistic freedom of emotional expression, by manliness. Roberts is a high-thinking, generous man. He speaks with a voice of power and leadership, and never with a mean note or one of heedless recklessness. This manliness and dignity render him particularly fitted for the great work which Canada at present offers her sons, and as he is only twenty-nine we hope to see his future a great one.

In point of time, however, the first important national poet was not Roberts, but nature-loving Charles Sangster, a born son of the Muses, and who was long the people's favourite. Sangster is a kind of Wordsworth, with rather more fire, and of course a great deal less metaphysical and technical skill. He has the unevenness and frequent flatness of Wordsworth, but is as close a personal friend of the mountains, lakes, and woods.

> "I have laid my cheek to Nature's, put my puny hands in hers."

Glowingly he takes us, in "St Lawrence and the Saguenay," down the grandeurs of that unrivalled tour—the great River, its rapids, cities, mountains, and "Isles of the Blest." Defective education in youth deprived him of the resources of modern art, which Roberts uses so freely, making a good deal of his poetry the curious spectacle of inborn strivings after perfect ideals driven to expression in abstractions rather than in concrete clothing of colours and forms; for instance:

> "All my mind has sat in state
>   Pondering on the deathless soul:
>   What must be the *Perfect Whole*
> When the atom is so great!
>
> God! I fall in spirit down,
>   Low as Persian to the sun;
>   All my senses, one by one,
> In the stream of *Thought* must drown."

Sangster's nervous system was broken down by the grind of newspaper toil and civil service tread-milling, and he has not written or published for twenty years; yet, though poetry has till lately been given a particularly small share of attention in Canada, his "Brock," "Song for Canada," his lines on Quebec, and many striking passages from his poems, are treasured in the popular memory.

But the most striking volume next to those of Roberts—indeed more boldly new than his—is that of the late brilliant Isabella Valancey Crawford. This wonderful girl, living in the "Empire" Province of Ontario, early saw the possibilities of the new field around her, and had she lived longer might have made a really matchless name. It was only in 1884 that her modest blue card-covered volume of two hundred and twenty-four pages came out. The sad story of unrecognised genius and death was re-enacted. "Old Spooks's Pass; Malcolm's Katie, and other Poems," as it was doubly entitled (the names at least were against it!), almost dropped from the press. Scarcely anybody noticed it in Canada. It made no stir, and in little more than two years the authoress died. She was a high-spirited, passionate girl, and there is very little doubt that the neglect her book received was the cause of her death. Afterwards, as usual, a good many people began to find they had overlooked work of merit. Miss Crawford's verse was, in fact, seen to be phenomenal. Setting aside her dialect poems, like "Old Spooks's Pass" (which, though the dialect is a trifle artificial, resulted in hitting off some good pictures of imaginary rustic characters), the style peculiarly her own has seldom been equalled for strength, colour, and originality:—

> "Low the sun beat on the land,
>   Purple slope and olive wood;
> With the wine cup in his hand,
>   Vast the Helot herdsman stood."
>
> * * * * *
>
> "Day was at her high unrest;
>   Fevered with the wine of light,
> Loosing all her golden vest,
>   Reeled she towards the coming Night."

INTRODUCTION.

Miss Crawford's poetry is packed with able stuff. It is worth a share of attention from the whole Anglo-Saxon world. The splendour of Canadian colour, the wonderful blue skies of that clear climate, the Heaven's-forests of its autumn, the matchless American sunsets and sunrises, imbued her like Roberts. A poetess of such original nature could not but strike boldly into Canadian subjects. "Malcolm's Katie; a Love Story," is an idyl of a true man who goes forth and cuts him a home with his axe, and of a maiden who remains true to him, until he returns for their union. Few finer bits were ever written by any one or anywhere than the passage which we give, from "Shanties grew," down to its glorious climax in the song, "O Love will build his lily walls." It seems to us that this is the most effective known use of a lyric introduced into a long poem. Her works, including a good deal never yet published, were to be brought before the English public in a new volume. A letter of hers, concerning the unpublished material, stated that it contained some of her best work.

The poets best known and most favourite next to Roberts and Sangster, are—besides Isabella Crawford—M'Lachlan, Kirby, and tender-hearted John Reade. Reade is one the charms of whose style are sweetness and culture. He is best known by his "Merlin, and Other Poems" (1870), composed of short lyrics, led off by "The Prophecy of Merlin," which is a Tennysonian Idyll of the King, foreshadowing the greatness of the British Empire. His style turns everything it touches into grace, but it appeals to the inner circle rather than the folk, and seems to shrink away from touching organ-keys. For examples of this grace of his, I should like to quote his "The Inexpressible," or "Good Night," but cannot do so here.

The claim of first place is awarded by the feelings of no small number to Alexander M'Lachlan, the human-hearted vigorous Scottish Radical, whose stanzas have such a singing rhythm and direct sympathy. They were a few years ago made a special feature of the great comic paper *Grip*, the *Punch* of Canada, and his popularity is shown by the presentation by his admirers a short time since of a homestead farm, upon which he now lives. His "Idylls of the Dominion," from which the poems quoted in this book are principally drawn, are so characteristic both of himself and of pioneerdom, that he is called "The Burns of Canada." He has lived the whole life of them, as a settler and a lover of the soil,—chopped his first tree, penetrated the mysterious "Hall of Shadows," listened to the cheerful bobolink's little aria, communed with "October" in her splendour and her sadness, and experienced the appalling sensations created by fire in the forest as he describes it.

William Kirby deserves a high position for his beautiful "Canadian Idylls" (based on history, while M'Lachlan's are upon life), from which the "Spina Christi," quoted here, is drawn. There are also some able descriptions in his long-known "U. E." (Loyalist) poem, from which is taken his passage on Niagara. Steeped in the romance of Canadian history, he wrote many years ago a magnificent novel founded upon the Quebec legend of the Chien d'Or, which has remained the most popular of Canadian stories. Kirby's strong point is his graphic descriptions.

One name I have not yet pronounced, though every Canadian no doubt has looked for it. A sombre shadow towers in the background of the group,—a man apart from the rest,—Charles Heavysege, author of the drama "Saul." When "Saul" came out in 1857, and a copy fell into the hands of Nathaniel Hawthorne, Heavysege became famous. He was pronounced the greatest dramatist since Shakespeare. The *North British Review* for August 1858 spoke of the book as follows :—

"Of 'Saul, a Drama, in three parts,' published anonymously at Montreal, we have before us perhaps the only copy which has crossed the Atlantic. At all events we have heard of no other, as it is probable we should have done, through some public or private notice, seeing that the work is indubitably one of the most remarkable English poems ever written out of Great Britain."

The *North British* reviewer was later, by no means alone, in its praise, and it became the fashion among tourists to Montreal to buy a copy of "Saul."

Heavysege had a very strange and original cast of mind. The following brief poem may be read as being characteristic of him :—

> "Open, my heart, thy ruddy valves;
>   It is thy master calls;
> Let me go down, and, curious trace
>   Thy labyrinthine halls.
> Open, O heart, and let me view
>   The secrets of thy den;
> Myself unto myself now show
>   With introspective ken.
> Expose thyself, thou covered nest
>   Of passions, and be seen;
> Stir up thy brood, that in unrest
>   Are ever piping keen.
> Ah! what a motley multitude,
>   Magnanimous and mean!"

He was originally a drama-composing carpenter, then a journalist in Montreal, and wore out his soul at the drudgery of the latter occupation and in poverty. To get out the third edition of "Saul" he was forced to borrow the money, which he was never able to repay. In person he was a small, very reticent man, who walked along the streets altogether locked up in himself, so that a literary acquaintance of his says Heavysege's appearance always reminded him exactly of "The Yellow Dwarf,"—

> "He walked our streets, and no one knew
> That something of celestial hue
> Had passed along; a toil-worn man
> Was seen,—no more; the fire that ran
> Electric through his veins, and wrought
> Sublimity of soul and thought,
> And kindled into song, no eye
> Beheld."

He died in 1869. A man apart he has remained. His work is in no sense distinctively Canadian. Canadians do not read him; but they claim him as perhaps their greatest, most original writer, if they could weigh him aright and appreciate him; and he will probably always command their awe, and refuse to be forgotten.

Sympathy with the prairie and the Indian has produced the

best verse of Charles Mair, who has dramatised the story of the immortal British ally Tecumseh, and lately from his North-West home gives us "The Last Bison;" and who has lived a life (some details of which you will find in the Biographical Notes) almost as Indian and North-West as his poems. "The Last Bison," he says, was suggested to him by what happened before his own eyes near the elbow of the North Saskatchewan some eight years ago. "Not a buffalo," so far as he knows, "has been seen on that river since. There are some animals in private collections; a small band perhaps exists in the fastnesses of Montana, and a few wood buffaloes still roam the Mackenzie River region; but the wild bison of the plains may now be looked upon as extinct." We may add, that it was lately reported by an Indian that he had tracked a herd of seven in the northerly region of the Peace River. He shot four bulls and a calf out of the seven! The North-West has also given happy inspirations to "Barry Dane" as a bird of passage.

John Hunter-Duvar, the author of "De Roberval" and Squire of "Hernewood," in Prince Edward Island, described in "The Emigration of the Fairies," derives his verse largely from the life and legends of the surrounding regions, shaped by his library.

George Martin, of Montreal, has digged in the gold mine of old French legend, with the result of "Marguerite; or, The Isle of Demons," a weird and sad story of De Roberval's desertion of his niece, in one of the early expeditions.

Arthur Wentworth Eaton and George Murray have explored the same mine with signal success,—the latter, who is very well known as a *litterateur*, producing the fine ballad "How Canada was Saved." (The same story has been well put in Martin's "Heroes of Ville-Marie.")

Bliss Carman has earned special honour for the originality and finish of his lyrics. Arthur John Lockhart, in his "Masque of Minstrels,"—particularly in "Gaspereau,"—sings as a bird of exile warbling towards home, for he lives just over the frontier. William Wilfred Campbell is the poet of the Great Lakes, which he has studied with a perfect love, resulting in those beautiful "Lake Lyrics" of his, which the reader will stop to admire. A bit of work of particular attractiveness has been done by William M'Lennan in his well-known translations of the old French *chansons*. Archibald Lampman has written perfectly exquisite pre-Raphaelite descriptions, with the finish and sparkle of jewellers' work.

I should have liked to quote more fully than has been possible from the "Lyrics on Freedom, Love, and Death" of the late George Frederick Cameron; but his fire and generosity of spirit belong rather to the world than to Canadian inspiration, and we are therefore confined here to a few lesser pieces of his. He died early, like so many other sons of genius.

Among names of special grace or promise are to be added those of "Laclède," John Talon-Lespérance, the well-known *littérateur*, and Fellow of the Royal Society of Canada; Barry Straton, Duncan Campbell Scott, Frederick George Scott, John Henry Brown, Dr Æneas M'Donald Dawson, F.R.S.C.; Arthur Weir (the author of "Fleurs de Lys"); Dr Charles Edwin Jakeway; the late Honourables d'Arcy M'Gee and Joseph Howe; Ernest J. Chapman, E. W. Thomson, Carroll Ryan, William Wye Smith, Phillips Stewart, J. J. Proctor, J. A. Richey; the aged but bright G. W. Wicksteed, Q.C.; H. L. Spencer; Evan M'Coll, the Gaelic-English "Bard of Lochfyne"; Messrs Dunn, Shanly, Haliburton, M'Donell, James M'Carroll, J. H. Bowes, K. L. Jones, S. J. Watson, T. G. Marquis, M'Alpine Taylor, the late Francis Rye, the late John Lowry Stuart, the late Charles Pelham Mulvaney, H. R. A. Pocock (author of spirited North-West pieces), Alexander Rae Garvie, and M'Pherson, the early Nova Scotia singer, whose "I Long for Spring, enchanting Spring," has a bell-like silveriness. Some of these I have been unable to get at. A bright and erratic name, which I am sorry I cannot represent, is that of the journalist George T. Lanigan ("Allid"),—"the most brilliant journalist who ever lived," says Mr George Murray. Lanigan wrote with equal felicity in French and English, and his humour was inexhaustible. I regret that space forbids me to add in the body of the book two good things by D. B. Kerr and Emily M'Manus. The latter's subject is the crescent province of the West :—

"MANITOBA.

" Softly the shadows of prairie-land wheat
 Ripple and riot adown to her feet;
 Murmurs all Nature with joyous acclaim,
 Fragrance of summer and shimmer of flame:
 Heedless she hears while the centuries slip:—
 Chalice of poppy is laid on her lip.

" Hark! From the East comes a ravishing note,—
 Sweeter was never in nightingale's throat,—
 Silence of centuries thrills to the song,
 Singing their silence awaited so long;
 Low, yet it swells to the heaven's blue dome,
 Child-lips have called the wild meadow-land ' Home!'

" Deep, as she listens, a dewy surprise
 Dawns in the languor that darkens her eyes;
 Swift the red blood through her veins, in its flow,
 Kindles to rapture her bosom aglow;
 Voices are calling, where silence had been,—
 ' Look to thy future, thou Mother of Men!'

" Onward and onward! Her fertile expanse
 Shakes as the tide of her children advance;
 Onward and onward! Her blossoming floor
 Yields her an opium potion no more;
 Onward! and soon on her welcoming soil
 Cities shall palpitate, myriads toil."

One peculiar feature of this literature, indeed, is its strength in lady singers. The number who have produced true poetry seems to indicate something special in the conditions of a new country. Verily one has not to read far in that noble, patriotic book, "Laura Secord," to acknowledge that Mrs Sarah Anne Curzon writes with the power and spirit of masculinity. How these women sympathise with the pluck of the heroes! The best war-songs of the late half-breed rebellion were written by Annie Rothwell, of Kingston, who had only a name for prose novels until the spirit of militarism was thus lit in her. "Fidelis" (Agnes Maude Machar), who is frequently given the credit of being the first of our poetesses, shows some of it, but excels in a graceful subjectivity which unfortunately is unfitted for representative quotation here; a remark which applies with still more hapless effect to the philosophic thought of Mary Morgan ("Gowan Lea"). Kate Seymour Maclean, authoress of "The Coming of the Princess," is mistress of a style of singular richness; and some of the brightest writing, both prose and verse, is done by "Seranus," of Toronto (Mrs S. Frances Harrison), who is working good service to our literature in a number of ways. Her "Old Régime," and "Rose Latulippe," express what has been called her "half-French heart," and breathe the air of the fertile, scarcely-wrought field of French Canadian life. Then there are "Fleurange," who wrote the best Carnival Poem, "The Italian Boy's Dream;" E. Pauline Johnson, daughter of Head-Chief Johnson, of the Mohawks of Brantford, who gives us poetry of a high stamp, and of great interest on account of her descent; "Esperance" (Alice Maud Ardagh); Mrs Leprohon; Mary Barry Smith; Helen Fairbairn; M. J. Katzmann Lawson; the late Miss E. M. Nash; Pamelia Vining Yule, "Clare Everest"; Janet Carnochan; Mrs Edgar Jarvis, "Jeanie Gray"; Isabel Macpherson; Louisa Murray, a well-known authoress, who, besides much fine prose, has written "Merlin's Cave," one of the best of Canadian undistinctive poems, and Ethelwyn Wetherald, authoress of many exquisite sonnets. Even from the beginning —fifty years ago, for there was no native poetry to speak of before that—we had Susanna Moodie, one of the famous Strickland sisters, authoress of "Roughing it in the Bush" (which book, by the way, did the country's progress a good deal of harm), who gave us the best verses we had during many years, and some of the most patriotic.

Some of those lines of "Fidelis" to which I referred, express so well the spirit of this preface, that I return to her name to quote them :—

CANADA TO THE LAUREATE.

"'And that true north, whereof we lately heard
A strain to shame us! keep you to yourselves,
So loyal is too costly! Friends, your love
Is but a burden: loose the bond and go,
Is this the tone of Empire?'
—*Tennyson's Ode to the Queen.*

"We thank thee, Laureate, for thy kindly words
Spoken for us to her to whom we look

With loyal love, across the misty sea;
Thy noble words, whose generous tone may shame
The cold and heartless strain that said ' Begone,
We want your love no longer; all our aim
Is riches—*that* your love can *not* increase!'
Fain would we tell them that we do not seek
To hang dependent, like a helpless brood
That, selfish, drag a weary mother down;
For we have British hearts and British blood
That leaps up, eager, when the danger calls!
Once and again, our sons have sprung to arms
To fight in Britain's quarrel,—*not our own*,—
And drive the covetous invader back,
Who would have let us, peaceful, keep our own.
So we had cast the British name away.
Canadian blood has dyed Canadian soil,
For Britain's honour, that we deemed our own,
Nor do we ask but for the right to keep
Unbroken, still, the cherished filial tie
That binds us to the distant sea-girt isle
Our fathers loved, and taught their sons to love,
As the dear home of freemen, brave and true,
And loving *honour* more than ease or gold!"

Many more writers than those above named, in all to a number which might be roughly placed at three hundred, have at various times produced really good verse.

A curious Indian song, representing a small but unique song-literature which has sprung up among the tribe at Caughnawaga Reservation, near Montreal, since barbaric times, "from the sheer necessity of singing when together," was translated specially for me by Mr John Waniente Jocks, the son of a Six-nation chief of that Reservation. Mr Jocks, who is a law student, is of pure Mohawk origin.

A few general remarks are now in order. The present is an imperfect presentation of Canadian poetry from a purely literary point of view, on account of the limitation of treatment; for it is obvious that if only what illustrates the country and its life *in a distinctive way* be chosen, the subjective and unlocal literature must be necessarily passed over, entraining the omission of most of the poems whose merit lies in perfection of finish. It is therefore greatly to be desired that a purely literary anthology may soon be brought together by someone. Such a collection was made in 1867, in the Rev. Edward Hartley Dewart's "Selections," which have ever since remained the standard book of reference for that period; but it has become antiquated, no longer represents what is being done, and most of the best authors, such as Roberts, Miss Crawford, Hunter-Duvar, Talon-Lespérance, and "Fidelis" have come into the field since its publication. Two or three other partial collections have been made, the best being Seranus's "Canadian Birthday Book," which affords a miniature survey of the chief verse-writers, both French and English. The most remarkable point of difference between the selections of Dewart and the poetry which has followed, is the tone of exultation and confidence which the singers have assumed since Confederation, for up to that epoch the verse was apologetic and depressed. Everything now points hopefully. Not only is the poetry more confident, but far better. A good deal of the best verse in American magazines is written in Canada.

The arrangement of the present collection has been devised in order to give a sketch of Canadian things in something like related order. I have introduced such broad principles of order as the contributions permitted, grouping them into sections, which respectively treat of the Imperial Spirit, the New Nationality, the Indian, the *Voyageur* and *Habitant*, Settlement Life, Historical Incidents, Places, and Seasons. They give merely, it should be understood, a sketch of the range of the subjects. Canadian history, for example, as anyone acquainted with Parkman will know, perfectly teems with noble deeds and great events, of which only a small share have been sung, whereof there is only space here for a much smaller share. The North-West and British Columbia, that Pacific clime of charm, —the gold-diggings Province, land of salmon rivers, and of the Douglas firs which hide daylight at noonday,—have been scarcely sung at all, owing to their newness. Pieces which take origin from them ought to be remarked as rare. The poetry of the Winter Carnival, splendid scenic spectacle of gay Northern arts and delights, is only rudimentary also. Those who have been present at the thrilling spectacle of the nocturnal storming of the Ice Palace in Montreal, when the whole city, dressing itself in the picturesque snow-shoe costume and arraying its streets in lights and colours, rises as one man in a tumultuous enthusiasm, must feel that something of a future lies before the poetry of these strange and wonderful elements. Here a word suggests itself concerning the climate of Canada. Winter is not perpetual, but merely, in most parts, somewhat long. It does not strike the inhabitants as intolerably severe. It is the season of most of their enjoyments; gives them their best roads; is indispensable to some industries, such as lumbering; and the clear nights and diamond days are sparklingly beautiful. Furthermore, the climate is not one but several. In British Columbia, it is so equable the whole year that roses sometimes bloom out of doors in January, and cactus is a native plant. In the Niagara peninsula, grapes and peaches are crops raised yearly in immense quantities, and the sycamore and acacia are so frequent as to have called out more than one poem. On the plains, temperature grows milder in proportion as you approach to the Rocky Mountains.

To omit a bow to the French would be ungracious. Forming about a fourth of the population, they have a literature which was within the last generation much more fecund than the English, and contains remarkable writing. We have devoted a special appendix to *ipsis verbis* specimens of Chauveau, Sulte, Fréchette, and Le May, leaders who have been very highly honoured in France. The charming old Chanson literature, in which numbers of medieval ballads brought over in past days from the *mère-patrie* are embalmed, is treated in another appendix, while in our text, the renderings of William M'Lennan are given for some of the best of them. "Entre Paris and St Denis," it is to be noted, preserves a remarkable machinery of sorcery; the quaintness and beauty of the others will speak for themselves.

In concluding, I desire to express my sense of shortcoming in the work, but believe it will be generally admitted that I have spared no necessary trouble.

The editor regrets to say that through an accidental cause unnecessary to explain, more MSS. were sent to the publishers

INTRODUCTION. xxxvii

than the volume required. As no time could be lost the general editor had no recourse except to undertake the difficult task of cutting down the matter, which he did in accordance with his best judgment, but guided by the sole criterion of the symmetry of the work. Some good poetry originally included has not found a place owing to the necessary reduction, and apology is tendered where unintentional injustice has resulted.

Acknowledgments are due to many kind persons, of whom the principal are duly mentioned in a note of thanks at the close of the volume.

And now, the canoes are packed, our *voyageurs* are waiting for us, the paddles are ready, let us start!

W. D. L.

MONTREAL, *September* 1888.

ENTRY OF THE MINSTRELS.

---—※———

From "THE MASQUE OF MINSTRELS."

Arthur J. Lockhart.

THEN came a company of wandering minstrels, without singing robes and garlands, up to the gate of the castle, which was opened readily enough to receive them. They were now only in the court-yard; but they went on —their harps in their hands—strengthened by the countenances of one another, and unabashed by the mighty band who had gone in before them. They were late in coming, and the choir of singers was already full; but of this they thought no ill, and when questioned of their act, they answered with a proud humility. They were near the door of the high hall, and in answer to their summons, it was thrown open, so that a herald stood before them.

HERALD.

And who be ye?

FIRST MINSTREL.

We be also of the Minstrelsy; we be Apprentices of the Muses; Secretaries of Love; Slaves of Beauty; Apostles of Desire; Disciples of Truth; Children of Nature; Followers of Aspiration; Servants of Song. We be uncrowned kings and queens in the realms of Music, coming to claim and win our sceptres. Crowns have been won and worn by others. Admit us.

HERALD.

Nay; ye claim too largely. Whose sons be ye, and whose daughters?

SECOND MINSTREL.

We be sons and daughters of fathers who were never cowards, and of mothers who were never ashamed; who loved valour and virtue even as their children love music.

I.—THE IMPERIAL SPIRIT.

I.—THE IMPERIAL SPIRIT.

HASTINGS.
John Reade.

I.

October's woods are bright and gay, a thousand colours vie
To win the golden smiles the Sun sends gleaming thro' the sky;
And tho' the flowers are dead and gone, one garden seems the earth,
For, in God's world, as one charm dies, another starts to birth.

II.

To every season is its own peculiar beauty given,
In every age of mortal men we see the Hand of Heaven;
And century to century utters a glorious speech,
And peace to war, and war to peace, eternal lessons teach.

III.

O grand old woods, your forest-sires were thus as bright and gay,
Before the axe's murderous voice had spoiled their sylvan play;
When other axes smote our sires, and laid them stiff and low,
On Hastings' unforgotten field, *eight hundred years ago.*

IV.

Eight hundred years ago, long years, before Jacques Cartier clomb
The Royal Height, where now no more the red men fearless roam!

Eight hundred years ago, long years before Columbus came
From stately Spain to find the world that ought to bear his
   name !

V.

The Sussex woods were bright and red on that October
   morn ;
And Sussex soil was red with blood before the next was
   born ;
But from that red united clay another race did start
On the great stage of destiny to act a noble part.

VI.

So God doth mould, as pleaseth Him, the nations of His
   choice ;
Now, in the battle-cry is heard His purifying voice ;
And now, with Orphic strains of peace he draws to nation-
   hood
The scattered tribes that dwell apart by mountain, sea, and
   wood.

VII.

He took the lonely poet Celt and taught him Roman lore ;
Then from the wealds of Saxony He brought the sons of
   Thor ;
Next from his craggy home the Dane came riding o'er the
   sea ;
And last, came William with his bands of Norman chivalry.

VIII.

And now, as our young nationhood is struggling into birth,
God grant its infant pulse may beat with our forefathers'
   worth !
And, as we gather into *one*, let us recall with pride
That we are of the blood of those who fought when Harold
   died.

ADVANCE OF THE EMPIRE.

Mary Barry Smith.

The march of the years is on, ever on to the guerdon,
    And the slow-paced deed and the wingèd steed are at one;
Crouching low in the valleys, shadows press like a burden;
    Up on the heights, sun-illumined, we stand in the sun.

Have we not crossed together the Rubicons of the nation,
    Shoulder to shoulder marching, a solid phalanx and strong?
Statesmen, Warriors, Sages, brave ones of every station?
    Here on this height, together, let the cheers be loud and
        long!

For from this hill of time, this vantage ground of position,
    Look we back o'er the past, and on to the coming years
And the signs of a nation's life, its Titan-throes of ambition,
    The ponderous strength of its toiling, its sweat and tears;

The laden hulks of its commerce, the glare of furnace fires,
    The noise of wheels and spindles and traffic's ceaseless
        hum;
Its many million aims and the thought that each inspires,
    Attest the past is great, but the greatest is yet to come!
        For so hath the gain been ever,
        Each step in the world's endeavour;
"It is naught; it is naught," saith the buyer of toil and
        thought,
But afterward goeth his way and boasteth the sum.

So commerce grows to its future, and science, Argus-visioned,
  Searches the earth and the heaven, miracles working still;
Giants of unguessed power people its fields elysianed,
  And magical deeds are wrought by a magical skill.

Marvels electric, sublime—the boast of a science still bright'ning,
  What are the bounds of Empire but the bounds of thought and skill?
England must foremost be, her sails all harbours whitening,
  Till the British brain is dull and the British hands are still.
        For the might of thought is believing,
        And the might of will is achieving,
  And God, who is over us all, hath the Infinite will!

CANADA TO ENGLAND.*

Anonymous.

Mother of many prosperous lands,
   Thy children in this far-off West,—
Seeing that vague and undefined
   A cloud comes up to mar our rest;
Fearing that busy tongues, whose speech
Is mischief, may have caused a breach,
And frayed the delicate links which bind
   Our people each to each,—
With loving hearts and outstretched hands
   Send greeting leal and kind.

Heed not the teachings of a school
Of shallow sophists who would part
The outlying members of thy rule;
   Who fain would lop, with felon stroke,
   The branches of our English oak,
And, wronging the great English heart,
   Would deem her honour cheaply sold
For higher prices on the mart,
   And increased hoard of gold.

---

* Appeared in *New Dominion Monthly*, 1869, with a statement that it had had a wide circulation "some years ago." Internal evidence shows it to have been written about 1861.

What though a many thousand miles
    Of boisterous waters ebb and flow
Between us and the favoured Isles,—
    The "inviolate Isles" which boast thy sway!
No time nor distance can divide
What gentlest bonds have firmest tied;
And this we fain would have thee know,
    The which let none gainsay.
Nay rather, let the wide world hear
That we so far are yet so near,
That, come what may, in weal or woe,
    Our hearts are one this day.

Thus late, when death's cold wings were spread,
    And when the nation's eyes were dim,
We also bowed the stricken head,
We too the eloquent teardrops shed
    In heartfelt grief for *him*.

  .   .   .   .

When recent danger threatened near,
    We nerved our hearts to play our part;
Not making boast, nor feeling fear;
    But as the news of insult spread
        Were none to dally or to lag;
For all the grand old Island spirit
Which Britain's chivalrous sons inherit
    Was roused, and as one heart, one head,
        We rallied round our flag.

And now as then unchanged, the same
    Though filling each our separate spheres;
Thy joys, thy griefs, and thy good name
Are ours, and or in good or ill;

Our pride of race we have not lost,
And aye it is our loftiest boast
   That we are Britons still!
And in the gradual lapse of years
We look, that 'neath these distant skies
Another England shall arise,—
   A noble scion of the old,—
Still to herself and lineage true,
   And prizing honour more than gold.
This is *our* hope, and as for you,
   Be just as you are generous, mother,
And let not those who rashly speak
Things that they know not, render weak
   The ties that bind us to each other.

EMPIRE FIRST.

Popular Song.

JOHN TALON-LESPÉRANCE—"LACLÈDE."

SHALL we break the plight of youth,
 And pledge us to an alien love?
No! We hold our faith and truth,
 Trusting to the God above.
   Stand, Canadians, firmly stand,
   Round the flag of Fatherland.

Britain bore us in her flank,
 Britain nursed us at our birth,
Britain reared us to our rank
 'Mid the nations of the earth.
   Stand, Canadians, &c.

In the hour of pain and dread,
 In the gathering of the storm,
Britain raised above our head
 Her broad shield and sheltering arm.
   Stand, Canadians, &c.

O triune kingdom of the brave,
 O sea-girt island of the free,
O empire of the land and wave,
 Our hearts, our hands, are all for thee.
   Stand, Canadians, &c.

THE CANADIANS ON THE NILE.

WILLIAM WYE SMITH.

O, THE East is but the West, with the sun a little hotter;
And the pine becomes a palm, by the dark Egyptian water:
And the Nile's like many a stream we know, that fills its
    brimming cup,—
We'll think it is the Ottawa, as we track the batteaux up!
    Pull, pull, pull! as we track the batteaux up!
    It's easy shooting homeward, when we're at the top!

O, the cedar and the spruce, line each dark Canadian
    river;
But the thirsty date is here, where the sultry sunbeams
    quiver;
And the mocking mirage spreads its view, afar on either
    hand;
But strong we bend the sturdy oar, towards the Southern
    land!
    Pull, pull, pull! as we track the batteaux up!
    It's easy shooting homeward, when we're at the top!

O, we've tracked the Rapids up, and o'er many a portage
    crossing;
And it's often such we've seen, though so loud the waves
    are tossing!

Then, it's homeward when the run is o'er! o'er stream, and
    ocean deep—
To bring the memory of the Nile, where the maple shadows
    sleep!
        Pull, pull, pull! as we track the batteaux up!
        It's easy shooting homeward, when we're at the top!

And it yet may come to pass, that the hearts and hands so
    ready
May be sought again to help, when some poise is off the
    steady!
And the Maple and the Pine be matched, with British Oak
    the while,
As once beneath Egyptian suns, the Canadians on the
    Nile!
        Pull, pull, pull! as we track the batteaux up!
        It's easy shooting homeward, when we're at the top!

II.—THE NEW NATIONALITY.

II.—THE NEW NATIONALITY.

DOMINION DAY.

"FIDELIS."

With *feu-de-joie* and merry bells, and cannon's thundering peal,
And pennons fluttering on the breeze, and serried rows of steel,
We greet, again, the birthday morn of our young giant's land,
From the Atlantic stretching wide to far Pacific strand;
With flashing rivers, ocean lakes, and prairies wide and free,
And waterfalls, and forests dim, and mountains by the sea;
A country on whose birth-hour smiled the genius of romance,
Above whose cradle brave hands waved the lily-cross of France;
Whose infancy was grimly nursed in peril, pain, and woe;
Whose gallant hearts found early graves beneath Canadian snow;
When savage raid and ambuscade and famine's sore distress,
Combined their strength, in vain, to crush the dauntless French *noblesse;*
When her dim, trackless forest lured, again and yet again,
From silken courts of sunny France, her flower, the brave Champlain.

And now, her proud traditions boast four blazoned rolls of
    fame,—
Crecy's and Flodden's deadly foes our ancestors we claim;
Past feud and battle buried far behind the peaceful years,
While Gaul and Celt and Briton turn to pruning-hooks
    their spears;
Four nations welded into one,—with long historic past,
Have found, in these our western wilds, one common life,
    at last;
Through the young giant's mighty limbs, that stretch from
    sea to sea,
There runs a throb of conscious life—of waking energy.
From Nova Scotia's misty coast to far Columbia's shore,
She wakes,—a band of scattered homes and colonies no
    more,
But a young nation, with her life full beating in her breast,
A noble future in her eyes—the Britain of the West.
Hers be the noble task to fill the yet untrodden plains
With fruitful, many-sided life that courses through her
    veins;
The English honour, nerve, and pluck,—the Scotsman's
    love of right,—
The grace and courtesy of France,—the Irish fancy bright,—
The Saxon's faithful love of home, and home's affections
    blest;
And, chief of all, our holy faith,—of all our treasures best.
A people poor in pomp and state, but rich in noble deeds,
Holding that righteousness exalts the people that it leads;
As yet the waxen mould is soft, the opening page is fair;
It rests with those who rule us now, to leave their impress
    there,—
The stamp of true nobility, high honour, stainless truth;
The earnest quest of noble ends; the generous heart of
    youth;

The love of country, soaring far above dull party strife;
The love of learning, art, and song—the crowning grace of life;
The love of science, soaring far through Nature's hidden ways;
The love and fear of Nature's God—a nation's highest praise.
So, in the long hereafter, this Canada shall be
The worthy heir of British power and British liberty;
Spreading the blessings of her sway to her remotest bounds,
While, with the fame of her fair name, a continent resounds.
True to her high traditions, to Britain's ancient glory
Of patient saint and martyr, alive in deathless story;
Strong, in their liberty and truth, to shed from shore to shore
A light among the nations, till nations are no more.

CANADA.

Charles G. D. Roberts.

O Child of Nations, giant-limbed,
    Who stand'st among the nations now
Unheeded, unadorned, unhymned,
    With unanointed brow,—

How long the ignoble sloth, how long
    The trust in greatness not thine own?
Surely the lion's brood is strong
    To front the world alone!

How long the indolence, ere thou dare
    Achieve thy destiny, seize thy fame,—
Ere our proud eyes behold thee bear
    A nation's franchise, nation's name?

The Saxon force, the Celtic fire,
    These are thy manhood's heritage!
Why rest with babes and slaves? Seek higher
    The place of race and age.

I see to every wind unfurled
    The flag that bears the Maple-Wreath;
Thy swift keels furrow round the world
    Its blood-red folds beneath;

Thy swift keels cleave the furthest seas;
    Thy white sails swell with alien gales;
To stream on each remotest breeze
    The black smoke of thy pipes exhales.

O Falterer, let thy past convince
    Thy future,—all the growth, the gain,
The fame since Cartier knew thee, since
    Thy shores beheld Champlain!

Montcalm and Wolfe! Wolfe and Montcalm!
    Quebec, thy storied citadel
Attest in burning song and psalm
    How here thy heroes fell!

O Thou that bor'st the battle's brunt
    At Queenston, and at Lundy's Lane,—
On whose scant ranks but iron front
    The battle broke in vain!—

Whose was the danger, whose the day,
    From whose triumphant throats the cheers,
At Chrysler's Farm, at Chateauguay,
    Storming like clarion-bursts our ears?

On soft Pacific slopes,—beside
    Strange floods that northward rave and fall,—
Where chafes Acadia's chainless tide—
    Thy sons await thy call.

They wait; but some in exile, some
  With strangers housed, in stranger lands;—
And some Canadian lips are dumb
  Beneath Egyptian sands.

O mystic Nile! Thy secret yields
  Before us; thy most ancient dreams
Are mixed with far Canadian fields
  And murmur of Canadian streams.

But thou, my Country, dream not thou!
  Wake, and behold how night is done,—
How on thy breast, and o'er thy brow,
  Bursts the uprising sun!

THE CONFUSED DAWN.

W. D. Lighthall.

YOUNG MAN.

What are the Vision and the Cry
That haunt the new Canadian soul?
  Dim grandeur spreads we know not why
O'er mountain, forest, tree and knoll,
  And murmurs indistinctly fly.—
  Some magic moment sure is nigh.
O Seer, the curtain roll!

SEER.

The Vision, mortal, it is this—
  Dead mountain, forest, knoll and tree
Awaken all endued with bliss,
  A native land—O think!—to be—
Thy native land—and ne'er amiss,
Its smile shall like a lover's kiss
  From henceforth seem to thee.

The Cry thou couldst not understand,
  Which runs through that new realm of light,
From Breton's to Vancouver's strand
  O'er many a lovely landscape bright,
It is their waking utterance grand,
  The great refrain, "A Native Land!"
    Thine be the ear, the sight.

(1882.)

NATIONAL HYMN.

W. D. Lighthall.

To Thee whose smile is might and fame,
    A nation lifts united praise
And asks but that Thy purpose frame
    A *useful* glory for its days.

We pray no sunset lull of rest,
    No pomp and bannered pride of war;
We hold stern labour manliest,
    The just side real conqueror.

For strength we thank Thee: keep us strong,
    And grant us pride of skilful toil;
For homes we thank Thee: may we long
    Have each some Eden rood of soil.

O, keep our mothers kind and dear,
    And make the fathers stern and wise;
The maiden soul preserve sincere,
    And rise before the young man's eyes.

Crush out the jest of idle minds,
    That know not, jesting, when to hush;
Keep on our lips the word that binds,
    And teach our children when to blush.

Forever constant to the good
   Still arm our faith, thou Guard Sublime,
To scorn, like all who have understood,
   The atheist dangers of the time.

Thou hearest!—Lo, we feel our love
   Of loyal thoughts and actions free
Toward all divine achievement move,
   Ennobled, blest, ensured, by Thee.

FROM "'85."

Barry Straton.

Shall we not all be one race, shaping and welding the nation?
  Is not our country too broad for the schisms which shake petty lands?
Yea, we shall join in our might, and keep sacred our firm Federation,
  Shoulder to shoulder arrayed, hearts open to hearts, hands to hands!

SONG FOR CANADA.

Charles Sangster.

Sons of the race whose sires
Aroused the martial flame
    That filled with smiles
    The triune Isles,
Through all their heights of fame!
With hearts as brave as theirs,
With hopes as strong and high,
    We'll ne'er disgrace
    The honoured race
Whose deeds can never die.
    Let but the rash intruder dare
        To touch our darling strand,
            The martial fires
            That thrilled our sires
        Would flame throughout the land.

Our lakes are deep and wide,
Our fields and forests broad;
    With cheerful air
    We'll speed the share,
And break the fruitful sod;
Till blest with rural peace,
Proud of our rustic toil,
    On hill and plain
    True kings we'll reign,
The victors of the soil.
    But let the rash intruder dare
        To touch our darling strand,
            The martial fires
            That thrilled our sires
        Would light him from the land

Health smiles with rosy face
Amid our sunny dales,
    And torrents strong
    Fling hymn and song
Through all the mossy vales;
Our sons are living men,
Our daughters fond and fair;
    A thousand isles
    Where Plenty smiles
Make glad the brow of Care.
  But let the rash intruder dare
    To touch our darling strand,
      The martial fires
      That thrilled our sires
    Would flame throughout the land.

And if in future years
One wretch should turn and fly,
    Let weeping Fame
    Blot out his name
From Freedom's hallowed sky;
Or should our sons e'er prove
A coward, traitor race,—
    Just heaven! frown
    In thunder down
T' avenge the foul disgrace!
  But let the rash intruder dare
    To touch our darling strand,
      The martial fires
      That thrilled our sires
    Would light him from the land.

HERE'S TO THE LAND.

William Wye Smith.

Here's to the Land of the rock and the pine :
    Here's to the Land of the raft and the river !
Here's to the Land where the sunbeams shine,
    And the night that is bright with the North-light's quiver !

Here's to the Land of the axe and the hoe !
    Here's to the hearties that give them their glory ;—
With stroke upon stroke, and with blow upon blow,
    The might of the forest has passed into story !

Here's to the Land with its blanket of snow,—
    To the hero and hunter the welcomest pillow !
Here's to the land where the stormy winds blow
    Three days ere the mountains can talk to the billow !

Here's to the buckwheats that smoke on her board ;
    Here's to the maple that sweetens their story ;
Here's to the scythe that we swing like a sword ;
    And here's to the fields where we gather our glory !

Here's to her hills of the moose and the deer ;
    Here's to her forests, her fields and her flowers ;
Here's to her homes of unchangeable cheer,
    And the maid 'neath the shade of her own native bowers !

CANADA NOT LAST.

W. D. LIGHTHALL.

AT VENICE.

Lo! Venice, gay with colour, lights and song,
   Calls from St Mark's with ancient voice and strange:
I am the Witch of Cities! glide along
   My silver streets that never wear by change
Of years; forget the years, and pain, and wrong,
And every sorrow reigning men among;
   Know I can soothe thee, please and marry thee
To my illusions   Old, and siren-strong,
   I smile immortal, while the mortals flee
   Who whiten on to death in wooing me!

AT FLORENCE.

Say, what more fair, by Arno's bridgèd gleam,*
   Than Florence, viewed from San Miniato's slope
At eventide, when west along the stream
   The last of day reflects a silver hope!—
Lo! all else softened in the twilight beam :—
The city's mass blent in one hazy cream;
   The brown Dome 'midst it, and the Lily Tower,
And stern Old Tower more near, and hills that seem
   Afar, like clouds to fade, and hills of power
   On this side, greenly dark with cypress, vine, and bower!

---

* " Sovra'l bel fiume d'Arno la gran villa."—DANTE.

AT ROME.

End of desire to stray I feel would come,
   Though Italy were all fair skies to me,
Though France's fields went mad with flowery foam,
   And Blanc put on a special majesty.
Not all could match the growing thought of home,
Nor tempt to exile. Look I not on ROME,—
   This ancient, modern, mediæval queen,—
Yet still sigh westward over hill and dome,
   Imperial ruin, and villa's princely scene,
     Lovely with pictured saints and marble gods serene!

REFLECTION.

Rome, Florence, Venice,—noble, fair, and quaint,
   They reign in robes of magic round me here;
But fading, blotted, dim, a picture faint,
   With spell more silent, only pleads a tear.
Plead not! Thou hast my heart, O picture dim!
   I see the fields, I see the autumn hand
Of God upon the maples! Answer Him
   With weird, translucent glories, ye that stand
Like spirits in scarlet and in amethyst!
I see the sun break over you; the mist
   On hills that lift from iron bases grand
     Their heads superb!—the dream, it is my native land!

AN ODE FOR THE CANADIAN CONFEDERACY.

Charles G. D. Roberts.

Awake, my country, the hour is great with change!
    Under this gloom which yet obscures the land,
From ice-blue strait and stern Laurentian range
    To where giant peaks our western bounds command,
A deep voice stirs, vibrating in men's ears
    As if their own hearts throbbed that thunder forth,
A sound wherein who hearkens wisely hears
    The voice of the desire of this strong North,—
        This North whose heart of fire
        Yet knows not its desire
    Clearly, but dreams, and murmurs in the dream.
The hour of dreams is done.   Lo, on the hills the gleam!

Awake, my country, the hour of dreams is done!
    Doubt not, nor dread the greatness of thy fate.
Tho' faint souls fear the keen, confronting sun,
    And fain would bid the morn of splendour wait;
Tho' dreamers, rapt in starry visions, cry,
    "Lo, yon thy future, yon thy faith, thy fame!"
And stretch vain hands to stars, thy fame is nigh,
    Here in Canadian hearth, and home, and name;—
        This name which yet shall grow
        Till all the nations know
    Us for a patriot people, heart and hand
Loyal to our native earth,—our own Canadian land!

O strong hearts, guarding the birthright of our glory,
    Worth your best blood this heritage that ye guard!
Those mighty streams resplendent with our story,
    These iron coasts by rage of seas unjarred,—
What fields of peace these bulwarks well secure!
    What vales of plenty those calm floods supply!
Shall not our love this rough, sweet land make sure,
    Her bounds preserve inviolate, though we die?
        O strong hearts of the North,
          Let flame your loyalty forth,
    And put the craven and base to an open shame,
Till earth shall know the Child of Nations by her name!

COLLECT FOR DOMINION DAY.

Charles G. D. Roberts.

FATHER of Nations! Help of the feeble hand,
    Strength of the strong! to whom the nations kneel!
Stay and destroyer, at whose just command
    Earth's kingdoms tremble and her empires reel!
Who dost the low uplift, the small make great,
    And dost abase the ignorantly proud;
Of our scant people mould a mighty state,
    To the strong stern, to Thee in meekness bowed!
Father of unity, make this people one!
    Weld, interfuse them in the patriot's flame,—
Whose forging on Thine anvil was begun
    In blood late shed to purge the common shame
That so our hearts, the fever of faction done,
    Banish old feud in our young nation's name.

III.—THE INDIAN.

III.—THE INDIAN.

A BLOOD-RED RING HUNG ROUND THE MOON.

"Barry Dane"—John E. Logan.

A BLOOD-RED ring hung round the moon,
   Hung round the moon. Ah me! Ah me!
I heard the piping of the Loon,
   A wounded Loon. Ah me!
And yet the eagle feathers rare,
I, trembling, wove in my brave's hair.

He left me in the early morn,
   The early morn. Ah me! Ah me!
The feathers swayed like stately corn,*
   So like the corn. Ah me!
A fierce wind swept across the plain,
The stately corn was snapt in twain.

They crushed in blood the hated race,
   The hated race. Ah me! Ah me!
I only clasped a cold, blind face,
   His cold, dead face. Ah me!
A blood-red ring hangs in my sight,
I hear the Loon cry every night.

---

* "Indian corn" is Maize.

THE DEPARTING OF CLOTE SCARP.

Charles G. D. Roberts.

It is so long ago ; and men well nigh
Forget what gladness was, and how the earth
Gave corn in plenty, and the rivers fish,
And the woods meat, before he went away.
His going was on this wise.

        All the works
And words and ways of men and beasts became
Evil, and all their thoughts continually
Were but of evil. Then he made a feast.
Upon the shore that is beside the sea
That takes the setting sun, he ordered it,
And called the beasts thereto. Only the men
He called not, seeing them evil utterly.
He fed the panther's crafty brood, and filled
The lean wolf's hunger ; from the hollow tree
His honey stayed the bear's terrific jaws ;
And the brown rabbit couched at peace, within
The circling shadow of the eagle's wings.
And when the feast was done, he told them all
That now, because their ways were evil grown,
On that same day he must depart from them,
And they should look upon his face no more.
Then all the beasts were very sorrowful.

It was near sunset, and the wind was still,
And down the yellow shore a thin wave washed
Slowly ; and Clote Scarp launched his birch canoe,
And spread his yellow sail, and moved from shore,
Though no wind followed, streaming in the sail,
Or roughening the clear waters after him.
And all the beasts stood by the shore, and watched.
Then to the west appeared a long red trail
Over the wave; and Clote Scarp sailed and sang
Till the canoe grew little like a bird,
And black, and vanished in the shining trail.
And when the beasts could see his form no more,
They still could hear him, singing as he sailed,
And still they listened, hanging down their heads
In long row, where the thin wave washed and fled.
But when the sound of singing died, and when
They lifted up their voices in their grief,
Lo ! on the mouth of every beast a strange
New tongue ! Then rose they all and fled apart,
Nor met again in council from that day.

CHANGE ON THE OTTAWA.

George Martin.

I.

Onward the Saxon treads. Few years ago,
    A chief of the Algonquins passed at dawn,
With knife and tomahawk and painted bow,
    Down the wild Ottawa, and climbed upon
A rocky pinnacle, where in the glow
    Of boyhood he had loved to chase the fawn;
Proudly he stood there, listening to the roar
Of rapids sounding, sounding evermore.

II.

All else was silence, save the muffled sound
    Of partridge drumming on the fallen tree,
Or dry brush crackling from the sudden bound
    Of startled deer, that snorts, and halts to see,
Then onward o'er the leaf-encumbered ground,
    Through his green world of beauty, ever free.
Such was the scene—no white man's chimney nigh,
And joy sat, plumed, in the young warrior's eye.

III.

No white man's axe his hunting-grounds had marred,
    The primal grandeur of the solemn woods,
When Summer all her golden gates unbarred,
    And hung voluptuous o'er the shouting floods,—
Or when stern Winter gave the rich reward,
    All suited with his uncorrupted moods,
For all was built, voiced, roofed with sun and cloud
By the Great Spirit unto whom he bowed.

IV.

The grey of morn was edging into white,
   When down the rugged rock the Indian passed,
Like a thin shadow. Soon the rosy light
   Lay on the maple leaf, the dew-drops cast
A lustrous charm on many a mossy height,
   And squirrels broke out in chatter, as the blast
Swayed the tall pine tops where they leaped, and made
Grand organ-music in the green-wood shade.

V.

Again the Indian comes—some years have rolled—
   Down the wild Ottawa, and stands upon
His boyhood haunt, and with an eye still bold
   Looks round, and sighs for glories that are gone;
For all is changed, except the fall that told,
   And tells its Maker still, and Bird-rock lone;
Sadly he leans against an evening sky,
Transfigured in its ebb of rosy dye.

VI.

He sees a city there:—the blazing forge,
   The mason's hammer on the shaping stone,
Great wheels along the stream revolving large,
   And swift machinery's whirr and clank and groan,
And the fair bridge that spans the yawning gorge,
   Which drinks the spray of Chaudière, leaping prone,—
And spires of silvery hue, and belfry's toll,
All strike, like whetted knives, the red man's soul.

VII.

Wide is the area of the naked space
    Where broods the city like a mighty bird,
And the grave Sachem from his rock can trace
    Her flock of villages, where lately stirred
The bear and wolf, tenacious of their place,
    And where the wild cat with her kittens purred;
Now while the shades of eve invest the land,
What myriad lights flash out on every hand!

VIII.

The dead day's crimson, interwove with brown,
    Has wrapped the watcher upon Oiseau Rock,
And o'er him hangs bright Hesper, like a crown,
    As if the hand of Destiny would mock
His soul's eclipse and sorrow-sculptured frown!—
    Thick as wild pigeons, dusky memories flock
O'er the wide wind-fall of his fated race,
And thus he murmurs to his native place:

IX.

" Here dwelt within the compass of my gaze,
    All whom I ever loved, and none remain
To cheer the languor of my wintry days,
    Or tread with me across the misty plain;
A solitary tree, the bleak wind strays
    Among my boughs, which moaningly complain;
Familiar voices whisper round and say,
Seek not to find our graves! Away! Away!

X.

"The sire who taught my hands to hold the bow,
　The mother who was proud of my renown,
On them no more the surly tempests blow,
　How little do they heed or smile or frown,
The summer's blossoms or the winter's snow!
　With them, at last, I thought to lay me down,
Where birds should sing, and wild deer safely play,
And endless woods fence out the glare of day.

XI.

"Friend of my youth, my 'Wa-Wa* Height,' adieu!
　No more shall I revisit thee, no more
Gaze from thy summit on the upper blue,
　And listen to the rapid's pleasing roar;—
I go,—my elder brother!—to pursue
　The Elk's great shadow on a distant shore,
Where Nature, still unwounded, wears her charms,
And calls me, like a mother, to her arms."

XII.

He ceased, and strode away; no tear he shed,
　A weakness which the Indian holds in scorn,
But sorrow's moonless midnight bowed his head,
　And once he looked around—Oh! so forlorn!
I hated for his sake the reckless tread
　Of human progress;—on *his* race no morn,
No noon of happiness shall ever beam;
They fade as from our waking fades a dream.

---

* "Wa-Wa," *the Wild Goose.*

From "TECUMSEH."—Act I., Scene 2.

Charles Mair.

LEFROY.

    This region is as lavish of its flowers
    As Heaven of its primrose blooms by night.

This is the Arum, which within its root
Folds life and death; and this the Prince's Pine,
Fadeless as love and truth—the fairest form
That ever sun-shower washed with sudden rain.
This golden cradle is the Moccasin Flower,
Wherein the Indian hunter sees his hound;
And this dark chalice is the Pitcher-Plant,
Stored with the water of forgetfulness.
Whoever drinks of it, whose heart is pure,
Will sleep for aye 'neath foodful asphodel,
And dream of endless love.
      .   .   .   .   .
    There was a time on this fair continent
When all things throve in spacious peacefulness.
The prosperous forests unmolested stood,
For where the stalwart oak grew there it lived
Long ages, and then died among its kind.
The hoary pines—those ancients of the earth—
Brimful of legends of the early world,
Stood thick on their own mountains unsubdued.
And all things else illumined by the sun,
Inland or by the lifted wave, had rest.

The passionate or calm pageants of the skies
No artist drew; but in the auburn west
Innumerable faces of fair cloud
Vanished in silent darkness with the day.
The prairie realm—vast ocean's paraphrase—
Rich in wild grasses numberless, and flowers
Unnamed save in mute Nature's inventory,
No civilised barbarian trenched for gain.
And all that flowed was sweet and uncorrupt.
The rivers and their tributary streams,
Undammed, wound on for ever, and gave up
Their lonely torrents to weird gulfs of sea,
And ocean wastes unshadowed by a sail.
And all the wild life of this western world
Knew not the fear of man; yet in those woods,
And by those plenteous streams and mighty lakes,
And on stupendous steppes of peerless plain,
And in the rocky gloom of canyons deep,
Screened by the stony ribs of mountains hoar
Which steeped their snowy peaks in purging cloud,
And down the continent where tropic suns
Warmed to her very heart the mother earth,
And in the congeal'd north where silence self
Ached with intensity of stubborn frost,
There lived a soul more wild than barbarous;
A tameless soul—the sunburnt savage free—
Free and untainted by the greed of gain,
Great Nature's man, content with Nature's food.

THE ARCTIC INDIAN'S FAITH.

Thomas D'Arcy M'Gee.

We worship the Spirit that walks unseen
    Through our land of ice and snow;
We know not His face, we know not His place,
    But His presence and power we know.

Does the Buffalo need the Pale-face word
    To find his pathway far?
What guide has he to the hidden ford,
    Or where the green pastures are?
Who teacheth the Moose that the hunter's gun
    Is peering out of the shade?
Who teacheth the doe and the fawn to run
    In the track the Moose has made?

Him do we follow, Him do we fear,
    The Spirit of earth and sky;
Who hears with the *Wapiti's* eager ear
    His poor red children's cry;
Whose whisper we note in every breeze
    That stirs the birch canoe;
Who hangs the reindeer-moss on the trees
    For the food of the Caribou.

The Spirit we worship, who walks unseen
    Through our land of ice and snow;
We know not His face, we know not His place,
    But His presence and power we know.

TAAPOOKAA: A HURON LEGEND.

CHARLES SANGSTER.

The clouds roll o'er the pine-trees,
   Like waves that are charged with ire;
Golden and glory-hued their crests,
   Ablaze with a gorgeous fire.

The sun has gone down in splendour,
   The heavens are wild with flame,
And all the horizon is burning
   With colours that have no name.

And over the mighty forests
   The mystical hues are spread,
As calm as the smiles of angels,
   As still as the peaceful dead.

And the lake, serene and thoughtful,
   And the river, deep in dreams,
And the purple cliff in the distance,
   Are robed with the glory gleams;

Until earth seems a sacred temple,
   Where spirits of light have trod,
Where man should not dare to enter,—
   Too sacred for aught but God.

Calm eve over lovely Huron,
    Calm eve in the sombre wild,
And over the rude bark wigwam
    Of the swarthy forest-child.

There's a gathering of the red-men,
    Of their youths and maidens fair,
Of the mothers of braves and heroes,
    And the feast is spreading there.

From the banks of Cadaraqui,
    From Niagara's solitudes,
Where the song of the Water Spirit
    Rolled vast through the primal woods.

From Superior's rocky defiles,
    Her grand and rugged shores,
From Utawa and blue-waved Erie,
    Came the Chiefs and Sagamores,

Bringing gifts from the distant lodges,
    Rare gifts for the lovely bride,—
Taapookaa, the fairest maiden
    That ever for true-love sighed.

Taapookaa, the loved, the lovely,
    No beauty was there like hers,
And through all the tribes of the forest
    The Braves were her worshippers.

But where is her young Sioux lover,
    The pride of her trusting heart?
The Brave that her love hath chosen,
    Whose life is of hers a part?

Away from the bridal revels,
    Away from the feast he roves,
Alone over lonely rivers,
    Alone in the lonely groves!

Taapookaa must wed another,
    The chief of a neighbour tribe;
Neither force nor friends can save her,
    Neither tears nor prayers can bribe!

For this have the Chieftains gathered,
    Great Chiefs from the wilds afar;
They have prayed to Manitou freely,
    And saluted the Bridal Star.

All things for the feast are ready,
    All ripe for the revelry,
And the bridegroom chief is waiting,
    But Taapookaa, where is she?

Like the zephyr that tends the flowers,
    That bendeth but may not break,
So, lightly, her footstep treadeth
    The cliff o'er the calmy lake.

The stars are all weeping for her,
    The moon hath a look forlorn,
For the beautiful maid, all blushes,
    All blushes, and truth, and scorn!

The breeze hath a mournful cadence,
    A sigh for the fairest fair;
It cooleth her maiden blushes,
    And fingereth her jetty hair.

Like a tragic queen she standeth,
    On the jagged cliff alone;
All nature has paused to shudder,
    And the stricken forests moan.

A prayer for her young Sioux lover,
    That wanders the wilds forlorn,
And she leaps from the cliff, all daring,
    And maidenly truth, and scorn.

At night when the stars are shining,
    And the moon, with silvery hue,
Illumines the lake with radiance,
    Is seen a white canoe.

Two shadowy forms within it,
    Two faces that seem to smile,—
The maid and her brave Sioux lover
    Returned from the Spirit-Isle.

THE CAUGHNAWAGA BEADWORK-SELLER.

W. D. Lighthall.

Kanawâki,—" By the Rapid,"—
   Low the sunset 'midst thee lies;
And from the wild Reservation
   Evening's breeze begins to rise.
Faint the Kōnoronkwa chorus
   Drifts across the currents strong;
Spirit-like the parish steeple
   Stands thine ancient walls among.

Kanawâki,—" By the Rapid,"—
   How the sun amidst thee burns!
Village of the Praying Nation,
   Thy dark child to thee returns.
All day through the palefaced city,
   Silent, selling beaded wares,
I have wandered with my basket,
   Lone, excepting for their stares.

They are white men; we are Indians:
   What a gulf their stares proclaim!
They are mounting; we are dying:
   All our heritage they claim.
We are dying, dwindling, dying!
   Strait and smaller grows our bound:
They are mounting up to heaven,
   And are pressing all around.

Thou art ours,—little remnant,
    Ours from countless thousand years,—
Part of the old Indian world:
    Thy breath from far the Indian cheers.
Back to thee, O Kanawâki!
    Let the rapids dash between
Indian homes and white men's manners,—
    Kanawâki and Lachine!

O, my dear! O Knife-and-Arrows!
    Thou art bronzed, thy limbs are lithe;
How I laugh when through the crosse-game
    Slipst thou like red elder-withe!
Thou art none of these palefaces!
    When with thee I'll happy feel;
For thou art the Indian warrior
    From thy head unto thy heel!

Sweet the Kōnoronkwa chorus
    Floats across the currents strong;
Clear behold the parish steeple
    Rise the ancient walls among!
Skim us deftly, noiseless paddle:
    In my shawl my bosom burns!
Kanawâki,—" By the Rapid,"—
    Thy own child to thee returns.

THE INDIAN'S GRAVE.

Bishop G. J. Mountain.

Bright are the heavens, the narrow bay serene;
    No sound is heard within the shelter'd place,
Save some sweet whisper of the pines,—nor seen
    Of restless man, or of his works, a trace :
    I stray, through bushes low, a little space :
Unlook'd for sight their parted leaves disclose :
    Restless no more, lo ! one of Indian race ;
His bones beneath that roof of bark repose.

Poor savage ! in such bark through deepening snows
    Once did'st thou dwell—in this through rivers move ;
Frail house, frail skiff, frail man ! Of him who knows
    His Master's will, not thine the doom shall prove :
What will be yours, ye powerful, wealthy, wise,
By whom the heathen unregarded dies?

WAHONOMIN.*—INDIAN HYMN TO THE QUEEN.

Frederick George Scott.

Great mother! from the depths of forest wilds,
From mountain pass and burning sunset plain,
We, thine unlettered children of the woods,
Upraise to thee the everlasting hymn
Of nature, language of the skies and seas,
Voice of the birds and sighings of the pine
In wintry wastes. We know none other tongue,
Nor the smooth speech that, like the shining leaves,
Hides the rough stems beneath. We bring our song,
Wood-fragrant, rough, yet autumn-streaked with love,
And lay it as a tribute at thy feet.
But should it vex thee thus to hear us sing,
Sad in the universal joy that crowns
This year of years, and shouldst thou deem our voice
But death-cry of the ages that are past,
Bear with us—say, " My children of the woods,
In language learnt from bird and wood and stream,
From changing moons and stars and misty lakes,
Pour forth their love, and lay it at my feet;
The voice is wild and strange, untuned to ear
Of majesty, ill-timed to fevered pulse
Of this young age, and meteor-souls that flash

---

* " Wahonomin" is an Indian cry of lamentation.

New paths upon night's dome; yet will I hear
This singing of my children ere they die."

Great mother! thou art wise, they say, and good,
And reignest like the moon in autumn skies,
The world about thy feet. We have not seen
Thy face, nor the wild seas of life that surge
Around thy throne; but we have stood by falls,
Deep-shadowed in the silence of the woods,
And heard the water-thunders, and have said,
Thus is the voice of men about our Queen.
What is the red man but the forest stream,
The cry of screech-owl in the desert wilds?
This flood that overflows the hills and plains
Is not for us. Back, Westward, Northward, ay,
Up to eternal winter 'neath the stars,
Our path must be in silence, till the snows
And sun and wind have bleached our children's bones.
The red must go; the axe and plough and plane
Are not for him. We perish with the pine,
We vanish in the silence of the woods;
Our footsteps, like the war-trail in the snow,
Grow fainter while the new spring buds with life.

Great mother! the white faces came with words
Of love and hope, and pointed to the skies,
And in the sunrise splendour set the throne
Of the Great Spirit, and upon the cross
Showed us His Son, and asked a throne for Him.
Their speech was music; but in camp at night
We brooded o'er the matter round the fire,
The shadowy pines about us, and the stars,

Set in the silent heavens, looking down.
We brooded o'er the matter days and years,
For thus each thought and thus each spake in words:
"We children of the woods have lived and died
In these our forests, since the first moon tipped
Their thousand lakes and rivers with her beams,
Pale silver in the fading sky of even.
Our fathers' faces kindled in the glow
Of setting suns; they read the starlit sky;
They heard the Spirit's breathing on the storm,
And on the quaking earth they felt His tread;
But never yet the story of His Son
Was wafted to them from the sighing woods,
Or bird or stream. Our fathers' God is ours;
And as for these new words, we watch and wait."

Great mother! we have waited days and years,
Thro' spring and summer—summer, autumn, spring;
Brooding in silence, for anon we dreamed
A bird's voice in our hearts half sung, "'Tis true."
We listened and we watched the pale face come,
When, lo! new gods came with them—gods of iron
And fire, that shook the forests as they rushed,
Filling with thunder and loud screeching, plains,
Mountains, and woods, and dimming with their breath
The shining skies. These new gods, who were they,
That came devouring all, and blackening earth
And sky with smoke and thunder? We knew not,
But fled in terror further from the face
Of these white children and their gods of iron;
We heard no more their story of the Son,
And words of love. Their own lives were not love,
But war concealed and fire beneath the ash.

Thus ever now the burden of our speech :—
We perish with the pine tree and the bird,
We vanish in the silence of the woods,
The white man's hunting-ground, it is not ours;
We care not for his gods of iron and fire;
Our home is in the trackless wilds, the depth
Of mountain solitudes, by starlit lakes,
By noise of waters in the unchanging woods.

Great mother! we have wondered that thy sons,
Thy pale sons, should have left thy side and come
To these wild plains, and sought the haunts of bears
And red men.   Why their battle with the woods?
Whither go they upon the gods of iron,
Out of the golden sunrise to the mists
Of purple evening in the setting west?
Their lives have scarce as many moons as ours,
Nor happier are.   We know not what they seek;
For death's cold finger chills their fevered life,
As in the wilds he stills the meanest worm,
And death flies with them over all their paths,
And waits them in the heart of wildest waste;
They cannot break his power.   Forgive these thoughts
If, as they rise like mists, they dim the gold
That zones thy brow.   They came to us at night,
As we have sat in council round the fire;
They seemed the echo of the sighing pines
Far in our soul.   One evening rose a chief,
White-headed, bowed with years, one hand on staff,
One on death's arm, preparing for the way.
" My sons," he said, " these people are not wise,
We bide our time, and they will pass away;
Then shall the red man come like a bird in spring,

And build the broken camp, and hunt and fish
In his old woods.   These people pass away ;
For I have thought through many nights and days
And wondered what they seek ; and now I know,
And knowing, say these people are not wise.
They found these plains beneath the burning west,
And westward, ever westward, still they press,
Seeking the shining meadows of the land
Where the sun sleeps, and, folded 'neath his wings,
The happy spirits breathe eternal day.
But I have lived thro' fivescore changing years,
And I have talked with wintry-headed chiefs,
And I have heard that kingdom is not reached
Thro' woods and plains, but by the bridge of death.
This people is not wise ; we bide our time."

Great mother ! they have told us that the snows
Of fifty winters sleep around thy throne,
And buds of spring now blossom with sweet breath
Beneath thy tread.   They tell us of the sea,
And other lands, where other children dwell ;
Of mighty cities and the gleam of gold,
Of empires wider than the shining plains
Viewed from giant hill, that lift thy throne above
The clouded mountain-tops.   They tell us, too,
Of wonders in the home of man ; of gods
Of iron and fire made servants, and of fire
Snatched from the clouds to flash man's swiftest
    thought ;
But these are not for us.   The forest flower
Droops in the haunts of man ; it needs the sky,
And smokeless air, and glances of the sun
Thro' rustling leaves.   We perish with the woods.

The plains are all before thee. Send thy sons
To plant and build, and drive thy flashing gods,
Startling the forests, till, like ocean's bounds,
Thine empire rolls in splendour from wide east
To widest west, broad fields of gold for thee
And thy white children; but our spirits wait
Amid the silent ages, and we pass
To where our fathers dwell, by silent streams,
And hunt in trackless wilds through cloudless days.
The wheels of thy great empire, as it moves
From east to west, from south to icy north,
Crush us to earth. We perish with the woods.

Great mother! if the changing moons have brought
Thee nearer to the darksome bridge that spans
The gulf between this and the eternal day;
If thy path and thy children's be the same,
And thy feet follow where thy fathers went,
Perchance thy soul upon earth's utmost verge,
The eternal sky about thee, and the deeps
Unfathomable beyond,—perchance thy soul,
Grown weary with the fever of thy life,
May yearn for song of bird, and sighing pine,
And silent meditation of the woods;
Perchance, when, looking back from infinite skies
To restless man, thy soul, too, echoes, "Why?"
"Where?" and "Whither?" and thy heart may love
This death-song of thy children, ere they pass
With birds and forests to the silent land.
Perchance the white face told us what was true,
And love and hope wait by the throne of God.
The ruffled lake gives out but broken gleams
Of the clear stars above; so, restless life

May be the troubled reflex of the skies.
The world rolls onward, ever on and on,
Through clouded vast and moans of dying years,
Into the depths of sunset; but the light
Blinds our dim eyes, we cannot see the goal.
The spirit of the world is not for us;
We perish with the pine tree and the bird;
We bow our head in silence. We must die.

WABANAKI SONG.

Tr. Charles G. Leland.

Now I am left on this lonely island to die—
No one to hear the sound of my voice.
Who will bury me when I die?
Who will sing my death-song for me?
My false friends leave me here to die alone;
Like a wild beast, I am left on this island to die.
I wish the wind spirit would carry my cry to my love!
My love is as swift as the deer; he would speed through the forest to find me;
Now I am left on this lonely island to die.
I wish the spirit of air would carry my breath to my love.
My love's canoe, like the sunlight, would shoot through the water to my side;
But I am left on this lonely island to die, with no one to pity me but the little birds.
My love is brave and strong; but, when he hears my fate, his stout heart will break;
And I am on this lonely island to die.
Now the night comes on, and all is silent but the owl. He sings a mournful song to his mate, in pity for me.
I will try to sleep. I wish the night spirit to hear my song; he will tell my love of my fate; and when I awake, I shall see the one I love.
I am on this lonely island to die.

WABANAKI SONG.

Tr. Charles G. Leland.

Come, my *moo sarge*, let us go up that shining mountain, and sit together on that shining mountain; there we will watch the beautiful sun go down from the shining mountain.

There we will sit, till the beautiful night traveller arises above the shining mountain; we will watch him, as he climbs to the beautiful skies.

We will also watch the little stars following their chief.

We will also watch the northern lights playing their game of ball in their cold, shiny country.

There we will sit, on the beautiful mountain, and listen to the thunder (*Badankac*) beating his drum.

We will see the lightning when she lights her pipe.

We will see the great whirlwind running a race with *betchi-vesay* (squall).

There we will sit, 'till every living creature feels like sleeping.

There we will hear the great owl sing his usual song, *teeg-lee-goo-wul-tique*, and see all the animals obey his song.

There we will sit on that beautiful mountain, and watch the little stars in their sleepless flight. They do not mind the song, *teeg-lee-goo-wul-tique;* neither will we mind it, but sit more closely together, and think of nothing but ourselves, on the beautiful mountain.

Again, the *teeg-lee-goo-wul-tique* will be heard, and the night traveller will come closer to warn us that all are dreaming, except ourselves and the little stars. They and their chief are coursing along, and our minds go with them. Then the owl sleeps; no more is heard *teeg-lee-goo-wul-tique;* the lightning ceases smoking; the thunder ceases beating his drum; and though we feel inclined to sleep, yet will we sit on the beautiful, shining mountain.

CAUGHNAWAGA SONG.

(Rinonwes, rinonwes, Rakeni.)

Tr. JOHN WANIENTE JOCKS.

CHORUS.

I LOVE him, I love him, father,—
That young man!

MAIDEN.

Well, father, what is thy word?
My spirit is now to marry.

FATHER.

Ashamed be thou, my child,—
Thou whom I hold my little one,—
Thou are yet too young;
Thou canst not get thee thy food.

MAIDEN (*in the words of the Chorus*)

I love him, I love him, father,—
That young man.

FATHER.

Hard drinks he, he thou lovest;
Great tears this would later make thee shed.

CHORUS (*passionately*).

I love him, I love him, father,—
That young man.

FATHER.

Thou askest for food; he will show thee a bottle.

CHORUS (*softly*).

Yet I love him, I love him, father,—
That young man.

IV.—THE VOYAGEUR AND HABITANT.

IV.—THE VOYAGEUR & HABITANT.

THE OLD RÉGIME.

(*From "Song of Welcome."*)

"SERANUS."

Yet survives a strain,
   One of saddest singing,
Chant of Habitant,
   On the river ringing;
Born in olden France,
All of dame and dance,
   Brought with golden lily.
From the distant pines,
From the northern waters,
From hardy sons and toiling daughters,
     Salutation; Salutation!

RECIT.

Strange visions of a land beyond the sea,
The quaint old towns and farms of Normandy,—
The land he never saw and ne'er will see!

Strange visions of a life as bright and gay
As his own now is quiet, dull and gray,—
The many-coloured life of Yesterday!

Strange visions of a past still dimly dear,
Since he, the toiler, cannot but revere
The past he may not see, nor feel, nor hear!

And strange for us the other sudden thought,
How without dreams that float across the foam
Of gray Atlantic, float, and float, and flash
At length on shores of Gallic name and fame
Into the actual glitter of old time—
We hold among our best possessions still,
E'en here in new and northern land—a past;
We have not many ruins, it is true,
And those we have, pray daily, but in vain,
For friendly green that grows not *gratis* here.
Not more than scraps of history, they have said!
They are enough to interest, kindle too,
If wisely we have learned to love our land,
But not enough to bore—no pedants here.
Here—tower and trophy, mound and monument,
The cairn and cuneiform of an Old World
Give place to Nature in her purity.
But what we have, we cling to. We would keep
All dear tradition; be it picturesque,
In the old *voyageur* with gay festoons
Of floating ribbons, happy, noisy, free;
Or polished, in the careful cavalier,
Fresh-furbelowed from out his sunny France;
Heroic, in the story of Verchères;
Or dark, in that of dismal Beaumanoir.
Through the long years we see as in a dream—
And will not part with it—the Old Régime.

Powdered tresses and rich brocade,
Stately matron and charming maid;

Flashing steel and stubborn rust,
Blood for blood and thrust for thrust;

Hand on heart in the good old style,
Courtly lips on lips without guile;

The young sweet land of *La Nouvelle France*,
Knew it all by a strange sweet chance;

All the charm of the dainty dressing,
All the force of a gay professing.

>CHORUS.—And still we seem
>   As in a dream,
>   To watch the Old Régime,
>   The Old Régime!

Crowned Quebec on her Citadel
Fierce wild tales of her youth can tell;

Tales of ghosts that still pursue
Scenes of riot and bloodshed too;

Tales of dark stains on the flooring,
Tales of woman's wild imploring;

The young sweet land of *La Nouvelle France*,
Had its share of Old World romance;

But sobered by Time are sword and gown,
And quiet reigns in the grey old town.

CHORUS.—Yet still we seem
    As in a dream,
    To watch the Old Régime,
    The Old Régime!

MALBROUCK.

(*Old Chanson.*)

Tr. WILLIAM M'LENNAN.

MALBROUCK has gone a-fighting,
Mironton, mironton, mirontaine,
Malbrouck has gone a-fighting,
But when will he return?

Perchance he'll come at Easter
Or else at Trinity Term.

But Trinity Term is over
And Malbrouck comes not yet.

My Lady climbs her watch-tower
As high as she can get.

She sees her page approaching
All clad in sable hue:

" Ah page, brave page, what tidings
From my true lord bring you?"

"The news I bring, fair Lady,
Will make your tears run down;

"Put off your rose-red dress so fine
And doff your satin gown;

"Monsieur Malbrouck is dead, alas!
And buried too, for aye;

"I saw four officers who bore
His mighty corse away.

"One bore his cuirass, and his friend
His shield of iron wrought;

"The third his mighty sabre bore,
And the fourth—he carried nought.

"And at the corners of his tomb
They planted rose-marie;

"And from their tops the nightingale
Rings out her carol free.

"We saw, above the laurels,
His soul fly forth amain;

"And each one fell upon his face
And then rose up again.

"And so we sang the glories
For which great Malbrouck bled ;

" And when the whole was ended
Each one went off to bed.

" I say no more my Lady,
     Mironton, mironton, mirontaine,
I say no more, my Lady,
As nought more can be said."

À LA CLAIRE FONTAINE.

(Old Chanson.)

Tr. W. D. LIGHTHALL.

UNTO the crystal fountain
  For pleasure did I stray;
So fair I found the waters
  My limbs in them I lay.

      Long is it I have loved thee,
      Thee shall I love alway,
        My dearest;
      Long is it I have loved thee,
      Thee shall I love alway.

II.

So fair I found the waters,
  My limbs in them I lay;
Beneath an oak tree resting,
  I heard a roundelay.
      Long is it, &c.

III.

Beneath an oak tree resting,
  I heard a roundelay,
The nightingale was singing
  On the oak tree's topmost spray.
      Long is it, &c.

IV.

The nightingale was singing
  On the oak tree's topmost spray :—
Sing, nightingale, keep singing,
  Thou who hast heart so gay!
      Long is it, &c.

V.

Sing, nightingale, keep singing,
  Thou hast a heart so gay,
Thou hast a heart so merry,
  While mine is sorrow's prey.
      Long is it, &c.

VI.

For I have lost my mistress,
  Whom I did true obey,
All for a bunch of roses,
  Whereof I said her nay.
      Long is it, &c.

VII.

I would those luckless roses
  Were on their bush to-day,
And that itself the rosebush
  Were plunged in ocean's spray.

    Long is it I have loved thee,
    Thee shall I love alway,
        My dearest;
    Long is it I have loved thee,
    Thee shall I love alway.

EN ROULANT MA BOULË.

(Old Chanson.)

Tr. WILLIAM M'LENNAN.

BEHIND the Manor lies the mere,
  En roulant ma boulë;
Three ducks bathe in its water clear,
  En roulant ma boulë.

   Rouli, roulant, ma boulë roulant,
   En roulant ma boulë roulant,
   En roulant ma boulë.

Three fairy ducks swim without fear:
The Prince goes hunting far and near.

The Prince at last draws near the lake;
He bears his gun of magic make.

With magic gun of silver bright,
He sights the Black but kills the White.

He sights the Black but kills the White:
Ah! cruel Prince, my heart you smite.

Ah! cruel Prince, my heart you break,
In killing thus my snow-white Drake.

My snow-white Drake, my Love, my King;
The crimson life-blood stains his wing.

His life-blood falls in rubies bright,
His diamond eyes have lost their light.

The cruel ball has found its quest,
His golden bill sinks on his breast.

His golden bill sinks on his breast,
His plumes go floating East and West.

Far, far they're borne to distant lands,
Till gathered by fair maidens' hands;

Till gathered by fair maidens' hands;
And form at last a soldier's bed.

And form at last a soldier's bed,
  En roulant ma boulë;
Sweet refuge for the wanderer's head,
  En roulant ma boulë.

    Rouli, roulant, ma boulë roulant,
    En roulant ma boulë roulant,
    En roulant ma boulë.

GAI LE ROSIER.

(*Old Chanson.*)

Tr. William M'Lennan.

Behind my aunt's there groweth
   A wood all greenery;
The nightingale's song filleth
   Its glades with melodie.
     Gai lon la, gai le rosier,
     Du joli mois de mai.

The nightingale's song filleth
   Its glades with melodie;
He sings for maids whose beauty
   No lover holds in fee.

He sings for maids whose beauty
   No lover holds in fee;
For me he singeth never,
   For my True-love loves me.

For me he singeth never
   For my True-love loves me;
He joins no more the dancers,
   Alas! he's far from me.

He joins no more the dancers,
    Alas! he's far from me;
A prisoner ta'en while fighting
    In distant Germanie.

A prisoner ta'en while fighting
    In distant Germanie;
" What wilt thou give, sweet maiden,
    An' I bring him back to thee?"

" What wilt thou give, sweet maiden,
    An' I bring him back to thee?"
" I'll give thee all Versailles,
    Paris, and St Denis.

" I'll give thee all Versailles,
    Paris and St Denis,
And the crystal fount that floweth
    In my garden clear and free."
        Gai lon la, gai le rosier,
        Du joli mois de mai.

ENTRE PARIS ET SAINT-DENIS.

(*Old Chanson.*)

Tr. WILLIAM M'LENNAN.

'TWIXT Paris fair and St Denis
The dance was up one day,
And all the ladies of the town
Looked on in brave array.
   Sur la feuille ron, . . . *don don don,*
   Sur la joli', joli' feuille ronde.

And all the ladies of the town
Looked on in brave array,
All save the Princess fair, who glanced
Adown the dusty way.

The Princess fair cast wistful looks
Adown the dusty way,
And soon she saw her messenger
Ride from where Nantés lay.

She saw her faithful messenger
His way from Nantés wing;
'Now, messenger, from Nantés town
What tidings do you bring?"

"Now, Messenger, bold Messenger,
What news from Nantés fair?"
"The only news I bring, fair Dame,
Your lover bade me bear.

"The only news I bring is this:
Your lover bade me say,
That he has found a sweetheart new,
Choose you a gallant gay.

"Choose you another gallant gay,
For I've a sweetheart rare."
"Now is she wiser far than I,
Or is her face more fair?"

"Now is she wiser far than I,
Or is her face more fair?"
"Although not near so fair as you,
Her wisdom's past compare.

"Her beauty is not like to yours,
But secret lore she knows;
She makes the snow, she makes the hail,
She makes the wind that blows.

"She makes the wind that blows so free,
She makes the snow so fine;
At midnight hour, within her bower,
She makes the sun to shine.

"She makes the sun to shine again
At midnight in her bower;
And on the borders of the sea
Makes rosemary to flower."

*Sur la feuille ron, . . . don don don,
Sur la joli', joli' feuille ronde.*

MARIANSON.

(Old Chanson.)

Tr. WILLIAM M'LENNAN.

"Ah! Marianson, my beauteous dame,
Where is your lord and master gone?"

"My lord rides to the battle-plain,
I know not if he'll come again."

"Ah! Marianson, my lady fair,
Lend me your rings of gold so rare."

"In the iron chest beside my bed,
You'll find the rings," she sweetly said.

"Now, Goldsmith, fashion me with care
Three golden rings of metal rare.

Three golden rings of fashion rare,
Like those that Marianson doth wear."

When he receives his golden rings
Upon his steed he lightly springs.

The first he meets upon the road
Is Marianson's haughty lord.

" Fair greeting now, bold cavalier,
What tidings do you bring me here?"

" Of tidings new I bring you none,
Save of the Lady Marianson."

" Ah! Marianson, my lady fair!
She's faithful aye, I'll boldly swear."

" I say not 'yes,'—I say not 'no,'
But see—the rings from her hands of snow."

" You lie! you lie! bold cavalier;
My wife is faithful, far or near."

His wife stood on the ramparts high;
She saw her lord ride wildly by.

Her heart stood still with a sudden fear
When she marked his face as he drew anear.

" Now, mother, show our new-born child,
Its grace will calm his anger wild."

"My son, behold your son and heir;
What name wilt thou give the babe to bear?"

He cried, "I'll give the child a name
That will fill its mother's life with shame."

He has seized the infant in its mirth,
And thrice has dashed it to the earth.

And Marianson, that lady fair,
He has tied to his horse by her golden hair.

Three days, three nights, he rode like wind,
And never cast a look behind.

Till, at close of the third long night,
He turned and looked on that awful sight.

"Ah! Marianson, my lady fair,
Where are your golden rings so rare?"

"In the iron chest, beside my bed,
You'll find the rings," she sadly said.

He has ta'en the keys with an evil grace,
And has found the rings in their hiding-place.

"Ah! Marianson, my lady fair,
You shall have the best chirurgeon's care."

"The best chirurgeon I would crave
Is a fine white sheet for my quiet grave."

"Ah! Marianson, my beauteous dame,
Will God e'er pardon all my shame?" *

"My death is pardoned now," she smiled,
"But never that of our helpless child."

THE RE-SETTLEMENT OF ACADIA.

Arthur Wentworth Eaton.

The rocky slopes for emerald had changed their garb of gray,
When the vessels from Connecticut came sailing up the bay,
There were flashing lights on every wave that drew the strangers on,
And wreaths of wild arbutus round the brows of Blomidon.

Five years in desolation the Acadian land had lain,
Five golden harvest moons had wooed the fallow fields in vain;
Five times the winter snows caressed, and summer sunsets smiled,
On lonely clumps of willows, and fruit trees growing wild.

There was silence in the forest, and along the Uniac shore,
And not a habitation from Canard to Beauséjour,
But many a ruined cellar and many a broken wall
Told the story of Acadia's prosperity, and fall!

And even in the sunshine of that peaceful day in June,
When Nature swept her harp, and found the strings in perfect tune,
The land seemed calling wildly for its owners, far away,
The exiles scattered on the coast from Maine to Charleston Bay.

Where, with many bitter longings for their fair homes and their dead,
They bowed their heads in anguish, and would not be comforted;
And like the Jewish exiles, long ago, beyond the sea,
They could not sing the songs of home in their captivity!

But the simple Norman peasant-folk shall till the land no more,
For the vessels from Connecticut have anchored by the shore,
And many a sturdy Puritan, his mind with Scripture stored,
Rejoices he has found at last his "garden of the Lord."

There are families from Jolland, from Killingworth and Lyme;
Gentle mothers, tender maidens, and strong men in their prime;
There are lovers who have plighted their vows in Coventry,
And merry children, dancing o'er the vessels' decks in glee.

They come as came the Hebrews into their promised land,
Not as to wild New England's shores came first the Pilgrim band,
The Minas fields were fruitful, and the Gaspereau had borne
To seaward many a vessel with its freight of yellow corn.

They come with hearts as true as their manners blunt and cold,
To found a race of noble men of stern New England mould,

A race of earnest people, whom the coming years shall teach
The broader ways of knowledge and the gentler forms of speech.

They come as Puritans, but who shall say their hearts are blind
To the subtle charms of Nature and the love of humankind!
The Blue Laws of Connecticut have shaped their thought, 'tis true,
But human laws can never wholly Heaven's work undo.

And tears fall fast from many an eye long time unused to weep,
For o'er the fields lay whitening the bones of cows and sheep—
The faithful cows that used to feed upon the broad Grand Pré,
And with their tinkling bells come slowly home at close of day.

And where the Acadian village stood, its roofs o'ergrown with moss,
And the simple wooden chapel with its altar and its cross,
And where the forge of Basil sent its sparks towards the sky,
The lonely thistle blossomed and the fire-weed grew high.

The broken dykes have been rebuilt a century and more,
The cornfields stretch their furrows from Canard to Beauséjour,

Five generations have been reared beside the fair Grand
  Pré
Since the vessels from Connecticut came sailing up the
  Bay.

And now across the meadows, while the farmers reap and
  sow,
The engine shrieks its discords to the hills of Gaspereau ;
And ever onward to the sea, the restless Fundy tide
Bears playful pleasure yachts and busy trade ships side by
  side.

And the Puritan has yielded to the softening touch of time,
Like him who still content remained in Killingworth and
  Lyme ;
And graceful homes of prosperous men make all the land-
  scape fair,
And mellow creeds and ways of life are rooted everywhere.

And churches nestle lovingly on many a glad hillside,
And holy bells ring out their music in the eventide ;
But here and there, on untilled ground, apart from glebe or
  town,
Some lone surviving apple-tree stands leafless, bare and
  brown.

And many a traveller has found, as thoughtlessly he strayed,
Some long-forgotten cellar in the deepest thicket's shade,
And clumps of willows by the dykes, sweet-scented, fair and
  green,
That seemed to tell again the story of Evangeline.

AT THE CEDARS.

DUNCAN CAMPBELL SCOTT.

You had two girls, Baptiste,
   One is Virginie ——
Hold hard, Baptiste,
   Listen to me.

The whole drive was jammed,
In that bend at the Cedars ;
The rapids were dammed,
With the logs tight rammed
And crammed ; you might know
The devil had clinched them below.

We worked three days—not a budge !
" She's as tight as a wedge,
On the ledge."
Says our foreman,
" Mon Dieu ! boys, look here,
We must get this thing clear."
He cursed at the men,
And we went for it then,
With our cant-dogs arow ;
We just gave " he yo ho,"
When she gave a big shove
From above.

The gang yelled, and tore
For the shore;
The logs gave a grind,
Like a wolf's jaws behind,
And as quick as a flash,
With a shove and a crash,
They were down in a mash.
But I, and ten more,
All, but Isaàc Dufour,
Were ashore.

He leaped on a log in front of the rush,
And shot out from the bind,
While the jam roared behind;
As he floated along,
He balanced his pole,
And tossed us a song.

But, just as we cheered,
Up darted a log from the bottom,
Leaped thirty feet, fair and square,
And came down on his own.

He went up like a block,
With the shock;
And when he was there,
In the air,
Kissed his hand
To the land.
When he dropped,
My heart stopped,
For the first logs had caught him,

And crushed him;
When he rose in his place
There was blood on his face.

There were some girls, Baptiste,
Picking berries on the hillside,
Where the river curls, Baptiste,
You know,—on the still side;
One was down by the water,
She saw Isaàc
Fall back.

She didn't scream, Baptiste;
She launched her canoe,—
It did seem, Baptiste,
That she wanted to die too,
For before you could think,
The birch cracked like a shell
In that rush of hell,
And I saw them both sink——

Baptiste!!——

He had two girls,
One is Virginie;
What God calls the other,
Is not known to me.

ROSE LATULIPPE.

(A French-Canadian Legend.)

"Seranus."

The story or ballad of Ma'amselle Rose,
Surnamed Latulippe, as the story goes.

Seventeen hundred and forty, I'm told,
The winter was long and dark and cold.

The frosts were hard, and the snows were deep,
Lake and river were wrapped in sleep.

The days so short, and the food so dear,
At Christmas-time made sorry cheer.

The drifts piled high, and the roads left bare,
Made New Year's Day a slow affair.

Yet Nöel and New Year's as Paradise were
To Lent with its vision of fasting and prayer.

And lively girls like Ma'amselle Rose,
In her dark-blue skirt and her scarlet hose,

All over the country felt the same,
With their restless feet and their eyes of flame,

Striving to make the most of their fun
Ere Mardi-Gras should behold it done.

The day before has Ma'amselle Rose,
Standing on tip of her little toes,

Petitioned her father with modest glance
To let her give—a little dance.

And here we know just what came about,
For Rose, too cunning to beg or pout,

At once is accorded—so frank, so sweet,
Who could refuse her?—the wished-for treat.

Great were the preparations then,
The asking of girls, the finding of men;

For partners are rare in this wild new land,
Where girls grow as ripe and ready to hand

As in any tropical island or town
(Lying becalmed 'neath a starry crown,

Rich with clustering fruit and flower,
With gaudy creeper and glowing bower),

Though few are as fair as Ma'amselle Rose,
In her dark-blue skirt and her scarlet hose.

As for Mardi-Gras—*ciel!* What a day,
The wind it blew this way, that way,—

All ways at once, you would have said,
Till the snow was whirled far over the head,

And towards the evening a storm uprose
Which frightened all save Ma'amselle Rose.

The windows rattled—what did she care?
She was upstairs plaiting her long brown hair.

The watch-dog howled, but she did not hear,
She was hanging an earring in either ear;

And, thinking of onyx and filigree,
And musing, of these, which shall it be,

She hardly observes old Mère Marmette,
Who has come in a tremble to look for her pet.

Old Mère Marmette, with her withered face,
Under the cap with its starched white lace,

Just as one sees, in a cold March wood,
An old brown leaf with its snowy hood

Pushed back a little, that one may know
Will melt full soon the frost and the snow.

"O Rose, *chèrie*, did you not hear me call?
I fear for you, child, and I fear for us all!

'Tis the wildest night the Curé has known,
And to hear that good dog howl and moan

Is enough to drive one on to one's knees,
Though there, to be sure, we all might freeze

Such a night as this!"   "Why, how you talk!"
Says Ma'amselle Rose, as she stops in her walk

To drape her flowered Indian shawl,
Thinking it makes her look quite tall.

"*Mon Dieu!* you talk," says Ma'amselle Rose,
With her laughing eye and her petulant pose,

"As if we had not seen nights as dark,
Or had never heard old Pierrot bark!"

Then to the window quick she flies—
"Look, Mère Marmette, look, look, what eyes!

What a figure! what grace! what a noble steed!
Now, who can it be?   Now who, indeed?"

"*Ciel!* I know not! Some stranger bold—
The town is full of such, I'm told;

And Rose Latulippe, look you, do not forget
The last advice of your old Marmette,

Dance, dance, little Rose, dance all you like
Till the midnight hour from the clock shall strike;

But to dance after twelve to-night is a *sin*,
Whether with stranger or kith or kin.

And the Curé says—."   "I know, I know,
Good mother Marmette, you tease one so!"

And with in the mirror a flying peep,
Away to the dance flies Rose Latulippe.

Already the guests are gathering all
In the long low room and the narrow hall,

Where hang the rude sticks and the stout raquettes,
And the great fur coats in patches wet

With the falling snow, that still outside
Is whirled aloft in an eddying tide!

There are the tenants from west and east,
From north to south, all bidden to feast

On pâtés, and fowls, and ragoûts immense,
All at their generous Seigneur's expense.

And here is old Jacques, the blind habitant,
Who can sing you the whole of *Le Juif Errant*,

And play on his fiddle such tunes so gay,
As *Le vent frivolant*, and *J'ai tant dansé*.

And now all the Seigneury forms in a line,
Then the *Grande Promenade* with an air so fine,

One can hardly believe it is "homespun grey"
And "*bottes sauvages*" who are leading the way.

And next they engage in a merry round dance,
Imported, of course, direct from France,

Which must surely gladden our gay little Rose,
In her dark-blue skirt and her scarlet hose.

But where is Rose? In the window seat
She seems to have found a cosy retreat,

And with her the stranger, tall and bold,
From her window she saw alight in the cold.

His eyes flash fire, and his brow is stern,
Yet his words with a thrilling music burn.

He knows her name, he has called her Rose,
Till her cheek with a brighter crimson glows;

He takes her hand, he holds it fast,
And into the circle they slip at last.

Then who so happy as little Rose,
While her red cheek redder and redder grows!

Again and again they dance like this,
And once has the stranger stolen a kiss,

That has almost frightened our brave little Rose—
Like a shudder of fire through her frame it goes—

Till the girls all stand in a whispering ring,
And deem it the very strangest thing,

That Rose should have known this cavalier,
And finish by deeming it *very queer*,—

As girls in all ages somehow do
When they have not been courted too.

But Mère Marmette is troubled still,
She follows her pet about until

The stranger has thrown her a wicked glance,
That might have sent her into a trance,

Had she not quickly crossed herself,
And gone on washing and drying the delf;

For now, the feasting and supper all done,
Is the very height of Mardi-Gras fun.

Soon it will be the midnight hour,
When to dance or play will be out of the power

Of all good Catholics, young and old,
Who wish to remain in the Church's fold.

But so proud and happy is Ma'amselle Rose,
In her dark-blue skirt and her scarlet hose,

With the stranger's arm around her waist,
And her hand on his shoulder lightly placed,

That when he beseeches for one turn more,
She slips on his arm out through the door

Into the dim and narrow hall,
Where creep the long shadows up the wall.

And lo, in a minute or less, that same Rose,
Surnamed Latulippe, as the story goes,

In the stranger's arms is spinning around
To a strange and diabolical sound,

Which cometh from no known instrument,
As old blind Jacques, in his corner intent

On a big pork pâté, very well knows :
Alas for poor little Ma'amselle Rose !

For presently, louder than Rose quite likes,
The tall old clock on the staircase strikes.

"*Mon Dieu !*" she cries, "you must let me go ;
'Tis twelve and after !" "Nay, nay, not so !

I have you, and hold you, and fold you tight,
You are mine," says the stranger, "from to-night.

Dance, dance, little Rose, a word in your ear,
You are dancing with Lucifer, what dost thou fear?"

. . . . . .

The Curé ! the Curé !   He takes it all in,
From Rose, in her peril of horrible sin,

To Mother Marmette and the agèd Seigneur,
The whispering girls and the dazed voyageur.

And breathing a hurried and silent prayer,
And making the sign of the cross in the air,

And saying aloud, "The Church hath power
To save her children in such an hour."

He taketh the maiden by both her hands,
Whilst Lucifer dark and discomfited stands;

Snorting and stamping in fiendish ire,
He gains his steed with the eyes of fire,

Who gives one loud and terrible neigh,
And then in the darkness thunders away.

ADIEU TO FRANCE.

(From " De Roberval.")

JOHN HUNTER-DUVAR.

ADIEU to France! my latest glance
    Falls on thy port and bay, Rochelle;
The sunrays on the surf-curls dance,
    And spring time, like a pleasing spell,
Harmonious holds the land and sea;
    How long, alas, I cannot tell,
Ere this scene will come back to me!

The hours fleet fast and on the mast
    Soon shall I hoist the parting sail;
Soon will the outer bay be passed,
    And on the sky-line eyes will fail
To see a streak that means the land.
    On then! before the tides and gale,
Hope at the helm and in God's hand.

What doom I meet, my heart will beat
    For France, the debonnaire and gay;
She ever will in memory's seat
    Be present to my mind alway.
Hope whispers my return to you,
    Dear land! But should Fate say me nay,
And this should be my latest view,
    Fair France, loved France, *my* France, adieu.
    Salut à la France! Salut!

V.—SETTLEMENT LIFE.

V.—SETTLEMENT LIFE.

SONG OF THE AXE.

Isabella Valancey Crawford.

High grew the snow beneath the low-hung sky,
And all was silent in the wilderness;
In trance of stillness Nature heard her God
Rebuilding her spent fires, and veil'd her face
While the Great Worker brooded o'er His work.

"Bite deep and wide, O Axe, the tree,
What doth thy bold voice promise me?"

"I promise thee all joyous things,
That furnish forth the lives of kings!

"For ev'ry silver ringing blow,
Cities and palaces shall grow!"

"Bite deep and wide, O Axe, the tree,
Tell wider prophecies to me."

"When rust hath gnaw'd me deep and red,
A nation strong shall lift his head!

"His crown the very Heav'ns shall smite,
Æons shall build him in his might!"

"Bite deep and wide, O Axe, the tree;
Bright Seer, help on thy prophecy!"

Max smote the snow-weigh'd tree, and lightly laugh'd.
"See, friend," he cried to one that look'd and smil'd,
"My axe and I—we do immortal tasks—
We build up nations—this my axe and I!"

FIRE IN THE WOODS; OR, THE OLD SETTLER'S STORY.

ALEXANDER M'LACHLAN.

WHEN first I settled in the woods,
  There were no neighbours nigh,
And scarce a living thing, save wolves,
  And Molly dear, and I.
We had our troubles, ne'er a doubt,
  In those wild woods alone;
But then, sir, I was bound to have
  A homestead of my own.

This was my field of battle, and
  The forest was my foe,
And here I fought with ne'er a thought,
  Save "lay the giants low."
I toiled in hope—got in a crop,
  And Molly watched the cattle;
To keep those "breachy" steers away,
  She had a weary battle.

The devil's dears were those two steers,—
  Ah, they were born fence-breakers!
And sneaked all day, and watched their prey,
  Like any salt-sea wreckers.
And gradually, as day by day,
  My crop grew golden yellow,
My heart and hope grew with that crop,—
  I was a happy fellow.

That crop would set me on my feet,
   And I'd have done with care;
I built away, the live-long day,
   Such "castles in the air!"
I'd beaten poverty at last,
   And, like a little boy
When he has got his first new coat,
   I fairly leapt for joy.

I blush to think upon it yet
   That I was such a fool;
But young folks must learn wisdom, sir,
   In old Misfortune's school.
One fatal night, I thought the wind
   Gave some unwonted sighs,
Down through the swamp I heard a tramp
   Which took me by surprise.

Is this an earthquake drawing near?
   The forest moans and shivers;
And then I thought that I could hear
   The rushing of great rivers;
And while I looked and listened there,
   A herd of deer swept by,
As from a close pursuing foe
   They madly seemed to fly.

But still those sounds, in long deep bounds,
   Like warning heralds came,
And then I saw, with fear and awe,
   The heavens were all aflame.

I knew the woods must be on fire,
    I trembled for my crop;
As I stood there, in mute despair,
    It seem'd the death of hope.

On, on it came, a sea of flame,
    In long deep rolls of thunder,
And drawing near, it seem'd to tear
    The heavens and earth asunder!
How those waves snored, and raged, and roared,
    And reared in wild commotion!
On, on they came, like steeds of flame
    Upon a burning ocean.

How they did snort, in fiendish sport,
    As at the great elms dashing;
And how they tore 'mong hemlocks hoar,
    And through the pines went crashing;
While serpents wound the trunks around,
    Their eyes like demons gleaming,
And wrapped like thongs around the prongs,
    And to the crests went screaming!

Ah! how they swept, and madly leapt,
    From shrinking spire to spire,
'Mid hissing hail, and in their trail
    A waving lake of fire!
Anon some whirlwind, all aflame,
    Growled in the ocean under;
Then up would reel a fiery wheel
    And belch forth smoke and thunder!

And it was all that we could do
  To save ourselves by flight,
As from its track we madly flew,—
  Oh! 'twas an awful night!
When all was past, I stood aghast,
  My crop and shanty gone,
And blackened trunks 'mid smouldering chunks
  Like spectres looking on!

A host of skeletons they seemed,
  Amid the twilight dim,
All standing there in their despair,
  With faces gaunt and grim;
And I stood like a spectre too,
  A ruined man was I,
And nothing left,—what could I do
  But sit me down and cry?

A heavy heart indeed was mine,
  For I was ruined wholly,
And I gave way that awful day
  To moping melancholy;
I lost my all, in field and stall,
  And nevermore would thrive,
All save those steers,—the devil's dears
  Had saved themselves alive.

Nor would I have a farm to-day,
  Had it not been for Molly,
She cheered me up, and charmed away
  My moping melancholy;

She schemed and planned to keep the land,
   And cultivate it too;
And how I moiled, and strained, and toiled,
   And fought the battle through.

Yes, Molly played her part full well;
   She's plucky, every inch, sir!
It seemed to me the " deil himsel' "
   Could not make Molly flinch, sir;
We wrought and fought, until our star
   Got into the ascendant;
At troubles past we smile at last,
   And now we're independent!

BURNT LANDS.

Charles G. D. Roberts.

On other fields and other scenes the morn
   Laughs from her blue,—but not such scenes are these,
   Where comes no summer cheer of leaves and bees,
And no shade mitigates the day's white scorn.
These serious acres vast no groves adorn;
   But giant trunks, bleak shapes that once were trees,
   Tower naked, unassuaged of rain or breeze,
Their stern grey isolation grimly borne.

The months roll over them, and mark no change;
   But when spring stirs, or autumn stills, the years,
     Surely some phantom leafage rustles faint
Thro' their parched dreams,—some old-time notes ring strange,
   When in his slender treble, far and clear,
     Reiterates the rain-bird his complaint.

ACRES OF YOUR OWN.

Alexander M'Lachlan.

Here's the road to independence!
Who would bow and dance attendance?
Who, with e'er a spark of pride,
While the bush is wild and wide,
Would be but a hanger-on,
Begging favours from a throne,
While beneath yon smiling sun
Farms, by labour, can be won?
    Up! be stirring, be alive,
    Get upon a farm and thrive!
    He's a king upon a throne
    Who has acres of his own!

Tho' the cabin's walls are bare,
What of that, if love is there?
What although your back is bent,
There are none to hound for rent;
What tho' you must chip and plough,
None dare ask, "What doest thou?"
What though homespun be your coat,
Kings might envy you your lot!
    Up! be stirring, be alive,
    Get upon a farm and thrive!
    He's a king upon a throne
    Who has acres of his own!

Honest labour thou would'st shirk—
Thou art far too good to work?
Such gentility's a fudge,
True men all must toil and drudge.
Nature's true Nobility
Scorns such mock gentility;
Fools but talk of blood and birth—
Ev'ry man must prove his worth!
   Up! be stirring, be alive,
   Get upon a farm and thrive!
   He's a king upon a throne
   Who has acres of his own!

From "MALCOLM'S KATIE."

Isabella Valancey Crawford.

The Land had put his ruddy gauntlet on,
Of Harvest gold, to dash in Famine's face.
And like a vintage wain, deep dy'd with juice,
The great moon falter'd up the ripe, blue sky,
Drawn by silver stars—like oxen white
And horn'd with rays of light.—Down the rich land
Malcolm's small valleys, fill'd with grain, lip-high,
Lay round a lonely hill that fac'd the moon,
And caught the wine-kiss of its ruddy light.
A cusp'd dark wood caught in its black embrace
The valleys and the hill, and from its wilds,
Spic'd with dark cedars, cried the whip-poor-will.
A crane, belated, sail'd across the moon ;
On the bright, small, close link'd lakes green islets lay,
Dusk knots of tangl'd vines, or maple boughs,
Or tuft'd cedars, boss'd upon the waves.
The gay enamell'd children of the swamp
Roll'd a low bass to treble tinkling notes
Of little streamlets leaping from the woods.
Close to old Malcolm's mills, two wooden jaws
Bit up the water on a sloping floor ;
And here, in season, rush'd the great logs down,
To seek the river winding on its way.
In a green sheen, smooth as a Naiad's locks,
The waters roll'd between the shudd'ring jaws
Then on the river level roar'd and reel'd

In ivory-arm'd conflict with itself.
"Look down," said Alfred, " Katie, look and see
How that but pictures my mad heart to you;
It tears itself in fighting that mad love
You swear is hopeless—hopeless—is it so?"
"Ah, yes!" said Katie, "ask me not again."
"But Katie, Max is false; no word has come,
Nor any sign from him for many months,
And—he is happy with his Indian wife."
She lifted eyes fair as the fresh grey dawn
With all its dews and promises of sun.
"O, Alfred!—saver of my little life—
Look in my eyes and read them honestly."
He laugh'd till all the isles and forests laugh'd.
"O simple child! what may the forest flames
See in the woodland ponds but their own fires?
And have you, Katie, neither fears nor doubts?"
She, with the flow'r-soft pinkness of her palm
Cover'd her sudden tears, then quickly said:
"Fears,—never doubts, for true love never doubts."

From "MALCOLM'S KATIE."

Isabella Valancey Crawford.

The South Wind laid his moccasins aside,
Broke his gay calumet of flow'rs, and cast
His useless wampun, beaded with cool dews,
Far from him, northward; his long ruddy spear
Flung sunward, whence it came; and his soft locks
Of warm fine haze grew silver as the birch.
His wigwam of green leaves began to shake;
The crackling rice-beds scolded harsh like squaws;
The small ponds pouted up their silver lips;
The great lakes ey'd the mountains,—whisper'd "Ugh!
Are ye so tall, O chiefs?" "Not taller than
Our plumes can reach,"—and rose a little way,
As panthers stretch to try their velvet limbs,
And then retreat to purr and bide their time.
At morn the sharp breath of the night arose
From the wide prairies, in deep-struggling seas,
In rolling breakers, bursting to the sky;
In tumbling surfs, all yellow'd faintly thro'
With the low sun; in mad, conflicting crests,
Voic'd with low thunder from the hairy throats
Of the mist-buried herds; and for a man
To stand amid the cloudy roll and moil,
The phantom waters breaking overhead,
Shades of vex'd billows bursting on his breast,
Torn caves of mist wall'd with a sudden gold,

Reseal'd as swift as seen,—broad, shaggy fronts,
Fire-ey'd and tossing on impatient horns
The wave impalpable,—was but to think
A dream of phantoms held him as he stood!
The late, last thunders of the summer crash'd
Where shrieked great eagles, lords of naked cliffs;
The pulseless Forest, lock'd and interlock'd
So closely, bough with bough, and leaf with leaf,
So serf'd by its own wealth, that while from high
The moons of summer kiss'd its green-gloss'd locks,
And round its knees the merry West Wind danc'd,
And round its ring-compacted emerald
The South Wind crept on moccasins of flame,
And the red fingers of th' impatient Sun
Pluck'd at its outmost fringes,—its dim veins
Beat with no life; its deep and dusky heart,
In a deep trance of shadow, felt no throb
To such soft wooing answer! Thro' its dream
Brown rivers of deep waters sunless stole;
Small creeks sprang from its mosses, and amaz'd,
Like children in a wigwam curtain'd close
Above the great dead heart of some red chief,
Slipp'd on soft feet, swift stealing through the gloom,
Eager for light and for the frolic winds.
In this shrill Moon the scouts of winter ran
From the ice-belted north, and whistling shafts
Struck maple and struck sumach, and a blaze
Ran swift from leaf to leaf, from bough to bough;
Till round the forest flash'd a belt of flame,
And inward lick'd its tongues of red and gold
To the deep tranced inmost heart of all.
Rous'd the still heart,—but all too late, too late!
Too late the branches, welded fast with leaves,
Toss'd, loosen'd to the winds; too late the Sun

Pour'd his last vigour to the deep dark cells
Of the dim wood! The keen two-bladed Moon
Of Falling Leaves roll'd up on crested mists;
And where the lush rank boughs had foiled the Sun
In his red prime, her pale sharp fingers crept
After the wind, and felt about the moss,
And seem'd to pluck from shrinking twig and stem
The burning leaves,—while groaned the shudd'ring wood!

. . . .

The mighty morn strode laughing up the land,
And Max, the labourer and the lover, stood
Within the forest's edge, beside a tree,—
The mossy king of all the woody tribes,—
Whose clatt'ring branches rattl'd, shuddering,
As the bright axe cleav'd moon-like thro' the air,
Waking strange thunders, rousing echoes link'd
From the full lion-throated roar to sighs
Stealing on dove-wings thro' the distant aisles.
Swift fell the axe, swift follow'd roar on roar,
Till the bare woodland bellow'd in its rage
As the first-slain slow toppl'd to his fall.
"O King of Desolation, art thou dead?"
Thought Max, and laughing, heart and lips, leap'd on
The vast prone trunk. "And have I slain a King?
Above his ashes will I build my house;—
No slave beneath its pillars, but—a King!"

. . . . . .

It was not all his own, the axe-stirr'd waste.
In these new days men spread about the earth,
With wings at heel,—and now the settler hears,
While yet his axe rings on the primal woods,
The shrieks of engines rushing o'er the wastes,
Nor parts his kind to hew his fortunes out.

And as one drop glides down the unknown rock,
And the bright-threaded stream leaps after it
With welded billions, so the settler finds
His solitary footsteps beaten out
With the quick rush of panting human waves,
Upheav'd by throbs of angry poverty,
And driven by keen blasts of hunger, from
Their native strands,—so stern, so dark, so drear!
O, then, to see the troubl'd, groaning waves,
Throb down to peace in kindly valley beds,
Their turbid bosoms clearing in the calm
Of sun-ey'd Plenty,—till the stars and moon,
The blessed sun himself, has leave to shine
And laugh in their dark hearts! So shanties grew
Other than his amid the blacken'd stumps;
And children ran with little twigs and leaves,
And flung them, shouting, on the forest pyres,
Where burn'd the forest kings,—and in the glow
Paus'd men and women when the day was done.
There the lean weaver ground anew his axe,
Nor backward look'd upon the vanish'd loom,
But forward, to the ploughing of his fields,
And to the rose of Plenty in the cheeks
Of wife and children, nor heeded much the pangs
Of the rous'd muscles tuning to new work;
The pallid clerk look'd on his blister'd palms,
And sigh'd and smil'd, but girded up his loins,
And found new vigour as he felt new hope;
The lab'rer, with train'd muscles, grim and grave,
Look'd at the ground, and wonder'd in his soul
What joyous anguish stirr'd his darken'd heart
At the mere look of the familiar soil,
And found his answer in the words—"*Mine own!*"
Then came smooth-coated men, with eager eyes,

And talk'd of steamers on the cliff-bound lakes,
And iron tracks across the prairie lands,
And mills to crush the quartz of wealthy hills,
And mills to saw the great wide-arméd trees,
And mills to grind the singing stream of grain;
And with such busy clamour mingled still
The throbbing music of the bold, bright Axe,—
The steel tongue of the Present, and the wail
Of falling forest,—voices of the Past.
   Max, social-soul'd, and with his practised thews,
Was happy, boy-like, thinking much of Kate,
And speaking of her to the women-folk;
Who, mostly, happy in new honeymoons
Of hope themselves, were ready still to hear
The thrice-told tale of Katie's sunny eyes
And Katie's yellow hair, and household ways;
And heard so often, "There shall stand our home,
On yonder slope, with vines about the door!"
That the good wives were almost made to see
The snowy walls, deep porches, and the gleam
Of Katie's garments flitting through the rooms.—
And the black slope, all bristling with burn'd stumps,
Was known amongst them all as "Max's House."

   O Love builds on the azure sea,
     And Love builds on the golden sand;
  And Love builds on the rose-wing'd cloud,
     And sometimes Love builds on the land.

   O if Love builds on sparkling sea,
     And if Love builds on golden strand,

And if Love builds on rosy cloud,—
   To Love, these are the solid land.

O Love will build his lily walls,
   And Love his pearly roof will rear,
On cloud or land, or mist or sea,—
   Love's solid land is everywhere!

THE SECOND CONCESSION OF DEER.

William Wye Smith.

John Tompkins lived in a house of logs,
    On the second concession of Deer;
The front was logs, all straight and sound—
The gable was logs, all tight and round—
The roof was logs, so firmly bound—
And the floor was logs, all down to the ground—
    The warmest house in Deer.

And John, to my mind, was a log himself,
    On the second concession of Deer;—
None of your birch, with bark of buff—
Nor basswood, weak and watery stuff—
But he was hickory, true and tough,
And only his outside bark was rough;—
    The grandest old man in Deer!

But John had lived too long, it seemed,
    On the second concession of Deer!
For his daughters took up the governing rein,
With a fine brick house on the old domain,
All papered, and painted with satinwood stain,
Carpeted stairs, and best ingrain—
    The finest house in Deer!

Poor John, it was sad to see him now,
   On the second concession of Deer!
When he came in from his weary work,
To strip off his shoes like a heathen Turk,—
Or out of the *company's* way to lurk,
And ply in the *shanty* his knife and fork—
      The times were turned in Deer!

But John was hickory to the last,
   On the second concession of Deer!
And out on the river-end of his lot.
He laid up the logs in a cosy spot,
And self and wife took up with a cot,
And the great brick house might swim or not—
      He was done with the pride of Deer!

But the great house could not go at all,
   On the second concession of Deer;
'Twas *mother* no more, to wash or bake,
Nor *father* the gallants' steeds to take—
From the kitchen no more came pie nor cake—
And even their butter they'd first to make!—
      There were lessons to learn in Deer!

And the lesson they learned a year or more,
   On the second concession of Deer!
Then the girls got back the brave old pair—
And gave the mother her easy chair—
She told them how, and they did their share—
And John the honours once more did wear
      Of his own domain in Deer!

THE SCOT ABROAD.

Sir Daniel Wilson.

Oh, to be in Scotland now,
When the yellow autumn smiles
  So pleasantly on knoll and howe;
  Where from rugged cliff and heathy brow
Of each mountain height you look down defiles
  Golden with the harvest's glow.

Oh, to be in the kindly land,
Whether mellow autumn smiles or no.
  It is well if the joyous reaper stand
  Breast-deep in the yellow corn, sickle in hand;
But I care not though sleety east winds blow,
  So long as I tread its strand.

To be wandering there at will,
Be it sunshine or rain, or its winds that brace;
  To climb the old familiar hill;
  Of the storied landscape to drink my fill,
And look out on the grey old town at its base,
  And linger a dreamer still.

Ah! weep ye not for the dead,
The dear ones safe in their native earth;
  Their fond hands pillowed the narrow bed
  Where fresh gowans, starlike, above their head
Spangle the turf of each spring's new birth
  For the living, loving tread.

Ah! not for them : doubly blest,
Safely home, and past all weeping ;
   Hushed and still, there closely pressed
   Kith to kin on one mother's breast
All still, securely, trustfully sleeping,
   As in their first cradled rest.

Weep rather, ay, weep sore,
For him who departs to a distant land.
   There are pleasant homes on the far-off shore ;
   Friends too, but not like the friends of yore
That fondly, but vainly, beckoning stand
   For him who returns no more.

Oh, to lie in Scottish earth,
Lapped in the clods of its kindly soil ;
   Where the soaring laverock's song has birth
   In the welkin's blue ; and its heavenward mirth
Lends a rapture to earth-born toil—
   What matter! Death recks not the dearth.

THE FARMER'S DAUGHTER CHERRY.

Isabella Valancey Crawford.

The Farmer quit what he was at,
    The bee-hive he was smokin':
He tilted back his old straw hat—
    Says he, "Young man, you're jokin'!
O Lordy!—(Lord, forgive the swar)—
    Ain't ye a cheeky sinner?
Come, if I give my gal thar,
    Where would *you* find her dinner?

"Now, look at *me;* I settl'd down
    When I was one and twenty,
Me, and my axe and Mrs Brown,
    And stony land a plenty.
Look up thar! ain't that homestead fine?
    And look at them thar cattle:
I tell ye, since that early time
    I've fit a tidy battle.

"It kinder wrestles down a man
    To fight the stuns and mire:
But I sort of clutch'd to thet thar plan
    Of David and Goliar.

Want was the mean old Philistine
    That strutted round the clearin';
Of pebbles I'd a hansum line,
    And flung 'em, nothin' fearin'.

"They hit him square, right whar they ought;
    Them times I *had* an arm!
I lick'd the giant, and I bought
    A hundred acre farm.
My gal was born about them days,—
    I was mowin' in the medder,
When some one comes along and says,
    "The wife's gone thro' the shadder!"

"Times thought it was God's will she went—
    Times thought she work'd too slavin';
And for the young one that was sent,
    I took to steady savin'.
Jest cast your eye on that thar hill
    The sugar bush just tetches,
And round by Miller Jackson's mill,
    All round the farm stretches.

"'Aint got a mind to give that land
    To any snip-snap feller
That don't know loam from mud or sand,
    Or if corn's blue or yaller.
I've got a mind to keep her yet;—
    Last Fall, her cheese and butter
Took prizes; sakes! I can't forget
    Her pretty pride and flutter.

"Why, you be off! her little face
    For me's the only summer;
Her gone, 'twould be a queer old place,—
    The Lord smile down upon her!
All goes with her, the house and lot,—
    You'd like to get 'em, very!
I'll give 'em when this maple bears
    A bouncin' ripe-red cherry!"

The Farmer fixed his hat and specks,
    And pursed his lips together;
The maple wav'd above his head,
    Each gold and scarlet feather:
The Teacher's honest heart sank down,—
    How could his soul be merry?
He knew—though teaching in a town—
    No maple bears a cherry.

Soft blew the wind; the great old tree,
    Like Saul to David's singing,
Nodded its jewelled crown, as he
    Swayed to the harp-strings' ringing;
A something rosy—not a leaf—
    Stirs up amid the branches;
A miracle *may* send relief
    To lovers fond and anxious!

O rosy is the velvet cheek
    Of one 'mid red leaves sitting!
The sunbeams played at hide-and-seek
    With the needles in her knitting.

"O Pa!"—the farmer prick'd his ears;
  Whence came that voice so merry?
The Teacher's thoughtful visage clears,—
  "The maple bears a cherry!"

The Farmer tilted back his hat:
  "Well, gal—as I'm a human,
I'll always hold as doctrine that
  Thar's nothin' beats a woman!
When crown'd that maple is with snow,
  And Christmas bells are merry,
I'll let you have her, Jack—that's so!
  Be sure you're good to Cherry!"

A CANADIAN FOLK-SONG.

William Wilfred Campbell.

The doors are shut, the windows fast,
Outside the gust is driving past,
Outside the shivering ivy clings,
While on the hob the kettle sings,—
Margery, Margery, make the tea,
Singeth the kettle merrily.

The streams are hushed up where they flowed,
The ponds are frozen along the road,
The cattle are housed in shed and byre,
While singeth the kettle on the fire,—
Margery, Margery, make the tea,
Singeth the kettle merrily.

The fisherman on the bay in his boat
Shivers and buttons up his coat;
The traveller stops at the tavern door,
And the kettle answers the chimney's roar,—
Margery, Margery, make the tea,
Singeth the kettle merrily.

The firelight dances upon the wall,
Footsteps are heard in the outer hall,
And a kiss and a welcome that fill the room,
And the kettle sings in the glimmer and gloom,—
Margery, Margery, make the tea,
Singeth the kettle merrily.

THE PIONEERS.

William Douw Lighthall.

All you who in your acres broad
    Know Nature in its charms,
With pictured dale and fruitful sod,
    And herds on verdant farms,
Remember those who fought the trees
    And early hardships braved,
And so for us of all degrees
    All from the forest saved.

And you who stroll in leisured ease
    Along your city squares,
Thank those who there have fought the trees,
    And howling wolves and bears.
They met the proud woods in the face,
    Those gloomy shades and stern;
Withstood and conquered, and your race
    Supplants the pine and fern.

Where'er we look, their work is there;
    Now land and man are free:
On every side the view grows fair,
    And perfect yet shall be.
The credit's theirs, who all day fought
    The stubborn giant hosts;
We have but built on what they wrought,
    Theirs were the honour-posts.

Though plain their lives and rude their dress,
   No common men were they;
Some came for scorn of slavishness
   That ruled lands far away;
And some came here for conscience' sake,
   For Empire and the King;
And some for Love a home to make,
   Their dear ones here to bring.

First staunch men left, for Britain's name,
   The South's prosperity;
And Highland clans from Scotland came—
   Their sires had aye been free;
And England oft her legions gave
   To found a race of pluck;
And ever came the poor and brave
   And took the axe and struck.

Each hewed, and saw a dream-like home!—
   Hewed on—a settlement!
Struck hard—through mists the spire and dome
   The distance rim indent!
So honoured be they midst your ease,
   And give them well their due;
Honour to those who fought the trees,
   And made a land for you!

"ROUGH BEN."

(An Incident of the North-West Rebellion.)

KATE B. SIMPSON.

"STARVED to death," sounds kind o' hard, eh?
    But its true's I'm holdin' this 'ere knife,
An' thet woman dumped in the grave to-day
    Jes' *starved to death*, sir, 'pon me life.

Ye wonder how in a land o' plenty,
    Where even Injuns wallop around
With their belts a-loosened of overfeedin',
    Fur a poor white critter grub ain't found.

Well; y'see ther's starvin' deeper'n eatin',
    An' thet ther' woman we slid to-day
Ain't died o' want of bannock and bacon;
    No! but a durned sight crueller way.

S'posin' ye sit on the fence rail, mister,
    Fur I ain't agoin' to plow nor sow.
See them there oxen—"G'long, ye beggars!"—
    (The flies is eatin' their heads off) "Whoa!"

Wal', some three years ago'r—no matter—
    When this yer' place w'ant much to see,
Me and Bill Martin and Bo'lin's brother
    Cum' an' squatted, jest whar' we be.

An' by'm'bye other folks, hearin'
    Land in the great Nor'-West had riz,
Cum' pourin' in top o' one another,
    Each squatter claimin' a patch as his.

An' among the lot thet came tom-foolin'
    Was an English chap as had no right
To 'speriment with a Nor'-West winter:
    The fool bro't his sister an' took up a site.

Wal', he pitched his tent ('twas a waggon cover),
    An' thar' they lived all summer thro',
An' managed some way by winter cummin'
    To knock up a shack,—jest them thar' two.

They didn't mix with the folk'ses gen'l,
    But kep' in like, an' read fine books;
An' after a spell the lad got ailin',
    With worrit an' fretted an' pinched like looks.

An' soon he stopped goin' out to water
    The cattle (two head o' steer he'd brought),
I see'd the gal a-tryin' to lead 'em,
    An' I up an offers to guide the lot.

She wasn't proud with me, sir, never,
    Her little hand 'ud lay in my own
Like a grasshopper's wing on an acre of fallow;
    An' her eyes? my God! they'd melt a stone.

Wal', he pinched, an' coughed, an' nigher'n nigher,
   What *she*, cryin', called " Death's Angel " cum,
An' off he went like a snuff o' candle,
   A-takin' a homestead beyond the sun.

We plowed him in—when the sun was settin'—
   On'y us na'bours around, you see ;
An' we left him covered, an' her a-cryin'
   Sumthin' about " Come back to me ! "

An' the cattle died—I'm blest if they didn't,
   Contrairy like—an' the claim he owned,
An' plow'd an' sow'd 'th his two gent's handles,
   W'ant worth a durn when the Injuns cum.

I found her sittin' and kinder cryin'
   By the hill as whar we had rolled him in ;
Lookin' so peaked an' white an' ghost-like
   I felt like wishin' she wus with him.

Wal' ! the cattle wus dead, the ground w'ant ready,
   An' the Injuns threat'nin' every day,
To hang our wigs to the belts as held 'em
   Chock full o' *rot-gut*, spite o' Hudson's Bay.

All at onc't I see'd her trouble,
   'Twas want o' wimmin to cuddle her in,
An' the nearest petticoat, too, by thunder !
   Thirty miles off—an' *she lived by sin.*

An' sooner'n *that*, I'd—wal', I'd give her
   The best I owned, sir, my land an' life:
It was shelter, you see, an' Injuns comin'
   Jest frightened her into a-bein' *my* wife.

Oh! ye may star' and handle yer shooter,
   But, afore high God, she was dear to me;
I toted her back to my old log cabin,
   An' worshipp'd the groun' she walked—an' she?

Wal', she *tried* to smile an' call me "Benny,"
   When all my life I'd been called "Rough Ben,"
An' I carted her roun' like you'd a luckpenny;
   An' th' Injuns? oh, Gov'ment settled them.

Ye mind the troops cum marchin' up here,
   An' the garrison we wus all shut in,
An' among the red-coats thet came paradin'
   Was as handsom' a chap as ever I seen.

An' while we popped at the redskins' top-knots,
   Them soldier fellows as saved our lives
Cum marchin' into the wood-pile barracks,
   An' what did I see with my own two eyes,

But my little girl as I took under cover
   Grow red an' white and fall like a star,
When out from the file that peart-faced stranger
   Shot like an arrow to whar' she war?

Uncle, sez I, or cousin, mebbe,
    As went to school whar' she got them books?
But when *he kissed my gal* I " tumbled,"
    And shook like the leaves that shadder the brooks.

An' then an' thar' I larned her story
    (Too late! for now she was straight my wife),
For the parson sed 'twas for ever an' ever,
    An' her nor me couldn't alter our life.

Wal', that evenin' I left them airly
    (I'm a-goin' to lead a duck, I sed),
But I know'd that wench's heart was breakin',
    An' I gave her a chance to skip 'th the lad.

But she didn't—I found her thar',
    Mendin' an' bakin' the usual way;
But a look in her eyes ther' was like unto
    A threat'nin' rain on a summer day.

He'd gone an' left her to me as took her
    Jest fur to give her shelter and care
(I know'd 'f the brother 'd lived, she'd never
    A-looked at me, mor'n them oxen thar.)

Somehow she kinder wilted, an' never
    Ask'd no question, but sort o' still;
With thet look o' hunger a-eaten' her heart out—
    Thet's the kind o' starvin' is sure to kill.

I fetch'd the best of eatin' an' drinkin'
    As wus to be bo't in them times out here;
But the days went slidin' into winter,
    An' mister, with snow-fly an empty cheer.

She slid away from me sort o' quiet,
    W' never a moan, but "Benny, good-night!"
An' me an' the neighbors, as allus loved her,
    Tuck'd her beside him, jest out o' sight.

An' the soldier-lover thet left her starvin',
    I'd like to put a ball through his hide.
What? honor! another's!! *You loved her!!!*
    My God! *You're the chap for who she died!*

Gimme your hand, and here above her,
    Altho' she *wus* mine by a parson's swar',
I hain't no right to that gal's ashes,—
    She died for you, an' you left her thar'.

Me and me oxen's movin' westward,
    You and the gal's best left alone;
She'll rest contenteder; good-bye, I'm goin';
    The claim is your'n, go claim your own.

"THE INJUN."

(An Incident in the Minnesota Massacre of 1862.)

JOHN E. LOGAN—"BARRY DANE."

Ye say the Injuns all alike,
   A bad an' sneakin' lot;
An' a'int no use for nuthin',
   So the cusses should be shot?

Well, p'raps they is, an' p'raps they a'int,
   A lazy, wuthless crowd;
Yet durn my skin ef I kin see
   Why white men chin so loud.

Ef some o' them poor devils kicks
   'Cause things a'int run quite squar',
An' jumps an Indian agent's ranch,
   An' yanks his bloomin' har,

Thar' a'int no thought uv causes,
   An' no one cares a cuss,
It's jes' call out the Blue Coats
   An' give 'em somethin' wuss.

Thar's good an' bad in Injun,
   An' thar's good an' bad in White;
But, somehow, they is always wrong,
   An' we is allus right.

But I'm an old, old timer,
   I've jes' bin here so long,
That I kin mostly allus tell
   The ones that's right an' wrong.

An' ye can bet yer sainted life,
   When things get steamin' hot,
That some white fool or knave has lit
   The fire that biles the pot.

Ye think the Injun isn't squar'?
   That's jes' whar' ye mistake;
Fer bein' true to them that's true
   The Injun scoops the cake.

Fer I kin tell ye what occurr'd
   Way back in 'sixty-two,
When things in Minnesota State
   Wuz lookin' kinder blue.

The Sioux wuz up an' on the shoot
   A-slingin' round their lead,
An' scalpin' every mother's son
   That wuzn't bald or dead.

Thar' warn't a livin' Yankee—
   An' lots wuz brave an' bold—
That would have crossed them plains alone
   For a waggon load uv gold.

'Cause why?   We know'd the Guv'ment
   Wuzn't treatin' Injuns fair;
That's why they riz an' painted things,
   An' raised the settlers' hair.

That summer a fur-trader
   Came up from Montreal,
An' on his way to Garry
   He landed at Saint Paul.

An' all the guides an' hunters said
   He couldn't cross the plains,
Fer them thar' painted devils
   Wuz layin' low fer trains.

He only laffed, and said, he know'd
   The Injuns all his life,
An' he wuz goin' to mosey through
   An' take along his wife.

An' she, you bet, wuz plucky,
   An' said she'd go along,
Fer Injuns only went fer them
   As allus done 'em wrong.

Now I should smile, 'twuz riskey—
   An' all the fellers sed
The chances of their gettin' through
   Warn't wuth an ounce uv lead.

But sure's yer born they started,
  Right out the northern trail,
Aboard a praree schooner,
  With a Texan steer fer sail.

An' right a-top that creekin' cart,
  Upon the highest rack,
That trader nailed a bloomin' rag—
  An English Union Jack.

So thar' he'd gone an' done it,
  Es stubborn as a mule;
An' knowin' fellers said we'd seen
  The last of that damn fool.

They wuzn't long upon the trail
  Before a band of Reds
Got on their tracks, an' foller'd up,
  A-goin' to shave their heads.

But when they seen that little flag
  A-stickin on that cart,
They jes' said, "Hudson Bay. Go on.
  Good trader with good heart!"

An' when they struck the river,
  An' took to their canoe,
'Twuz that thar' bit uv culler
  That seen 'em safely through.

Fer thar' that cussed little rag
   Went floatin' through the State—
A-flappin' in the face of uv death,
   An' smilin' right at fate.

That wuz the way them 'tarnal fools
   Crossed them thar' blazin' plains,
An' floated down the windin' Red
   Through waves with bloody stains.

What give that flag its virtoo?
   What's thar' in red an' blue,
To make a man an' woman dar'
   What others daesn't do?

Jes' this—an' Injuns know'd it—
   That whar' them cullers flew,
The men that lived beneath them
   Wuz mostly straight an' true.

That when they made a bargain,
   'Twuz jes' as strong an' tight
As if 't were drawn on sheep-skin
   An' signed in black an' white.

That's how them Hudson traders done
   Fer mor'n two hundred year;
That's why that trader feller crossed
   Them plains without a fear.

An' jes' so long es white men
  Don't try some little game,
To euchre out the red man,
  So long he'll act the same.

But when the men beneath that flag
  Tries any monkey ways,
Then, good-bye, old time friendship,
  For the Injuns goin' ter raise.

But jes' believe me, onst for all,
  To them that treats him fair,
The Injun mostly allus wuz,
  And is, and will be, square.

SHAKESPEER AT DEAD-HOS' CRICK.

(A Romance of the North-West.)

JOHN E. LOGAN—"BARRY DANE."

It wuz way out west o' the praree,
    Whar the mountins begins to raise,
Pokin' holes in the snowy blankets
    Uv clouds that acrost 'em lays.

We wuz washin' down in the gulches,
    An' the culler wuz commin' well;
An' the fellers wuz crowdin' from east and west,
    Till the place wuz es full es hell.

I've bin in some dandy places,
    Whar things wuz a kinder hot;
But I never, in my hul mortal days,
    Struck so near to the real old spot.

It aint no use to tell yer
    The names uv the boys that wuz thar;
But they wuz the hardest crowd uv pills
    That ever wuz straight an' squar.

I mean thar warn't no skulkin',
    An' shootin' behind a plank;
Er plantin' a cold-deck up on a pal,
    An' standin' in with the bank.

Thar wuz plenty uv cold-decks planted,
    An' plenty uv shootin' done ;
But the fust wuz all in the way uv biz,
    An' the other wuz straight es a gun.

Ef thar wuz a row, it wuz up-an'-up,
    An' the fust that draw'd cud bark,
An' we gen'ly lifted the other chap,
    An' planted him out in the dark.

But I wuz agoin' to tell yer
    A thing that occurr'd one night,
Jes' to show yer the kinder chaps them wuz,
    In their trew an' proper light.

The biggist strikes wuz by Dead-Hos' Crick,
    An' thar, on a summer's day,
We wuz all at work, when we heerd the bells
    Uv the mule teams up the way.

In another minit they come in sight,
    A-joggin' down the road ;
An' I reckon it made them boys' eyes stare
    To see what they had fer load.

They was sittin' on trunks an' boxes,
    An' bumpin' right along,—
A gal, four men, an' a woman,
    An' the gal wuz singin' a song,

An' lookin' es pleased an' happy
  Es if ridin' a Pulman car;
An' when she ketched sight uv the boys' red shirts,
  She hollered out "Thar they are."

An' kep' on clappin' her little han's,
  An' laffin' jes' like a bird;
I guess them boys jes' thought that laff
  The sweetest they'd ever heard;

Fer they all quit work, an' foller'd
  Them teams, with their starin' eyes,
Till they turned the corner at Tucker's dam,
  An' then, I think, the skies

Grow'd jes' a trifle darker,—
  Though the sun wuz a kinder strong,—
An' I noticed that some o' the younger boys
  Didn't work, that day, so long.

When I come down from the gulch that night,
  I was tired an' wet an' mad;
Fer I hadn't got quite the pile o' dust
  That I thought I oughter had.

An' when I come to the "Dead-Hos' House"
  (The biggest bar in the town),
The boys wuz standin' in threes an' fours
  A-jawin' each other down.

I hadn't heerd no shootin',
  An' no one was givin' chin;
An' they all wuz lookin' so ser'us like,
  That I couldn't take it in.

So I jes' turns into the bar an' calls
  For a finger uv whisky white,
When the shinger sez, es he antied the stuff,
  "Er ye goin' to the show to-night?"

An' thar, hung up on the bar-room wall,
  An' printed in black an' yeller,
I reads the bill uv the play that night:
  It wuz Shakspeer's play "Otheller."

I knowed it es soon es I seen the name,
  Fer I'd seen it onct before
Way down in Frisco, in '62,
  The year I jined the war;

But the boys know'd nuthin' better
  Than the snidest nigger show,
Er a dance hall in behind a bar,
  With a faro bank below.

So them wuz the player people
  That passed us that very day,
An' I snicker'd to think how the boys would stare
  When they seen a fust-class play.

That hall wuz crowded fer standin' room,
    An' they scoop'd the dust, you bet;
An' lots uv the boys give double weight,
    Fer that laff wuz a-ringing' yet.

The boys wuz rather startled
    When they seen the nigger coon,
What jumped with the Gran' Dook's dater,
    But they took to him pooty soon.

But they wuz down on the feller
    What scoopt the nigger in,
An' hissed an' hollered so loud at last,
    Ye could hardly hear him chin.

I seen the boys wuz nervus,
    An' a kinder wicked too;
So I edges my way along to see
    Jes' what they wuz goin' to do.

The play wuz about nigh over,
    Es well es my mem'ry went,
An' the laffin' gal waz lyin' asleep
    In a bed like a little tent,

When in jumps the nigger feller,
    A-ravin', full's a goat,
An' chuekin' a bowie-knife on the floor,
    He grips her 'roun the throat.

She jes' gave one little holler;
    But that wuz mor'n enuff;
Fer I know'd them boys wuz nervus,
    An' wouldn't stand no guff.

It waz ping—ping—ping—es quick es flash,
    An' the nigger, he fell back dead;
An' the gal lep' up with a skeert white face,
    An' lifted his lifeless head,

An' called out "Father! father!"
    An' kiss'd his eyes an' lips;
But when she seen them stains uv blood
    A rednin' her finger tips,

She jes' riz up like a spectre,
    Es white an' es cold an' tall,
That a shiver went right through every man
    That wuz standin' in that hall.

Her voice wuz low, but every word
    Wuz es clear es a bell at night,
"May his red blood drip for ever
    Before his murderers' sight."

'Thar warn't no talk uv lynchin',
    For we wuzn't up to fun;
It wuz rough on her, but es for them,
    We know'd how the thing wuz done.

That night, es I rolled my blankets out,
    I found three bags uv dust;
An' I knowed the boys what put them thar,
    An' they know'd I'd keep their trust.

I sometimes wonder ef that thar gal
    Can ever sing er laff;
Perhaps she don't, an' perhaps she do;
    Fer she don't know only half.

She don't know that me an' another chap,
    In the early mornin' light,
Went up the road by Tucker's dam,
    Where fust she come in sight,

An' found three bodies lyin'
    A-restin' peacefully,
Jes' like three miners sleepin',
    Under a cedar tree.

She don't know that they luv'd her,
    An' I guess she never will;
But them wuz the kinder tuffs that worked
    In the gulch by Dead-Hos' Hill.

That's all I know uv Shakspeer,
    An' it's all I want to know;
I've never bin to a play since then,
    An' I never want to go.

They say he's made lots uv heros;
    Well, gimme my chice an' pick,
An' I'll take the three he made that night
    In the gulch at Dead-Hos' Crick.

VI.—SPORTS AND FREE LIFE.

VI.—SPORTS AND FREE LIFE.

THE WRAITH OF THE RED SWAN.*

Bliss Carman.

Why tarries the flash of his blade?
    At morning he sailed from me;
From the depth of our high beech glade,
    To the surge and the sea
I followed the gleam of his blade.

The cherries were flowering white,
    And the Nashwaak Islands flooded,
When the long Red Swan took flight;
    On a wind she scudded
With her gunwale buried from sight,
Till her sail drew down out of sight.

He shouted, "A northward track,
    Before the swallows have flown!"
And now the cherries are black,
    And the clover is brown,
And the Red Swan comes not back.

---

* "The Red Swan" is the author's favourite birch bark canoe, so named by him from the phenomenal rosiness of its bark material.

The stream-bends, hidden and shy,
    With their harvest of lilies are strewn ;
The gravel bars are all dry,
    And warm in the noon,
Where the rapids go swirling by,—
Go singing and rippling by.

Through many an evening gone,
    Where the roses drank the breeze,
When the pale slow moon outshone
    Through the slanting trees,
I dreamed of the long Red Swan.

How I should know that one
    Great stroke, and the time of the swing
Urging her on and on,
    Spring after spring,
Lifting the long Red Swan,
Lifting the long Red Swan !

How I should drink the foam—
    The far white lines from her swift
Keen bow, when, hurrying to come,
    With lift upon lift
The long Red Swan came home !

Here would I crouch down low,
    And watch the Red Swan from far,
A speck in the evening, grow
    To a flaming star
In the dusk as of ages ago,
In the dusk of ages ago.

I would lean, and with lips apart,
    See the streak of the Red Swan's fire
Glow dim at the twilight's heart,—
    Feel the core of desire
From the slumber of years upstart.

How soon should the day grow wan,
    And a wind from the south unfold,
Like the low beginning of dawn,—
    Grow steady and hold
In the race of the long Red Swan,
In the race of the long Red Swan!

How glad of their river once more
    Would the crimson wings unfurl,
And the long Red Swan, on the roar
    Of a whitecap swirl,
Steer in to the arms of her shore!

But the wind is the voice of a dirge!
    What wonder allures him, what care,
So far on the world's bleak verge?
    Why lingers he there,
By the sea and the desolate surge,
In the sound of the moan of the surge?

Last midnight the thunder rode
    With the lightning astride of the storm
Low down in the east, where glowed
    The fright of his form
On the ocean-wild rack he bestrode.

The hills were his ocean wan,
   And the white tree tops foamed high,
Lashed out of the night, whereon
     In a gust fled by
A wraith of the long Red Swan,
A wraith of the long Red Swan.

Her crimson bellying sail
   Was fleckered with brine and spume;
Its taut wet clew, through the veil
     Of the driving fume,
Was sheeted home on the gale.

The shoal of the fury of night
   Was a bank in the fog, wherethrough
Hissed the Red Swan in her flight;
     She shrilled as she flew,
A shriek from the seething white,
In the face of the world grown white.

She laboured not in the sea,
   Careened but a handbreadth over,
And, the gleam of her side laid free
     For the drift to cover,
Sped on to the dark in her lee.

Through crests of the hoarse tide swing,
   Clove sheer the sweep of her bow;
There was loosed the ice-roaring of Spring
     From the jaws of her prow,—
Of the long Red Swan full wing,
The long Red Swan full wing.

Where the rake of her gunwale dipped
  As the spent black waves ran aft,
In a hand for helm there was gripped
  The sheen of a haft,
Which sang in the furrows it ripped.

Then I knew and was glad, for what foam
  Could the rush of her speed o'erwhelm
If Louis and his Whitehaulm
  Were steersman and helm,
When the long Red Swan drave home,
When the long Red Swan drave home?

Yet ever the sweeping mist
  Was a veil to his face from me,
Though yearning I well half wist
  What his look might be
From the carven bend of his wrist.

Then a break, and the cloud was gone,
  And there was his set keen face
Afire with smouldering dawn
  In the joy of her race,
In the flight of the long Red Swan,
In the flight of the long Red Swan!

Though drenched in the spray-drift hoar,
  As of old it was ruddy and warm
Through the black hair, grizzled and frore,
  Whipped out on the storm;
Then "Louis!" I launched on the roar.

L

O'er night and the brawl of the stream
    The hail of my cry flew on;
He turned, with a smile supreme,
      And the long Red Swan
Grew dim as the wraith of a dream,
As the blown white wraith of a dream.

Look! Burnished and blue, what a sweep
    Of river outwinds in the sun;
What miles of shimmering deep,
      Where the hills grow one
With their shadow of summer and sleep!

I gaze from the cedar shade
    Day long, high over the beach,
And never a ripple is laid
      To the long blue reach,
Where faded the gleam of that blade,
The far gold flash of his blade.

I follow and dream and recall,
    Forget and remember and dream;
When the interval grass waves tall,
      I move in the gleam
Where his blade-beats glitter and fall.

Yet never my dream gets clear
    Of the whispering bodeful spell
The aspen shudders to hear,
      Yet hurries to tell,—
How the long Red Swan draws near,
How the long Red Swan draws near.

BIRCH AND PADDLE.

(*To Bliss Carman.*)

CHARLES G. D. ROBERTS.

FRIEND, those delights of ours
Under the sun and showers,—

Athrough the noonday blue
Sliding our light canoe,

Or floating, hushed, at eve,
When the dim pine-tops grieve!

What tonic days were they
Where shy streams dart and play,—

Where rivers brown and strong
As caribou bound along,

Break into angry parle
Where wildcat rapids snarl,

Subside, and like a snake
Wind to the quiet lake!

We've paddled furtively,
Where giant boughs hide the sky,—

Have stolen, and held our breath,
Thro' coverts still as death,—

Have left, with wing unstirred,
The brooding phœbe-bird,

And hardly caused a care
In the water-spider's lair.

For love of his clear pipe
We've flushed the zigzag snipe,—

Have chased in wilful mood
The wood-duck's flapping brood,—

Have spied the antlered moose
Cropping the young green spruce,

And watched him till betrayed
By the kingfisher's sharp tirade.

Quitting the bodeful shades,
We've run thro' sunnier glades,

And dropping craft and heed
Have bid our paddles speed.

Where the mad rapids chafe
We've shouted, steering safe,—

With sinew tense, nerve keen,
Shot thro' the roar, and seen,

With spirit wild as theirs,
The white waves leap like hares.

And then, with souls grown clear
In that sweet atmosphere,

With influences serene,
Our blood and brain washed clean,

We've idled down the breast
Of broadening tides at rest,

And marked the winds, the birds,
The bees, the far-off herds,

Into a drowsy tune
Transmute the afternoon.

So, Friend, with ears and eyes,
Which shy divinities

Have opened with their kiss,
We need no balm but this,—

A little space for dreams
On care-unsullied streams,—

'Mid task and toil, a space
To dream on Nature's face!

THE NOR'-WEST COURIER.

"Barry Dane"—John E. Logan.

I.

Up, my dogs, merrily,
  The morn sun is shining,
    Our path is uncertain,
    And night's sombre curtain
May drop on us, verily,
  Ere time for reclining;
  So, up, without whining,
You rascals, instanter,
    Come into your places
    There, stretch out your traces,
And off, at a canter.

II.

Up, my dogs, cheerily,
  The noon sun is glowing,
    Fast and still faster,
    Come, follow your master;
Or to-night we may wearily,
Tired and drearily,
    Travel, not knowing
    What moment disaster
May sweep in the storm-blast,
And over each form cast
  A shroud in its blowing.

III.

On, my dogs, steadily,
   Though keen winds are shifting
   The snowflakes, and drifting
     Them straight in your faces;
Come, answer me readily,
Not wildly nor headily,
   Plunging and lifting
     Your feet, keep your paces;
For yet we shall weather
The blizzard together,
     Though evil our case is.

IV.

Sleep, my dogs, cosily,
   Coiled near the fire,
   That higher and higher
Sheds its light rosily
Out o'er the snow and sky;
    Sleep in the ruddy glow,
    Letting Keewaydin blow
   Fierce in his ire.
    Sleep, my dogs, soundly;
    For to-morrow we roundly
Must buffet the foe.

THE HALL OF SHADOWS.

Alexander M'Lachlan.

The sun is up, and through the woods
    His golden rays are streaming;
The dismal swamp, and swale so damp,
    With faces bright are beaming.
And in the wind-fall, by the creek,
    We hear the partridge drumming;
And strange bright things, on airy wings,
    Are all around us humming.

The merry schoolboys, in the woods
    The chipmunk are pursuing;
And as he starts, with happy hearts
    They're after him hallooing.
The squirrel hears the urchins' cheers,—
    They never catch him lagging,—
And on the beech, beyond their reach,
    Hear how the fellow's bragging!

The redbird pauses in his song,—
    The face of man aye fearing,—
And flashes, like a flame, along
    The border of the clearing.

The humming-bird, above the flower,
   Is like a halo bending;
Or like the gleams we catch in dreams
   Of heavenly things descending.

And hear the bugle of the bee
   Among the tufted clover!
This day, like thee, I'll wander free,
   My little wild-wood rover!
Through groves of beech, and maple green,
   And pines of lofty stature;
By this lone creek, once more we'll seek
   The savage haunts of nature.

See there a noble troop of pines
   Have made a sudden sally,
And all, in straight, unbroken lines,
   Are rushing up the valley;
And round about the lonely spring
   They gather in a cluster,
Then off again, till on the plain,
   The great battalions muster.

And there the little evergreens
   Are clust'ring in the hollows,
And hazels green, with sumachs lean,
   Among the weeping willows;
Or sit in pride the creek beside,
   Or through the valley ramble;
Or up the height, in wild delight,
   Among the rocks they scramble.

And here a gorge, all reft and rent,
    With rocks in wild confusion,
As they were by the wood-gods sent
    To guard them from intrusion;
And gulfs, all yawning wild and wide,
    As if by earthquakes shattered;
And rocks that stand—a grizzly band!—
    By time and tempest battered.

Some great pines, blasted in their pride,
    Above the gorge are bending;
And rock-elms, from the other side
    Their mighty arms extending.
And midway down the dark descent
    One fearful hemlock's clinging;
His headlong fall he would prevent,
    And grapnels out he's flinging.

One ash has ventured to the brink,
    And tremblingly looks over
That awful steep, where shadows sleep,
    And mists at noonday hover.
But further in the woods we go,
    Through birch and maple valleys,
And elms that stand, like patriarchs grand,
    In long dark leafy alleys.

Away, away! from blue-eyed day,
    The sunshine and the meadows;
We find our way, at noon of day,
    Within the Hall of Shadows.

How like a great cathedral vast!
   With creeping vines roofed over,
While shadows dim, with faces grim,
   Far in the distance hover.

Among the old cathedral aisles,
   And Gothic arches bending,
And ever in the sacred pales
   The twilight gloom descending.
And let me turn where'er I will,
   A step is aye pursuing;
And there's an eye upon me still
   That's watching all I'm doing.

And in the centre there's a pool,
   And by that pool is sitting
A shape of Fear, with shadows drear
   For ever round her flitting.
Why is her face so full of woe?
   So hopeless and dejected?
Sees she but there, in her despair,
   Nought but herself reflected?

Is it the gloom within my heart,
   Or lingering superstition,
Which draws me here three times a year
   To this weird apparition?
I cannot tell what it may be!
   I only know that seeing
That shape of Fear, draws me more near
   The secret soul of being.

CANADIAN HUNTER'S SONG.

Susanna (Strickland) Moodie.

The Northern Lights are flashing
  On the rapids' restless flow;
But o'er the wild waves dashing
  Swift darts the light canoe,
    The merry hunters come,—
      "What cheer? What cheer?"
      "We've slain the deer!"
    "Hurrah! you're welcome home!"

The blithesome horn is sounding,
  And the woodsman's loud halloo;
And joyous steps are bounding
  To meet the birch canoe.
    "Hurrah! the hunters come!"
      And the woods ring out
      To their noisy shout,
    As they drag the dun deer home!

The hearth is brightly burning,
  The rustic board is spread;
To greet their sire returning
  The children leave their bed.
    With laugh and shout they come,
      That merry band,
      To grasp his hand,
    And bid him welcome home!

CANADIAN CAMPING SONG.

James D. Edgar.

I.

A WHITE tent pitched by a glassy lake,
    Well under a shady tree,
Or by rippling rills from the grand old hills,
    Is the summer home for me.
I fear no blaze of the noontide rays,
    For the woodland glades are mine,
The fragrant air, and that perfume rare,—
    The odour of forest pine.

II.

A cooling plunge at the break of day,
    A paddle, a row or sail;
With always a fish for a midday dish,
    And plenty of Adam's ale;
With rod or gun, or in hammock swung,
    We glide through the pleasant days;
When darkness falls on our canvas walls,
    We kindle the camp-fire's blaze.

III.

From out the gloom sails the silv'ry moon,
    O'er forests dark and still;
Now far, now near, ever sad and clear,
    Comes the plaint of whip-poor-will;
With song and laugh, and with kindly chaff,
    We startle the birds above;
Then rest tired heads on our cedar beds,
    And dream of the ones we love.

THE FISHERMAN'S LIGHT.

Mrs Susanna (Strickland) Moodie.

The air is still,—the night is dark,—
   No ripple breaks the dusky tide;
From isle to isle the fisher's bark,
   Like fairy meteor, seems to glide,—
Now lost in shade,—now flashing bright;
   On sleeping wave and forest tree,
We hail with joy the ruddy light,
Which far into the darksome night
   Shines red and cheerily.

With spear high poised, and steady hand,
   The centre of that fiery ray
Behold the skilful fisher stand,
   Prepared to strike the finny prey;
"Now, now!" the shaft has sped below,—
   Transfixed the shining prize we see;
On swiftly glides the birch canoe,
The woods send back the long halloo
   In echoes loud and cheerily!

Around yon bluff, whose pine crest hides
   The noisy rapids from our sight,
Another bark, another glides,—
   Red spirits of the murky night,—
The bosom of the silent stream
   With mimic stars is dotted free;
The tall woods lighten in the beam,
   Through darkness shining cheerily.

THE KINGFISHER.

Charles Lee Barnes.

When the summer's bright and tender sunbeams fill the land with splendour,
In his robes of blue and purple, and his crown of burnished green,
Lone the kingfisher sits dreaming, with his dark eyes brightly gleaming,
While he peers for chub and minnows in the water's limpid sheen.

And he haunts the river's edges, oozy flats, and rustling sedges,
Till he sees his prey beneath him in the waters clear and cool;
Then he quickly dashes nearer, and he breaks the polished mirror
That was floating on the surface of the creek or hidden pool.

Where the nodding reeds are growing, and the yellow lilies blowing,
In our little boat we slowly glide along the placid stream;
And we know he's coming after, by the music of his laughter,
And the flashing of his vesture in the sun's effulgent beam.

Well he knows the alder bushes, and the slender slimy rushes,
And the swamp, and pond, and lakelet, and the ice-cold crystal spring;
And the brooklet oft he follows through the meadows and the hollows,
Far within the shadowy woodland where the thrush and robin sing.

Oh, he well can flutter proudly, and he well can laugh so loudly,
For he lives within a castle where he never knows a care!
And his realm is on the water, and his wife a monarch's daughter;
And his title undisputed is on earth, or sea, or air!

THE CANOE.

Isabella Valancey Crawford.

My masters twain made me a bed
Of pine-boughs resinous, and cedar;
Of moss, a soft and gentle breeder
Of dreams of rest; and me they spread
With furry skins, and, laughing, said,—
" Now she shall lay her polish'd sides,
As queens do rest, or dainty brides,
Our slender lady of the tides!"

My masters twain their camp-soul lit,
Streamed incense from the hissing cones;
Large crimson flashes grew and whirl'd,
Thin golden nerves of sly light curl'd,
Round the dun camp, and rose faint zones
Half-way about each grim bole knit,
Like a shy child that would bedeck
With its soft clasp a Brave's red neck;
Yet sees the rough shield on his breast,
The awful plumes shake on his crest,
And fearful drops his timid face,
Nor dares complete the sweet embrace.

Into the hollow hearts of brakes
Yet warm from sides of does and stags,
Pass'd to the crisp dark river flags,
Sinuous, red as copper, snakes,—
Sharp-headed serpents, made of light,
Glided and hid themselves in night.

My masters twain the slaughter'd deer
Hung on fork'd boughs—with thongs of leather.
Bound were his stiff slim feet together,—
His eyes like dead stars cold and drear;
The wand'ring firelight drew near
And laid its wide palm, red and anxious,
On the sharp splendour of his branches;
On the white foam grown hard and sere
   On flank and shoulder,—
Death, hard as breast of granite boulder,—
     And under his lashes
Peer'd thro' his eyes at his life's grey ashes.

My masters twain sang songs that wove
(As they burnish'd hunting blade and rifle)
A golden thread with a cobweb trifle,—
Loud of the chase, and low of love.

"O Love! art thou a silver fish,
Shy of the line, and shy of gaffing?
Which we do follow, fierce, yet laughing,
Casting at thee the light-wing'd wish;
And at the last shall we bring thee up
From the crystal darkness under the cup
    Of lily folden,
    On broad leaves golden?

"O Love! art thou a silver deer?
Swift thy starr'd feet as wing of swallow,
While we with rushing arrows follow;
And at the last shall we draw near,
And over thy velvet neck cast thongs,
Woven of roses, of stars, of songs,—
    New chains all moulden
    Of rare gems olden?"

'They hung the slaughter'd fish like swords
On saplings slender,—like scimitars
Bright, and ruddied from new-dead wars,
Blaz'd in the light,—the scaly hordes.

They pil'd up boughs beneath the trees,
Of cedar-web and green fir tassel ;
Low did the pointed pine tops rustle,
The camp fire blush'd to the tender breeze.

The hounds laid dew-laps on the ground,
With needles of pine, sweet, soft, and rusty,—
Dream'd of the dead stag, stout and lusty ;
A bat by the red flames wove its round.

The darkness built its wigwam walls
Close round the camp, and at its curtain
Press'd shapes, thin woven and uncertain,
As white locks of tall waterfalls.

CANOE SONG,

Isabella Valancey Crawford.

O LIGHT canoe! where dost thou glide?
Below thee gleams no silver'd tide,
But concave heaven's chiefest pride.

Above thee burns eve's rosy bar;
Below thee throbs her darling star;
Deep 'neath thy keel her round worlds are!

Above, below, O sweet surprise!
To gladden happy lover's eyes;
No earth, no wave,—all jewelled skies!

THE WALKER OF THE SNOW.

Charles Dawson Shanly.

Speed on, speed on, good Master !
  The camp lies far away ;
We must cross the haunted valley
  Before the close of day.

How the snow-blight came upon me
  I will tell you as I go,—
The blight of the Shadow-hunter,
  Who walks the midnight snow.

To the cold December heaven
  Came the pale moon and the stars,
As the yellow sun was sinking
  Behind the purple bars.

The snow was deeply drifted
  Upon the ridges drear,
That lay for miles around me
  And the camp for which we steer.

Twas silent on the hill-side,
  And by the solemn wood
No sound of life or motion
  To break the solitude,

Save the wailing of the moose-bird
    With a plaintive note and low,
And the skating of the red leaf
    Upon the frozen snow.

And said I, "Though dark is falling,
    And far the camp must be,
Yet my heart it would be lightsome,
    If I had but company."

And then I sang and shouted,
    Keeping measure, as I sped,
To the harp-twang of the snow-shoe
    As it sprang beneath my tread;

Nor far into the valley
    Had I dipped upon my way,
When a dusky figure joined me,
    In a capuchon of grey,

Bending upon the snow-shoes,
    With a long and limber stride;
And I hailed the dusky stranger,
    As we travelled side by side.

But no token of communion
    Gave he by word or look,
And the fear-chill fell upon me
    At the crossing of the brook.

For I saw by the sickly moonlight,
   As I followed, bending low,
That the walking of the stranger
   Left no footmarks on the snow.

Then the fear-chill gathered o'er me,
   Like a shroud around me cast,
As I sank upon the snow-drift
   Where the Shadow-hunter passed.

And the otter-trappers found me,
   Before the break of day,
With my dark hair blanched and whitened
   As the snow in which I lay.

But they spoke not as they raised me;
   For they knew that in the night
I had seen the Shadow-hunter,
   And had withered in his blight.

Sancta Maria speed us!
   The sun is falling low,—
Before us lies the valley
   Of the Walker of the Snow!

IN THE SHADOWS.

E. Pauline Johnson.

I am sailing to the leeward,
Where the current runs to seaward
    Soft and slow,
Where the sleeping river grasses
Brush my paddle, as it passes
    To and fro.

On the shore the heat is shaking,
All the golden sands awaking
    In the cove;
And the quaint sandpiper, winging
O'er the shallows, ceases singing
    When I move.

On the water's idle pillow
Sleeps the overhanging willow,
    Green and cool;
Where the rushes lift their burnished
Oval heads from out the tarnished
    Emerald pool.

Where the very water slumbers,
Water lilies grow in numbers,
    Pure and pale ;
All the morning they have rested,
Amber crowned, and pearly crested—
    Fair and frail.

Here, impossible romances,
Indefinable sweet fancies,
    Cluster round ;
But they do not mar the sweetness
Of this still September fleetness
    With a sound.

I can scarce discern the meeting
Of the shore and stream retreating,
    So remote ;
For the laggard river, dozing,
Only wakes from its reposing
    Where I float.

Where the river mists are rising,
All the foliage baptising
    With their spray ;
There the sun gleams far and faintly,
With a shadow soft and saintly
    In its ray.

And the perfume of some burning
Far-off brushwood, ever turning
    To exhale ;

All its smoky fragrance, dying,
In the arms of evening lying,
    Where I sail.

My canoe is growing lazy,
In the atmosphere so hazy,
    While I dream ;
Half in slumber I am guiding
Eastward, indistinctly gliding
    Down the stream.

ON THE CREEK.

C‍HARLES G. D. ROBERTS.

DEAR Heart, the noisy strife
   And bitter carpings cease;
Here is the lap of life,
   Here are the lips of peace.

Afar from stir of streets,
   The city's dust and din,
What healing silence meets
   And greets us gliding in!

Our light birch silent floats;
   Soundless the paddle dips;
Yon sunbeam thick with motes
   Athro' the leafage slips.

To light the iris wings
   Of dragon-flies alit
On lily-leaves, and things
   Of gauze that float and flit.

Above the water's brink
   Hush'd winds make summer riot;
Our thirsty spirits drink
   Deep, deep, the summer quiet.

We slip the world's gray husk,
    Emerge, and spread new plumes
In sunbeam-fretted dusk,
    Thro' populous golden glooms.

Like thistledown we slide,
    Two disembodied dreams,—
With spirits, alert, wide-eyed,
    Explore the perfume-streams.

For scents of various grass
    Stream down the veering breeze;
Warm puffs of honey pass
    From flowering linden-trees;

And fragrant gusts of gum
    From clammy balm-tree buds,
With fern-brake odours, come
    From intricate solitudes.

The elm-trees are astir
    With flirt of idle wings;
Hark to the grackles' chirr
    Whene'er the elm-bough swings!

From off yon ash-limb sere,
    Out thrust amid green branches,
Keen like an azure spear
    A kingfisher down launches.

Far up the creek his calls
   And lessening laugh retreat;
Again the silence falls,
   And soft the green hours fleet.

They fleet with drowsy hum
   Of insects on the wing :—
We sigh—the end must come!
   We taste our pleasure's sting.

No more, then, need we try
   The rapture to regain;
We feel our day slip by,
   And cling to it in vain.

But, Dear, keep thou in mind
   These moments swift and sweet!
Their memory thou shalt find
   Illume the common street.

And thro' the dust and din,
   Smiling, thy heart shall hear
Quiet waters lapsing thin,
   And locusts shrilling clear.

THE RAPID.

Charles Sangster.

All peacefully gliding,
    The waters dividing,
The indolent bátteau moved slowly along,
    The rowers, light-hearted,
    From sorrow long parted,
Beguiled the dull moments with laughter and song:
    "Hurrah for the Rapid! that merrily, merrily,
    Gambols and leaps on its tortuous way;
    Soon we will enter it, cheerily, cheerily,
    Pleased with its freshness, and wet with its spray."

    More swiftly careering,
    The wild Rapid nearing,
They dash down the stream like a terrified steed;
    The surges delight them,
    No terrors affright them,
Their voices keep pace with their quickening speed:
    "Hurrah for the Rapid! that merrily, merrily
    Shivers its arrows against us in play;
    Now we have entered it cheerily, cheerily,
    Our spirits as light as its feathery spray."

Fast downward they're dashing,
Each fearless eye flashing,
Though danger awaits them on every side;
Yon rock—see it frowning!
They strike—they are drowning!
But downward they speed with the merciless tide:
No voice cheers the Rapid, that angrily, angrily
Shivers their bark in its maddening play;
Gaily they entered it—heedlessly, recklessly,
Mingling their lives with its treacherous spray!

THE WINTER SPIRIT.

(*The Origin of the Ice Palace.*)

Helen Fairbairn.

The winter night was full of wind and storm,
   The Christian's festal season close at hand,
With frosty, glistening, snow-besprinkled form,
   The Winter Spirit roamed throughout the land.

Beneath, his flying footsteps froze the ground;
   And with his garments' rustling fell the snow;
His lightest touch made icicles abound;
   His breath, as when the keenest north winds blow.

He paused above the river, dull and gray,
   Turbid and chafing with a restless pain,
And soon in icy quietness it lay,
   Bound, bank to bank, within his Arctic chain.

He roamed along the leafless mountain side,
   And whereso'er he found a solemn spruce,
Or stately fir, or hemlock rich and wide,
   He paused, and shook his gleaming garments loose.

And from their ample folds came softly down
   A cloud of snowflakes like a starry mist,
That gave each evergreen a spotless crown,
   For faithful keeping of its winter tryst.

Amid the storm-tossed pines his voice was heard,
   A wild soft sighing in their depths profound,
Like notes of some strange ghostly winter bird,
   Whose white wings fluttered with a muffled sound.

To lighter, more fantastic work, anon
   He turned, and, with a skill that art surpassed,
Drew strange designs and fairy forms upon
   The casements closed against the winter blast.

At one he longer paused than all the rest,
   And whispered in a frosty monotone,
"This work shall be my rarest and my best,
   Rarest and best is she for whom 'tis done."

He knew the girlish face with heavenly eyes,
   The fair sweet face whose eyes, so deep and blue,
Would kindle to their depths with glad surprise,
   At sight of what his frosty skill could do.

Without a sound the wintry work was done,
   With wondrous haste the icy picture grew,
And when at last the crowning point was won,
   From ragged clouds the moon burst forth to view.

With crystal towers and glittering battlement,
   A pictured castle in the moonlight gleamed,
In silver set, a gem of Occident,
   Like clustered starry jewels brightly beamed.

Now, when the Winter Spirit's fair design,
　　In beauty rare, complete before him lay,
"Farewell," he sighed, "the frosty gem be thine!
　　While I in storm and darkness fly away."

Once more to darkling storm the night was given,
　　Once more the wild wind whistled through the town,
Like myriad blessings sent to earth from Heaven,
　　The air was thick with snowflakes coming down.

SNOWSHOEING SONG.

Arthur Weir.

Hilloo, hilloo, hilloo, hilloo !
Gather, gather ye men in white ;
The winds blow keenly, the moon is bright,
The sparkling snow lies firm and white ;
Tie on the shoes, no time to lose,
We must be over the hill to-night.

Hilloo, hilloo, hilloo, hilloo !
Swiftly in single file we go,
The city is soon left far below,
Its countless lights like diamonds glow ;
And as we climb, we hear the chime
Of church bells stealing o'er the snow.

Hilloo, hilloo, hilloo, hilloo !
Like winding-sheet about the dead,
O'er hill and dale the snow is spread,
And silences our hurried tread ;
The pines bend low, and to and fro
The maples toss their boughs o'erhead.

Hilloo, hilloo, hilloo, hilloo !
We laugh to scorn the angry blast,
The mountain top is gained and past.
Descent begins, 'tis ever fast—
One short quick run, and toil is done,
We reach the welcome inn at last.

Shake off, shake off the clinging snow;
Unloose the shoe, the sash untie;
Fling tuque and mittens lightly by;
The chimney fire is blazing high,
And, richly stored, the festive board
Awaits the merry company.

Remove the fragments of the feast!
The steaming coffee, waiter, bring.
Now tell the tale, the chorus sing,
And let the laughter loudly ring;
Here's to our host, drink down the toast,
Then up! for time is on the wing.

Hilloo, hilloo, hilloo, hilloo!
The moon is sinking out of sight,
Across the sky dark clouds take flight,
And dimly looms the mountain height;
Tie on the shoes, no time to lose,
We must be home again to-night.

SKATING.

John Lowry Stuart.

Come to the moonlit lake,
   Where rays of silver bright
Their slender arrows break
   On the glassy pavement bright !
For hearts are gay, and joy is rife ;
And youth and beauty, love and life,
   Are out on the ice to-night.

Not in the crowded hall,
   Where earth-lit tapers gleam,
We'll hold our festival,
   But out on the frozen stream ;
No dull faint air, or heated room,
Shall rob thy cheek of beauty's bloom,
   Thine eye of its sparkling beam.

Bright is the fairy scene ;
   The ringing steels resound ;
And gleams the glowing sheen
   To feet of beauty bound ;
And health, with rosy pencil, seeks
To paint the blush on beauty's cheeks,
   And the echoing laugh rings round.

Ne'er such a pavement spread
  Glittered in marble halls;
Ne'er gleamed such lamps o'erhead
  To gladden their carnivals;
The circling hills, whose tree-clad brows
Upbear the dome on cornice boughs,
  Are our lofty palace walls.

Whence foaming waters roar
  That winter could not bind
(Their brothers called on Huron's shore,
  And they would not stay confined).
As free and gay, and wild as they,
We'll speed e'en to the mystic way
  Of the isle with cedars lined.

Earth and its cares forgot,
  Our hearts we'll then reveal;
And spurn each colder thought,
  As the ice the flashing steel.
Who, 'neath the sway of Luna's ray,
Love's sweet commands could disobey,
  Or its brighter beams conceal?

THE WINTER CARNIVAL.

JOHN READE.

I.

WE fear thee not, O Winter!
  Though stern thy face and grim;
Though vast thy strength to crush and rend
  Our bodies, limb from limb.
On Scandinavian mountains,
  On stormy northern seas,
Our fathers braved thy wrath of yore,
And heeded not thy sullen roar
  Amid the bending trees.

II.

They loved thy gusty music,
  And from full chests and throats
Rivalled, in happy recklessness,
  The Storm-King's boisterous notes;
They made thee now their playmate,
  They made thee now their slave;
Thy frost-built roads for them to ride,
With fair-haired lemans side by side,
  Above the rushing wave.

III.

Over the snows they trod apace,
    Adown the drifts they sped;
They met thy fury face to face,
    And all thy shapes of dread.
And though thy wild sport sometimes left
    Sights that were sad to see,
Health, beauty, courage, giant thews,
Well braced by salutary use,
    Came of their fight with thee.

IV.

Such were the hardy Northmen,
    By land and sea renowned;
Such gifts they brought where'er their feet
    New resting-places found.
Such gifts to France, to England,
    To Scotia's shores, they brought;
And many a thrice-encircled rath
Still shows on Erin's hills the path
    By which they came and fought.

V.

Such gifts to this new Northland
    All we of Northern blood,
Tempered by other gentler strains,
    Brought with us o'er the flood
To this broad land, where Winter
    Is Summer's best ally;
And with his robe, so soft and white,
Her tender children shields from blight
    Beneath the brumal sky.

VI.

Ages ago, in battle,
　We fairly won the day ;
And, though we still may call him king,
　He bears disputed sway.
We make his mighty forces
　Obedient to our will ;
Beneath our hands his ice and snow
To wondrous shapes of beauty grow,
　Triumphs of art and skill.

VII.

Out of his frozen torrents
　We carve the glittering mass,
And raise a dome, whose fairy charms
　Old Greece could not surpass.
Upon its fair proportions
　Men gaze in silent awe,
As those who in a dream behold
The streets of pearl and gates of gold
　Which John in Patmos saw.

VIII.

And who that loveth Nature
　Feels not his heart aglow
In presence of our winter woods,
　Tinselled with ice and snow !
'Twas just such woodland visions,
　With moonlight glimmering down,
Gave pious hearts the rapt desire
To raise the grand cathedral spire
　In many a feudal town.

IX.

O Winter! if thy anger
    Affrights the poor of heart,
Best humoured and most cheery
    Of playfellows thou art.
E'en Summer cannot rival
    Thy many-sided glee;
For young and old, for maid and boy,
Thou hast a store of healthy joy
    To bind our hearts to thee.

X.

Now, in thy festal season,
    We celebrate thy praise;
For our Canadian Carnival
    Send us auspicious days.
All ills that flesh is heir to
    Be banished from our train;
And may the pleasures of the scene
Keep in each heart its memory green
    Until we meet again!

THE SPIRIT OF THE CARNIVAL.

"Fleurange."

Onward! the people shouted,
    Let merriment be king!
Fling out your crimson banners,
    Your fragrant roses fling;
Fly faster, maddened horses,
    Through din of trumpets loud;
Crash down the dusty Corso,
    Cheered by the frantic crowd!

Sweep onward, gaudy pageant,
    In wild uproarious glee;
Dark goblins, elves fantastic,
    Strange shapes from land and sea;
Wave high the flaming torches!
    Clang loud the brazen bells!
The great enchanter, Carnival,
    Hath Rome within his spells.

Weary of heat and clamour
    A young Italian lay
Beneath the ilex shadow,
    When closed the burning day;
Faint as his faded garlands
    His drowsy eyelids seem,—
The Spirit of the Carnival
    Comes to him in his dream:

"Awake, oh youth, arouse thee,
  And follow where I lead;
I know thy ardent nature,
  Thy soul is strong indeed;
It loathes the gilded folly,
  The childish pranks and play,
The weak excited populace
  Wild with a holiday.

"And here, indeed, *I* linger
  To laugh and jest awhile;
But as a king may pause to greet
  A wilful beauty's smile,
Yet guardeth ever in his heart
  An image pure and fair,
And hastening homeward to his queen
  Finds life and love are there,—

"So follow, follow where I lead,
  Across the western sea,
Where thou shalt learn thy manhood might,
  From farce and folly free."
The youth sighed in his sleep,—his soul
  Obeyed the strange command,—
The great enchanter, Carnival,
  Still led him by the hand.

And soon the groves of olives
  Are fading from his sight,
The dim blue shores of Italy
  Melt into deeper night;

Fresh draughts of light inhaling,
   Where northern breezes blow,
Vast regions lie before him
   All white with frost and snow.

"Behold!" th' enchanter whispered,
   "Gaze on, and thou shalt see
Why Canada, my kingdom,
   My chosen home should be;
Here all my sports and merriment,
   To noble ends allied,
Teach manly strength and fortitude,
   A nation's truest pride.

See! like a jewel burning
   Upon a silver band,
Fair Montreal is shining
   Upon the snowy land;
Its stately mansions glowing
   With hospitable cheer,
The merry sleigh-bells ringing
   Re-echo far and near."

The city keeps high festival,
   The icy air, like wine,
Quickens each pace to bounding glee,
   Bright eyes with gladness shine.
With merry laughter following fast
   From countless summits high—
Like flashing arrows from a bow,
   The swift toboggans fly!

Then, as the youth gazed on, he sees
    A fairy palace rise,
Seeming of mist and moonbeams born,
    Or poet's fantasies ;
Within it throbs a soul of fire,
    That glows through every part,
Softly as shines the light of love
    Within a maiden's heart.

A moment, and the magic scene
    Grows strangely bright as day,
For, see! an army storms the fort,
    Oh, guard it while ye may!
Hurrah! the rockets leap aloft,
    The waving torches flare—
A rainbow shower of golden stars
    Breaks into glory there!

And far on yonder mountain side
    A chain of living light!
Each link a stalwart snow-shoer
    With torch that blazes bright,—
A jewelled order proudly flung
    On old Mount Royal's breast,
A starry circlet from the skies
    Dropt on his snowy crest.

Then lights and city faded,
    And the dreamer woke at last,
O'er him hung the old-world languor,
    Faint with mem'ries of the past;

But his spirit glowed within him,
   And he left the careless throng,
Lived and wrought in earnest fashion,
   Toil or pastime, brave and strong.

So may faint hearts ever gather
   From Canadian sports and play,
Something of the force that, working,
   Hewed the forests, cleared the way:
For the tree shows fairer blossom
   Where the roots are wide and deep,
And the pleasure turns to glory
   When the victors revel keep;

And the Carnival no longer wears
   The bells as Fancy's Fool,—
He is a King, whose subjects free,
   Are loyal to his rule;
Each merry heart beats true and fast,
   And knows, amid his play,
To-morrow he can meet the foe
   Who tries his strength to-day.

Then guard it well, fair Canada,
   Thy festival of snow,
Proving old Winter, stern and grim,
   Thy friend and not thy foe;
And may thy sons build steadfastly
   A nation great and free,
Whose vast foundations stretch abroad
   From mighty sea to sea.

Long may Canadians bear thy name
　　In unity and pride,—
Their progress, like thy rushing streams,
　　Roll a resistless tide ;
Their hearts be tender as the flowers
　　That o'er thy valleys grow ;
Their courage rugged as thy frost
　　When winds of winter blow ;
Their honour brilliant as thy skies,
　　And stainless as thy snow !

THE FOOTBALL MATCH.

I.

O WILD kaleidoscopic panorama of jaculatory arms and legs.
The twisting, twining, turning, tussling, throwing, thrusting, throttling, tugging, thumping, the tightening thews.
The tearing of tangled trousers, the jut of giant calves protuberant.
The wriggleness, the wormlike, snaky movement and life of it;
The insertion of strong men in the mud, the wallowing, the stamping with thick shoes;
The rowdyism, and *élan*, the slugging and scraping, the cowboy Homeric ferocity.
(Ah, well kicked, red legs! Hit her up, you muddy little hero, you!)
The bleeding noses, the shins, the knuckles abraded:
That's the way to make men! Go it, you border ruffians, I like ye.

II.

Only two sorts of men are any good, I wouldn't give a cotton hat for no other—
The Poet and the Plug Ugly. They are picturesque. O, but ain't they?
These college chaps, these bouncing fighters from M'Gill and Toronto,
Are all right. I must have a fighter, a bully, somewhat of a desperado;
Of course, I prefer them raw, uneducated, unspoiled by book rot;

I reckon these young fellows, these howling Kickapoos of
    the puddle, these boys,
Have been uneducated to an undemocratic and feudal-aris-
    tocratic extent;
Lord! how they can kick, though! Another man slugged
    there!

III.

Unnumbered festoons of pretty Canadian girls, I salute you;
Howl away, you non-playing encouragers of the kickers!
Rah, Rah, Rah, Rah, Rah, Rah, M'Gill!
Rah, Rah, Rah, Sis. Boom, Toronto! Lusty-throated give it!
O, wild, tumultuous, multitudinous shindy. Well, this *is*
    the boss;
This is worth coming twenty miles to see. Personally, I
    haven't had so much fun since I was vaccinated.
I wonder if the Doctor spectates it. Here is something
    beyond his plesiosauri.
Purely physical glow and exultation this of abundantest
    muscle:
I wish John Sullivan were here.

IV.

O, the kicking, stamping, punching, the gore and the glory
    of battle!
Kick, kick, kick, kick, kick, kick. *Will* you kick!
You kickers, scoop up the mud, steam plough the field,
Fall all over yourselves, squirm out! Look at that pile-
    driver of a full-back there!
Run, leg it, hang on to the ball; say, you big chump, don't
    you kill that little chap
When you are about it.
Well, I'd like to know what a touch down is, then? Draw?
Where's your draw?
Yer lie!

VII.—THE SPIRIT OF CANADIAN HISTORY.

VII.—THE SPIRIT OF CANADIAN HISTORY.

JACQUES CARTIER.

Hon. Thomas D'Arcy M'Gee.

In the seaport of St Malo, 'twas a smiling morn in May,
When the Commodore Jacques Cartier to the westward sailed away;
In the crowded old Cathedral, all the town were on their knees,
For the safe return of kinsmen from the undiscovered seas;
And every autumn blast that swept o'er pinnacle and pier,
Filled many hearts with sorrow, and gentle hearts with fear.

A year passed o'er St Malo—again came round the day,
When the Commodore Jacques Cartier to the westward sailed away;
But no tidings from the absent had come the way they went,
And tearful were the vigils that many a maiden spent;
And manly hearts were filled with gloom, and gentle hearts with fear,
When no tidings came from Cartier at the closing of the year.

But the earth is as the Future, it hath its hidden side,
And the Captain of St Malo was rejoicing in his pride ;
In the forests of the North—while his townsmen mourned his loss—
He was rearing on Mount Royal the *fleur-de-lis* and cross ;
And when two months were over, and added to the year,
St Malo hailed him home again, cheer answering to cheer.

He told them of a region, hard, iron-bound, and cold,
Nor seas of pearl abounded, nor mines of shining gold ;
Where the wind from Thulé freezes the word upon the lip,
And the ice in spring comes sailing athwart the early ship ;
He told them of the frozen scene, until they thrilled with fear,
And piled fresh fuel on the hearth to make them better cheer.

But when he chang'd the strain,—he told how soon is cast
In early Spring the fetters that hold the waters fast ;
How the Winter causeway, broken, is drifted out to sea,
And the rills and rivers sing with pride the anthem of the free ;
How the magic wand of Summer clad the landscape to his eyes,
Like the dry bones of the just when they wake in Paradise.

He told them of the Algonquin braves—the hunters of the wild ;
Of how the Indian mother in the forest rocks her child ;
Of how, poor souls, they fancy in every living thing
A spirit good or evil, that claims their worshipping ;

Of how they brought their sick and maim'd for him to
    breathe upon ;
And of the wonders wrought for them, thro' the Gospel of
    St John.

He told them of the river, whose mighty current gave
Its freshness for a hundred leagues to ocean's briny wave ;
He told them of the glorious scene presented to his sight,
What time he reared the cross and crown on Hochelaga's
    height ;
And of the fortress cliff, that keeps of Canada the key ;—
And they welcomed back Jacques Cartier from the perils
    over sea.

L'ISLE STE. CROIX.

Where the first French Settlement in America was made.

Arthur Wentworth Eaton.

With tangled brushwood all o'ergrown,
And here and there a lofty pine,
Around whose form strange creepers twine,
And crags that mock the sea's wild moan;

And little bays, where no ships come,
Though many a white sail passes by;
And many a white cloud in the sky
Looks down and shames the sleeping foam.

Unconscious on the waves it lies,
While, mid the golden reeds and sedge
That southward line the water's edge,
The thrush sings her shrill melodies.

No human dwelling now is seen
Upon its rude unfertile slopes;
Though many a summer traveller gropes
For ruins 'midst the tangled green;

And seeks, upon the northern shore,
The graves of that adventurous band
That followed to this western land
Champlain, De Monts, and Poutrincourt.

There stood the ancient fort that sent
Fierce cannon echoes through the world;
There waved the Bourbon flag that told
The mastery of a continent;

Where through the pines, with groan and moan,
The winter wind swept, as at eve
The arches of St Genevieve
Had echoed the great organ's tone;

There Huguenots, and cassocked priests,
And noble born, and sons of toil,
Together worked the barren soil,
And shared each other's frugal feasts;

And heard, across the sailless sea,
A strange, prophetic harvest tune;
And saw, beneath the yellow moon,
The golden reapings that should be.

Till stealthy Winter, through the reeds,
Crept, crystal-footed, to the shore;
And to the little hamlet bore
His hidden freight of deathly seeds.

Spring came at last, and o'er the waves
The welcome sail of Pontgravé;
But half the number silent lay,
Death's pale first-fruits, in western graves.

Sing on, wild sea, your sad refrain
For all the gallant sons of France,
Whose songs and sufferings enhance
The romance of the western main.

Sing requiems to these tangled woods,
With ruined forts and hidden graves;
Your mournful music history craves
For many of her noblest moods.

THE CAPTURED FLAG.

Arthur Weir.

Loudly roared the English cannon, loudly thundered back
    our own,
Pouring down a hail of iron from their battlements of
    stone,
Giving Frontenac's proud message to the clustered British
    ships:
"I will answer your commander only by my cannons' lips."
Through the sulphurous smoke below us, on the Admiral's
    ship of war,
Faintly gleamed the British ensign, as through cloud-wrack
    gleams a star;
And above our noble fortress, on Cape Diamond's rugged
    crest,—
Like a crown upon a monarch, like an eagle in its nest,—
Streamed our silken flag, emblazoned with the royal *fleur-
    de-lys*,
Flinging down a proud defiance to the rulers of the sea.
As we saw it waving proudly, and beheld the crest it bore,
Fiercely throbbed our hearts within us, and with bitter
    words we swore,
While the azure sky was reeling at the thunder of our guns,
We would strike that standard never, while Old France had
    gallant sons.

Long and fiercely raged the struggle, oft our foes had sought
    to land,
But with shot and steel we met them, met and drove them
    from the strand;

Though they owned them not defeated, and the stately Union Jack,
Streaming from the slender topmast, seemed to wave them proudly back.
Louder rose the din of combat, thicker rolled the battle smoke,
Through whose murky folds the crimson tongues of thundering cannon broke;
And the ensign sank and floated in the smoke-clouds on the breeze,
As a wounded fluttering sea-bird floats upon the stormy seas.
While we looked upon it sinking, rising, through the sea of smoke,
Lo! it shook, and bending downwards, as a tree beneath a stroke,
Hung one moment o'er the river, then precipitously fell,
Like proud Lucifer descending from high heaven into hell.
As we saw it flutter downwards, till it reached the eager wave,
Not Cape Diamond's loudest echo could have matched the cheer we gave;
Yet the English, still undaunted, sent an answering echo back;
Though their flag had fallen conquered, still their fury did not slack,
And with louder voice their cannon to our cannonade replied,
As their tattered ensign drifted slowly shoreward with the tide.

There was one who saw it floating, and within his heart of fire,
Beating in a Frenchman's bosom, rose at once a fierce desire,

That the riven flag thus resting on the broad St Lawrence tide
Should, for years to come, betoken how France humbled England's pride.
As the stag leaps down the mountain, with the baying hounds in chase,
So the hero, swift descending, sought Cape Diamond's rugged base,
And within the water, whitened by the bullets' deadly hail,
Springing, swam towards the ensign with a stroke that could not fail.
From the shore and from the fortress we looked on with bated breath,
For around him closer, closer, fell the messengers of death;
And as nearer, ever nearer, to the floating flag he drew,
Thicker round his head undaunted still the English bullets flew.
He has reached and seized the trophy! Ah! what cheering rent the skies,
Mingled with deep English curses, as he shoreward brought his prize!
Slowly, slowly, almost sinking, still he struggled to the land,
And we hurried down to meet him as he reached the welcome strand;
Proudly up the rock we bore him, with the flag that he had won,
And that night the English vessels left us with the setting sun.

HOW CANADA WAS SAVED.

(*May 1660.*)

George Murray.

"'Il faut ici donner la gloire à ces dix-sept François de Montréal, et honorer leurs cendres d'un éloge qui leur est deu avec justice, et que nous ne pouvons leur réfuser sans ingratitude. Tout estait perdu, s'ils n'eussent péri, et leur malheur a sauvé ce pais."—Rélations des Jesuites, 1660, p. 17.

Beside the dark Utawa's stream, two hundred years ago,
A wondrous feat of arms was wrought, which all the world should know:
'Tis hard to read with tearless eyes that record of the past,
It stirs the blood, and fires the soul, as with a clarion's blast.
What though no blazoned cenotaph, no sculptured columns, tell
Where the stern heroes of my song, in death triumphant, fell;
What though beside the foaming flood untombed their ashes lie,
All earth becomes the monument of men who nobly die.

A score of troublous years had passed since on Mount-Royal's crest
The gallant Maisonneuve upreared the Cross devoutly bless'd,
And many of the saintly Guild that founded Ville-Marie
With patriot pride had fought and died—determined to be free.

Fiercely the Iroquois had sworn to sweep, like grains of sand,
The Sons of France from off the face of their adopted land,
When, like the steel that oft disarms the lightning of its power,
A fearless few their country saved in danger's darkest hour.

Daulac, the Captain of the Fort—in manhood's fiery prime—
Hath sworn by some immortal deed to make his name sublime,
And sixteen "Soldiers of the Cross," his comrades true and tried,
Have pledged their faith for life and death—all kneeling side by side;
And this their oath :—On flood or field, to challenge face to face
The ruthless hordes of Iroquois, the scourges of their race;
No quarter to accept or grant,—and, loyal to the grave,
To die like martyrs for the land they shed their blood to save.

Shrived by the priest within the Church where oft they had adored,
With solemn fervour they partake the Supper of the Lord;
And now, those self-devoted youths from weeping friends have passed,
And on the Fort of Ville-Marie each fondly looks his last.
Unskilled to steer the frail canoe, or stem the rushing tide,
On through a virgin wilderness, o'er stream and lake they glide,
Till, weary of the paddle's dip, they moor their barks below
A Rapid of Utawa's flood—the turbulent Long-Sault.

There, where a grove of gloomy pines sloped gently to the
    shore,
A moss-grown Palisade was seen—a Fort in days of yore;
Fenced by its circle, they encamped; and on the listening air,
Before those staunch Crusaders slept, arose the voice of
    prayer.
Sentry and scout kept watch and ward, and soon, with glad
    surprise,
They welcomed to their roofless hold a band of dark allies,—
Two stalwart chiefs and forty "braves,"—all sworn to strike
    a blow
In one great battle for their lives against the common foe.

Soft was the breath of balmy Spring in that fair month of
    May,
The wild flower bloomed, the wild bird sang on many a
    budding spray,—
A tender blue was in the sky, on earth a tender green,
And Peace seemed brooding, like a dove, o'er all the sylvan
    scene;
When, loud and high, a thrilling cry dispelled the magic
    charm,
And scouts came hurrying from the woods to bid their
    comrades arm,
And bark canoes skimmed lightly down the torrent of the
    Sault,
Manned by three hundred dusky forms—the long expected
    foe.

They spring to land—a wilder brood hath ne'er appalled the
    sight—
With carbines, tomahawks, and knives that gleam with
    baleful light;

Dark plumes of eagles crest their chiefs, and broidered deerskins hide
The blood-red war-paint that shall soon a bloodier red be dyed.
Hark! to the death-song that they chant,—behold them as they bound,
With flashing eyes and vaunting tongues, defiantly around;
Then, swifter than the wind, they fly the barrier to invest,
Like hornet-swarms that heedless boys have startled from a nest.

As Ocean's tempest-driven waves dash forward on a rock,
And madly break in seething foam, hurl'd backward by the shock,
So onward dashed that surging throng, so backward were they hurl'd,
When from the loopholes of the Fort flame burst and vapour curl'd.
Each bullet aimed by bold Daulac went crashing through the brain,
Or pierced the bounding heart of one who never stirred again;
The trampled turf was drenched with blood—blood stained the passing wave—
It seemed a carnival of death, the harvest of the grave.

The sun went down—the fight was o'er—but sleep was not for those
Who, pent within that frail redoubt, sighed vainly for repose;
The shot that hissed above their heads, the Mohawks' taunting cries,
Warned them that never more on earth must slumber seal their eyes.

In that same hour their swart allies, o'erwhelmed by craven
    dread,
Leaped o'er the parapet like deer and traitorously fled;
And, when the darkness of the night had vanished, like a
    ghost,
Twenty and two were left—of all—to brave a maddened host.

Foiled for a time, the subtle foes have summoned to their aid
Five hundred kinsmen from the Isles, to storm the Palisade;
And, panting for revenge, they speed, impatient for the fray,
Like birds of carnage from their homes allured by scent of
    prey.
With scalp-locks streaming in the breeze, they charge,—but
    never yet
Have legions in the storm of fight a bloodier welcome met
Than those doomed warriors, as they faced the desolating
    breath
Of wide-mouthed musketoons that poured hot cataracts of
    death.

Eight days of varied horrors passed! What boots it now to
    tell
How the pale tenants of the Fort heroically fell?
Hunger, and thirst, and sleeplessness—death's ghastly aids
    —at length
Marred and defaced their comely forms, and quelled their
    giant strength.
The end draws nigh—they yearn to die—one glorious rally
    more
For the dear sake of Ville-Marie, and all will soon be o'er;
Sure of the martyr's golden Crown, they shrink not from
    the Cross,
Life yielded for the land they love they scorn to reckon loss!

The Fort is fired, and through the flames, with slippery, splashing tread,
The Redmen stumble to the camp o'er ramparts of the dead;
There, with set teeth and nostril wide, Daulac the dauntless stood,
And dealt his foes remorseless blows 'mid blinding smoke and blood,
Till, hacked and hewn, he reeled to earth, with proud unconquered glance,
Dead—but immortalised by death—Leonidas of France!
True to their oath, that glorious band no quarter basely craved;—
So died the peerless Twenty-two, so Canada was saved!

MADELEINE DE VERCHÈRES.

John Reade.

I.

"Oh! my country, bowed in anguish 'neath a weight of bitter woe,
Who shall save thee from the vengeance of the desolating foe?
They have sworn a heathen oath, that every Christian soul must die,—
God of Heaven, in mercy shield us! Father, hear thy children's cry."

II.

Thus prayed Madeleine, the daughter of an old heroic line,—
Grecian poet, had he seen her, would have deemed her race divine;
But as the golden sun transcends the beauty of the brightest star,
Than all the charms of face or form her maiden heart was lovelier far.

III.

We can see her now in fancy, through the dim years gazing back
To those stormy days of old, the days of valiant Frontenac,
When the thinly settled land was sadly wasted far and near,
And before the savage foe the people fled like stricken deer.

IV.

'Tis the season when the forest wears its many-coloured dress,
And a strange foreboding whisper answers back the wind's caress
As the swaying pines repeat the murmurs of the distant waves,
While the children of the Summer flutter softly to their graves.

V.

But—was that another whisper, warning *her* of ill to come,
As she stands beside the river, near her father's fortress-home?
Hark! the sound of stealthy footsteps creeps upon the throbbing ear—
Maiden, fly! the foe approaches, and no human aid is near.

VI.

Surely He who decked with beauty this fair earth on which we dwell,
Never meant that men should change it by their madness into hell!
He who gave the trees their glory, gave the birds their gift of song,
Cannot smile from out yon heavens at the sight of human wrong.

VII.

But those savage hearts no beauty wins to thoughts of tender ruth—
Mother fond, or gentle maid, or smiling innocence of youth.
See! with fierce exulting yells the flying maiden they pursue—
Hear her prayer, O God, and save her from that wild vindictive crew.

VIII.

Never ere that day or since was such a race by maiden run,
Never 'gainst such fearful odds was wished-for goal so swiftly won ;
Fifty foes are on her track, the bullets graze her floating hair—
But worse than vain is all their rage, for God has heard her prayer.

IX.

Madeleine has reached the Fort,—the gates are closed against the foe,
But now, a stricken throng sends up to heaven a wail of woe—
Feeble men, and fainting women, without heart or hope or plan—
Then it was that God gave courage to a maid to act the man.

X.

Then it was that Madeleine bethought her of her father's name :
" Never shall a soldier's daughter die the coward's death of shame ;
Never, in the days to come, when Canada is great and proud,
Be it said a Christian maiden by a heathen's threat was cowed.

XI.

"He is but a craven wretch would bid me yield in such an hour—
Never yet my country's sons in peril's face were known to cower!
No, my people! God is with us; 'tis our homes that we defend—
Let the savage do his worst, we will oppose him to the end.

XII.

"Women, I am but a girl, but heroes' blood is in my veins,
And I will shed it drop by drop before I see my land in chains;
Let them tear me limb from limb, or strew my ashes to the wind,
Ere I disgrace the name I bear, or leave a coward's fame behind.

XIII.

"Brothers mine, though young in years, you are old enough to know
That to shed your blood is noble, fighting with your country's foe!
Be the lesson unforgotten that our noble father gave,
Whether glory be its guerdon, or it wins us but a grave.

XIV.

"Come, my people, take your places, every one as duty calls;
Death to every foe who ventures to approach these fortress walls!

Let no point be unprotected, leave the rest to God on high,
That we shall have done our duty, even if we have to die."

XV.

Thus she raised their drooping courage, matchless maiden, Madeleine;
And the cry, "To arms!" re-echoed, till the roof-trees rang again;
Cannons thundered, muskets rattled, and the clank of steel was heard,
Till the baffled foe retreated, like a wolf untimely scared.

XVI.

Seven days and seven nights, with sleepless eye and bated breath,
They held the Fort against the foe that lurked around them plotting death!
At last a joyous challenge came, it was the brave La Monnerie,
And up to heaven arose a shout, "The foe has fled, and we are free!"

THE BATTLE OF LA PRAIRIE.

(*1691.*)

(*A Ballad.*)

WILLIAM DOUW LIGHTHALL.

I.

THAT was a brave old epoch,
   Our age of chivalry,
When the Briton met the Frenchman
   At the Fight of La Prairie ;
And the manhood of New England,
   And the Netherlanders true,
And Mohawks sworn, gave battle
   To the Bourbon's lilied blue.

II.

That was a brave old Governor,
   Who gathered his array,
And stood to meet, he knew not what,
   On that alarming day.
Eight hundred, against rumours vast
   That filled the wild wood's gloom,
With all New England's flower of youth,
   Fierce for New France's doom.

III.

And the brave old scarce three hundred!
    Theirs should in truth be fame;
Borne down the savage Richelieu
    On what emprise they came!
Your hearts are great enough, O few:
    Only your numbers fail!
New France asks more for conquerors,
    All glorious though your tale.

IV.

It was a brave old battle
    That surged around the fort,
When D'Hosta fell in charging,
    And 'twas deadly strife and short;
When in the very quarters
    They contested face and hand,
And many a goodly fellow
    Crimsoned yon La Prairie sand.

V.

And those were brave old orders
    The colonel gave to meet
That forest force, with trees entrenched,
    Opposing the retreat:
" De Callières' strength's behind us,
    And beyond's your Richelieu:
We must go straightforth at them;
    There is nothing else to do."

VI.

And then the brave old story comes,
    Of Schuyler and Valrennes,*
When "Fight!" the British colonel called,
    Encouraging his men,
"For the Protestant Religion,
    And the honour of our King!"—
"Sir, I am here to answer you!"
    Valrennes cried, forthstepping.

VII.

Were those not brave old races?—
    Well, here they still abide;
And yours is one or other,
    And the second's at your side.
So when you hear your brother say,
    "Some loyal deed I'll do;"
Like old Valrennes, be ready with,
    "I'm here to answer you!"

---

* Pronounced "Skyler" and "Valrenn."

THE BATTLE OF GRAND PRÉ.

(February 9th, 1746.)

M. J. Katzmann Lawson.

Room for the dead, the honoured dead, in this fair year of grace;
In the Valhalla of the brave, give them a glorious place!
The loyal men who crossed the sea, and came with battle ring,
To hold this free fair land of ours a province for their king.
When winter's iron fetters bound river and lake and bay,
And snow-drifts, piled in fleecy white, on plain and mountain lay,
Where Blomidon's blue crest looks down upon the valley land,
And the great waves of Fundy lap the grey stones on the strand;
Here, where the scattered homesteads stood, from time and labour won,
The brave commander of the force quartered his garrison,
Retaining for his citadel the old French stone house, set
Where the ripple of the Gaspereaux sighs round its ruins yet.

Down from the heights of Cobequid, on noiseless snow-shoes borne,
Slowly the crafty foeman came, by march and travel worn;

Lightly the low toboggans swept, bearing their motley freight,
Food for the rebels on the march, shot for the brave who wait ;
Broad rivers, all unknown to name, their stealthy footsteps crossed,
The Shubenacadie, Ste Croix, and Avon bridged by frost ;
For sixteen weary days they crept over these leagues of snow,
As the grim panther tracks his prey, so stole they on the foe.
In the deep stillness of the night,—out from the cold, black cloud,
The snowflakes, falling one by one, the hemlock branches bowed ;
Forest, and plain, and hamlet, all hushed in slumber deep,
And still before the driving blast the freezing Frenchmen creep ;
With panting breath and weary tread, through midnight's icy blast,
With murder in their hearts, they reach the Grand Pré camp at last.
The sentinels were at their post, within the watchers slept,
Hushed in the tumult which the storm and cruel snow-drift kept ;
Oh, God! that brave men thus should die, no time to rouse or stir!
One hundred English soldiers fell in that dread massacre,
Guarding the colours of their king in this new province land,—
Scalped by the Indians' tomahawk, hewn down by alien hand !

Roused by the din at dead of night, piercing the stone house then,
Brave Noble faced, with sword in hand, those fierce and blood-stained men ;

The bitter wind in fury swept around his half-clad form,
And flash of steel and sweep of shot, more cruel than the storm;
The Red Cross flag of England waved above his fortress rude,
And brave, as all her loyal sons, he well her foes withstood;
All worn and faint, from battle sore, wounded in heart and frame,
From dying lips the valiant shout of "No surrender!" came.
Nor nobler names can Britain write upon her glorious scroll
Than those who held the fort that night where Minas' waters roll,—
Surprised, and overpowered and slain, yet heroes every one,
Those cold, set faces, white and still, turned to the rising sun.
Though many a score of years has marked this earth with loss and gain,
Since Noble fought his last long fight on Grand Pré's snowy plain,
No stone is raised to mark the place where his brave comrades fell,
No monument above his grave, of valiant deeds to tell.
Room for the honoured dead to-day, in memory's tender grace.
To chronicle their glorious deeds above their burial-place.
Crimean heroes, all our own, Lucknow and Kars still tell
That Nova Scotia's sons can serve their Queen and country well!
But, with their fame, let us recall the battle long ago,
When English soldiers met the French at daybreak in the snow;
And held the fort, and kept the flag, as only heroes could,
Where, in this orchard land of ours, the old grey stone house stood.

Now, in this year of Jubilee, when living deeds are read,
Glance backward through the centuries which hold our honoured dead,—
Where Lechmere sank, and Pickering died, where the brave Noble fell,
Under our own old English flag, the flag they loved so well;
Where sunny Gaspereaux sweeps on amid the apple trees,
And the blue waves of Minas chant a requiem to the breeze;
Raise shaft or column to the dead, let some memorial fair
Tell to our children's children still that *Heroes* slumber there!

SPINA CHRISTI.

WILLIAM KIRBY.

PART I.

> "There is a thorn—it looks so old,
> In truth you'd find it hard to say
> How it could ever have been young,
> It looks so old and grey."
> —WORDSWORTH.

The city walls of Avignon are built of stone, and high
The houses stand, with balconies above the streets that lie
Around the old cathedral, whose sweet bells were ringing
    clear
A merry tune, one day in June
Of seventeen hundred year,
And half a hundred years beside, while crowding far and
    near,
Beneath the flags and tapestries, the people loudly cheer;—
The regiment of Rousillon is ordered to the war,
A thousand strong, the pick among
The mountaineers of Var.

The great Church portals open wide, the crowd goes surg-
    ing in,
The soldiers tramp with measured tread—the services begin,
A blessing is invoked upon the King's Canadian war;
Beyond the seas there is no ease,
And all things are ajar.

The English in America do boldly break and mar
The peace they made ; but we will keep the treaties as they
    are !
And now the Royal Rousillon take up the route with joy,
And march away while bugles play—
Mid shouts of " Vive le Roy ! "

There lives a lady beautiful as any Provence rose,
The chatelaine of Bois le Grand, who weepeth as she goes—
For sleep has left her eyelids on the banks of rapid Rhone :
" But three months wed ! alas," she said,
" To live my life alone !
Pining for my dear husband, in his old chateau of stone,
While he goes with his regiment, and I am left to moan :
That his dear head, so often laid at rest upon my knee,
No pillow kind, but stones, shall find—
No shelter but a tree ! "

" Weep not, dear wife ! " replied the count, and took her in
    his arms,
And kissed her lovingly, and smiled to quiet her alarms ;
They stood beneath the holy thorn of the old Celestine,
Pope Clement brought with blessing fraught
And planted it between
The wall and wall beside the cross, where he was daily seen
To kneel before it reverently. It came from Palestine,
A plant from that which cruelly the crown of thorns supplied,
Christ wore for me, when mocked was He,
And scourged and crucified.

" I'll take a branch of it," he said, " across the stormy sea
    That roars between New France and Old, and plant it
        solemnly

In that far country where I go campaigning for the King;
It will remind and teach mankind
Of pains that blessing bring."
Above his head he plucked a spray acute with many a sting,
And placed it on his plumed chapeau, in token of the thing
Alone can turn the sinful man—the piercing of the thorn—
The healing smart—the contrite heart—
Of penitence new born.

Despairingly she kissed his lips: "O welcome sharpest pain,
That cuts the heart to bleeding, and bids hope revive again!
O Spina Christi! to my heart I press thee wet with tears—
If love outlast as in the past
Each parting that endears!
Our sky has been so bright and filled with music of the spheres,
So gloomy now in sad eclipse it suddenly appears!
For joy dies out in silence like sweet singing that is done,
If men forget their sacred debt
To women they have won."

PART II.

Atlantic gales come winged with clouds and voices of the sea,
The misty Capes uncap to hear the ocean melody;
In broad St Lawrence rise and fall the everlasting tides,
Which come and go with ebb and flow—
While every ship that rides
At anchor swings, and east or west the passing flood divides,
Or westward ho! mid seamen's shouts still onward gently glides,

Tasting the waters sweet from lakes, of boundless solitude,
Where thousand isles break into smiles
Of nature's gladdest mood.

A hundred leagues and many more towards the glowing west,
Amid the forests' silences, Ontario lay at rest—
Keel rarely ploughed or paddle dipt its wilderness of blue ;
Where day by day life passed away
In peace that irksome grew.
In old Niagara fort, a cross stood loftily in view,*
And *Regnat. Vincit. Imperat. Christus* the words did show
Carved on it, when the Rousillon came up in early spring
To close the port, and guard the fort,
And keep it for the King.

O! fair in summer time it is, Niagara plain to see,
Half belted round with oaken woods and green as grass can be!
Its levels broad in sunshine lie, with flowerets gemmed and set
With daisy stars, and red as Mars
The tiny sanguinet,
The trefoil with its drops of gold, white clover heads, and yet
The sweet grass, commonest of all God's goodnesses we get!
The dent-de-lions, downy globes a puff will blow away,
Which children pluck to try good luck,
Or tell the time of day.

---

*In the centre of the fort stood a cross eighteen feet high, with the inscription "Regn. Vinc. Imp. Chrs." The interpretation of which admits of as much ambiguity as a Delphic oracle.

Count Bois le Grand sought out a spot of loveliness, was full
Of sandworts, silvered leaf and stem, with down of fairy
    wool;
Hard by the sheltering grove of oak he set the holy thorn,
Where still it grows and ever shows
How sharp the crown of scorn
Christ wore for man, reminding him what pain for sin was
    borne,
And warning him he must repent before his sheaf is shorn,
When comes the reaper, Death, and his last hour of life is
    scored,—
Of all bereft, and only left
The mercy of the Lord.

The thorn was planted, leafed and bloomed, as if its sap
    were blood
That stained its berries crimson which fell dropping where
    it stood,
And seeded others like it,—as on Golgotha befell,
An awful sight, if seen aright,
The trees that root in hell! *
Contorted, twisted, writhing, as with human pain to tell
Of cruel spines and agonies that God alone can quell.
A cluster like them Dante saw, and never after smiled;
A grove of doom, amid whose gloom
Were wicked souls exiled.

---

* A number of these thorns, old and weird of aspect, are still standing on the plains of Niagara, near the grove of Paradise; they were formerly called the "French thorns," a designation now nearly forgotten.

Niagara fort was bravely built with bulwarks strong and
    high,
A tower of stone, and pallisades with ditches deep and dry;
And best of all, behind them lay Guienne and Rousillon,*
La Sarre and Béarn, 'neath Pouchot stern—
A wall of men like stone—
De Villiers and Bois le Grand of old Avignon ;
And over all, the flag of France waved proudly in the sun.
Prepared for it, they met the war with gaiety and zest—
And every day barred up the way
That opened to the west.

Discord was rampant now and hate, and peace lay like a
    yoke,
That galled the necks of both of them ; and French and
    English broke,
With mutual wrath and rivalry, the treaty they had made ;
Too proud to live and each one give
Sunshine as well as shade.
From Louisburg to Illinois they stood as foes arrayed,
And east and west war's thunder rolled,—the soldier's
    polished blade
Flashed 'mid the savage tomahawks that struck and never
    spared,
While fort and field alternate yield
The bloody laurels shared.

The clouds of war rolled redder from the north, and English pride

---

* Portions of the regiments of Rousillon, La Sarre, Béarn, and Guienne, formed the garrison of Niagara during the memorable siege of 1759.

Was stung to desperation at the turning of the tide,
When Montcalm the heroic, wise in council, struck the blow,
Won Chouaguen, and conquered then
At Carillon the foe.
But with his very victories his armies melted slow.
No help from France obtained he—and his heart sank very low ;
He knew that England's courage flames the fiercest in defeat,
And in the day she stands at bay
Most dangerous to meet.

" Help us, O France ! to save thy fair dominion in the west,
Which for thy sake we planted, and have carved thy royal crest
Of golden lilies on the rocks beside the streams that flow
From mountain rills and past the hills
Of far off Ohio ;
Then down leagues by the hundred, where bayous meander slow,
Though orange groves and sugar canes, and flowers that ever blow,
In fair Louisiana. We will take and hold the land
For Francia's crown of old renown,
If she will by us stand."

So spake Montcalm, and message sent : " My armies melt away
With victories—my beaten foes grow stronger every day ;
In vain Monongahela and Carillon piled with slain,
If France forget to pay the debt
Of honour without stain,

She owes her sons who willingly are bleeding every vein
For sake of her white flag and crown, on fortress and on
    plain.
If we can keep Niagara safe that guards the western door,
Then in the east Quebec may feast
In quiet evermore."
Vain were Montcalm's appeals for aid, Voltaire's cold spirit
    ruled
The Court—while noisy doctrinaires a gallant nation
    schooled
In selfishness and unbelief, and cowardice and ease,
Which manhood daunt, while women flaunt
Their idle hours to please.
Degenerately they drank the wine of life mixed with the lees;
The Spartan virtues, that make nations free and famous,
    these
Were mocked, derided, set at nought, while fatuous states-
    men stand,
Whose feeble will, potent for ill,
Yields where it should command.

PART III.

Remote amid the trackless woods and waters of the west,
No enemy had broken yet Niagara's quiet rest.
The fifth year of the war came in—a change was nigh at
    hand;
The order ran to raise the ban
And make a final stand.
Prideaux and Johnson honoured were with new and high
    command,
From Albany a hundred leagues to march across the land,
While Wolfe besieged Quebec, and its defences battered in;
So they elate took bond of fate
Niagara to win.

But not before June's leafy days, when all the woods are
    green,
And skies are warm and waters clear, the English scouts
    were seen.
A lull before the tempest fell with weeks of steady calm,
Of golden hours when blooming flowers
Filled all the air with balm.
The garrison were now prepared to struggle for the palm,
To win the wreath of victory or die without a qualm ;
So passed their time in jollity and ease, as if the day
Of bloody strife with life for life
Was continents away.

A fleet of swift canoes came up, all vocal with the song
Of voyageurs, whose cadences kept even time among
The dipping paddles, as they flashed along Ontario's shore,
Past headlands high and coasts that lie
In mistiness, and bore
A bevy of fair wives who loved their husbands more and
    more,—
Who could not bear their absence, and defiant of the roar
Of forests and of waters, came to comfort and caress,
As women may—and only they—
Man's solitariness.

In these Capuan days they basked in pleasure's sunny
    beams,
The Provence home of Bois le Grand was rarer in his
    dreams,
The chatelaine of his chateau fast by the rapid Rhone,
A memory dim became to him—
Nor loved he her alone.

A dame of charms most radiant—the cynosure that shone
Amid the constellations of Quebec's magnetic zone,
Drew him with force and held him fast, a captive with her eyes,
Which, dark and bright as tropic night,
Loved him without disguise.

And he remembered not the thorn he planted by the grove
Of Paradise, where he forgot, in his forbidden love,
The chatelaine of Bois le Grand, the purest wife and best
Of womankind he left behind,
And ventured, like the rest,
To sport with woman's loveliness—as for a passing jest.
His heart was very lonely, too, while all beside were blest;
Like Samson in Delilah's lap, his lock of strength was shorn;
He loved again, despite the pain
And stinging of the thorn.

One day when he a-hunting went in the Norman Marsh,* and she
The dame he loved rode with him, as Diana fair to see
In green and silver habited, and silken bandoleer,
With dainty gun—by it undone!—
And bugle horn so clear;
While riding gaily up and down to turn the timid deer
And meet the joyance of his glance, when she should reappear,
She vanished in the thicket, where a pretty stag had flown—
Saw something stir—alas for her!
She shot her lover down!

---

* The "*Marais Normand,*" so called during the French occupation of Niagara. It is now covered with farms, but is still called the swamp.

Bleeding he fell—"O, Madelaine!" his cry turned her to
    stone,
"What have you done unwittingly?" he uttered with a
    groan,
As she knelt over him with shrieks sky-rending, such as rise
From women's lips on sinking ships,
With death before their eyes.
She beat her breast despairingly; her hair dishevelled flies;
She kissed him madly, and in vain to stanch the blood she
    tries,
Till falling by him in a swoon they both lay as the dead—
A piteous sight! love's saddest plight!
With garments dabbled red.

Their servants ran, and hunters pale, and raised them from
    the ground;
Restored the dame to consciousness, and searched his fatal
    wound.
They pitched for him a spacious tent the river bank above,
With boundless care for ease and air
And tenderness of love.
She waited on him night and day; plucked off her silken
    glove
With self-accusing grief and tears—lamenting, as a dove
Bewails her wounded mate—so she—and in her bosom
    wore
A spike of thorn which every morn
She gathered—nothing more.

She cast her jewels off and dressed in robe of blackest hue,
Her face was pale as look the dead, and paler ever grew.
Smiles lit no more her rosy lips where sunbeams used to
    dance;

A withering blight that kills outright
Fell on her like a trance;
For Bois le Grand was dying, and it pierced her like a lance
To hear him vainly calling on his chatelaine in France,
And not for her who knelt by him, and lived but in his breath—
Remorse and grief without relief
Were hastening her death.

Far, far away in Avignon, beneath the holy thorn,
The chatelaine of Bois le Grand knelt down at eve and morn;
And prayed for him in hope and trust long witless of his fate;
But never knew he was untrue
And had repented late.
As caught between two seas his bark was in a rocky strait,
And with his life went down the lives of those two women. Fate
Bedrugged the love, betrayed them both—and one by Laura's shrine
Took her last rest—the other best,
Drank death with him like wine.

Niagara's doom long threatened came—the roll of English drums
Was heard deep in the forest as Prideaux's stout army comes.
They sap and trench from day to day, the cannon fierce roar,
The hot attack when beaten back
Again comes to the fore.
The pallisades are red with fire, the ramparts red with gore,

Its brave defenders on the walls die thickly more and more,
Mid rack and ruin overwhelmed—no help above—below,
The few remain—not of the slain—
Surrender to the foe.

But not before all hope had fled, when gathered far and wide
From prairie, forest, fort, and field—with every tribe allied
To France, throughout the west they came, the fatal siege to raise,
And marched along, a mingled throng,
Amid the forest maze.
They halted in the meadows, where they stood like stags at gaze,
The English and the Iroquois confronting them for days,
Till Brant and Butler, wary chiefs, with stratagem of war
Broke up their host, and captured most,
While fled the rest afar.

The last day came, and Bois le Grand beheld with misty eyes
The flag of France run down the staff, and that of England rise.
It was the sharpest thorn of all that 'neath his pillow lay—
"O, Madelaine!" he cried, "my men!
My Rousillon so gay!
Fill graves of honour,—while I live to see this fatal day!
But not another! No!" he cried, and turned as cold as clay.
She kissed his mouth the last long kiss the dying get alone—
"O, Spina!" cried—fell by his side,
And both lay dead as stone.

THE LOYALISTS.

Sarah Anne Curzon.

O ye, who with your blood and sweat
   Watered the furrows of this land,—
See where upon a nation's brow,
   In honour's front, ye proudly stand!

Who for her pride abased your own,
   And gladly on her altar laid
All bounty of the older world,
   All memories that your glory made.

And to her service bowed your strength,
   Took labour for your shield and crest;
See where upon a nation's brow.
   Her diadem, ye proudly rest!

BROCK.

Charles Sangster.

One voice, one people, one in heart,
    And soul, and feeling, and desire!
    Re-light the smouldering martial fire,
    Sound the mute trumpet, strike the lyre,
    The hero deed can not expire,
        The dead still play their part.

Raise high the monumental stone!
    A nation's fealty is theirs,
    And we are the rejoicing heirs,
    The honoured sons of sires whose cares
    We take upon us unawares,
        As freely as our own.

We boast not of the victory,
    But render homage, deep and just,
    To his—to their—immortal dust,
    Who proved so worthy of their trust,—
    No lofty pile nor sculptured bust
        Can herald their degree.

No tongue need blazon forth their fame,—
    The cheers that stir the sacred hill
    Are but mere promptings of the will
    That conquered then, that conquers still;
    And generations yet shall thrill
        At Brock's remembered name.

Some souls are the Hesperides
    Heaven sends to guard the golden age,
    Illuming the historic page
    With records of their pilgrimage ;
    True Martyr, Hero, Poet, Sage :
        And he was one of these.

Each in his lofty sphere sublime
    Sits crowned above the common throng,
    Wrestling with some Pythonic wrong,
    In prayer, in thunder, thought, or song ;
    Briareus-limbed, they sweep along,
        The Typhons of the time.

CAPTURE OF FORT DETROIT, 1812.

Charles Edwin Jakeway.

The summons spread throughout the land, the summons to the brave;
It speeded west to far St Clair, and north to Huron's wave.
And fast into the forest wild its thrilling notes did float;
It called the woodman from his toil, the fisher from his boat.
And high upon the mountain, lone and deep within the dell,
The red man heard its stirring notes and answered to them well.
In haste they came responsive to their country's call for aid,—
The young, the old, the white, the red, for Truth and Right arrayed;
Their arms were strong, their mettle true, but few in numbers they—
To cope in arms upon the field against the great array.

. . . . . .

On marched the force invading, looking at their foe in scorn,
And sure that they would vanish like the mist before the morn;

But hearts of giant might were there that knew not how to fear,
And willing hands were waiting to provide a bloody bier;
And warmly did they welcome the approach of that proud band
That came to conquer and subdue their fair, free, noble land.
And then, in haste and terror, back unto their native shore,
The boastful host went surging,—their advance was quickly o'er;
Behind them thronged the heroes, while a bright chivalric glow
Went flashing o'er their faces as they chased the beaten foe.
"No time for rest!" cried Brock the Brave; "Let's conquer now or die!"
And swart Tecumseh at his side re-echoed back the cry.
And fast and far, from rank to rank, the thrilling orders came,
That they must cross the river in the face of shot and flame,
And on they went undaunted, they, the bravest of the brave,
And thought then but of honour, and they thought not of the grave.
The leader's towering figure stood erect in his canoe,
And o'er him England's banner out upon the breezes blew.
Ah! who at such a moment, and with such a leader there,
With such a flag above him, would of victory despair?
Not one I ween who followed, through the midst of shot and shell,
The grand heroic figure they knew and loved so well.
They reached the shore, they scaled the beach, and from a favoured post,

They hurled, like chaff before the wind, the huge opposing host;
These fled for shelter to the fort, where shelter there was none,
The flashing fire on ev'ry side boomed out each leaguer's gun.
"Advance! advance!" rang out the cry along the line of red;
"Advance! advance!" in trumpet tones their noble leader said.
With answering cheers upon their lips obeyed the willing men,
While far and wide, on every side, upstarting from the glen,
The painted Indians whooping came, and raised a dreadful din,
And rushed along with bounding step the carnage to begin.
But oh! what now? the charge is checked, and all along the line
The men in wonder see, and stop in answer to the sign
That by their leader's hand is made. My country, can it be
That he is craven-hearted turned? No craven heart is he!
See high above yon bastioned wall that flutt'ring flag of white,
Where Stripes and Stars a moment since were glitt'ring on the sight!
And list, adown the joyous ranks the thrilling tidings go,
"The fort has fallen into our hands, and with it all the foe!"
A cheer triumphant rang aloud o'er forest, field, and plain,
And distant echoes caught its notes and pealed them forth again.
Right proudly beat the hearts, I trow, of all that gallant few,

As flaunting o'er the battlements the flag of England flew,
While clad in blue, with looks as blue, long lines of captives came,
Who answered back with sullen looks the victors' loud acclaim,
As from the ramparts of the fort they made the welkin ring
With plaudits loud for Brock the Brave, and cheers for England's King.

TECUMSEH'S DEATH.

Major Richardson.

Amid that scene, like some dark towering fiend,
   With death-black eyes and hands all spotted o'er,
The fierce Tecumseh on his tall lance leaned,
   Fired with much spoil and drunk with human gore;
And now his blasting glance ferocious gleamed—
   The chief who leads the eagles to his shore—
When, with one scream that devils might appal,
Deep in his breast he lodged the whizzing ball.

Like the quick bolt that follows on the flash
   Which rends the mountain oak in fearful twain,
So springs the warrior with infernal dash
   Upon the Christian writhing in his pain;
High gleamed his hatchet, ready now to crash
   Along the fibres of his swimming brain,
When from the adverse arm a bullet flew
With force resistless, and with aim too true.

The baffled Chieftain tottered, sunk, and fell,
   Rage in his heart, and vengeance in his glance;
His features ghastly pale—his breast was hell;
   One bound he made to seize his fallen lance,
But quick the death-shades o'er his vision swell,
   His arm dropped nerveless, straining to advance;
One look of hatred, and the last, he gave,
Then sunk and slumbered with the fallen brave.

Forth from the copse a hundred foemen spring,
    And pounce like vultures on the bleeding clay;
Like famished bloodhounds to the corse they cling,
    And bear the fallen hero's spoils away;
The very covering from his nerves they wring,
    And gash his form, and glut them o'er their prey,—
Wild hell-fiends all, and revelling at his death,
With bursting shrieks and pestilential breath.

A BALLAD FOR BRAVE WOMEN.

Charles Mair.

A story worth telling our annals afford,
'Tis the wonderful journey of Laura Secord!
Her poor crippled spouse hobbled home with the news,
That Bœrstler was nigh! "Not a minute to lose,
Not an instant," said Laura, "for stoppage or pause—
I must hurry and warn our brave troops at Decaw's."
"What! you!" said her husband, "to famish and tire!"
"Yes, me!" said brave Laura, her bosom on fire.
"And how will you pass the gruff sentry?" said he,
"Who is posted so near us?"

                              " Just wait till you see;
The foe is approaching, and means to surprise
Our troops, as you tell me. Oh, husband, there flies
No dove with a message so needful as this—
I'll take it, I'll bear it. Good-bye, with a kiss."
Then a biscuit she ate, tucked her skirts well about,
And a bucket she slung on each arm, and went out.

'Twas the bright blush of dawn, when the stars melt from sight,
Dissolved by its breath like a dream of the night;
When Heaven seems opening on man and his pain,
Ere the rude day strengthens and shuts it again.

But Laura had eyes for her duty alone—
She marked not the glow and the gloom that were thrown
By the nurslings of morn, by the cloud-lands at rest,
By the spells of the East, and the weirds of the West.
Behind was the foe, full of craft and of guile ;
Before her, a long day of travel and toil.
"No time this for gazing," said Laura, as near
To the sentry she drew.

                      "Halt! You cannot pass here."
"I cannot pass here! Why, sirrah, you drowse,
Are you blind? Don't you see I am off to my cows?"
"Well, well, you can go." So she wended her way
To the pasture's lone side, where the farthest cow lay,
Got her up, caught a teat, and, with pail at her knees,
Made her budge, inch by inch, till she drew by degrees
To the edge of the forest. "I've hoaxed, on my word,
Both you and the sentry," said Laura Secord.

With a lingering look at her home, then away
She sped through the wild wood—a wilderness gray—
Nature's privacy, haunt of a virgin sublime,
And the mother who bore her, as ancient as Time ;
Where the linden had space for its fans and its flowers,
The balsam its tents, and the cedar its bowers ;
Where the lord of the forest, the oak, had its realm,
The ash its domain, and its kingdom the elm ;
Where the pine bowed its antlers in tempests, and gave
To the ocean of leaves the wild dash of the wave ;
And the mystical hemlock—the forest's high-priest—
Hung its weird, raking, top-gallant branch to the east.

And denser and deeper the solitude grew,
The underwood thickened, and drenched her with dew;
She tripped over moss-covered logs, fell, arose,
Sped, and stumbled again by the hour, till her clothes
Were rent by the branches and thorns, and her feet
Grew tender and way-worn and blistered with heat.
And on, ever on, through the forest she passed,
Her soul in her task, but each pulse beating fast,
For shadowy forms seemed to flit from the glades,
And beckon her into their limitless shades;
And mystical sounds—in the forest alone,
Ah! who has not heard them?—the voices, the moan
Or the sigh of mute nature, which sinks on the ear,
And fills us with sadness or thrills us with fear?
And who, lone and lost in the wilderness deep,
Has not felt the strange fancies, the tremors which creep
And assemble within, till the heart 'gins to fail,
The courage to flinch, and the cheeks to grow pale,
Midst the shadows which mantle the spirit that broods
In the sombre, the deep haunted heart of the woods?

She stopped—it was noonday. The wilds she espied
Seemed solitudes measureless. "Help me!" she cried;
Her piteous lips parched with thirst, and her eyes
Strained with gazing. The sun in his infinite skies
Looked down on no creature more hapless than she,
For woman is woman where'er she may be.
For a moment she faltered, then came to her side
The heroine's spirit—the Angel of Pride.
One moment she faltered. Beware! What is this?
The coil of the serpent! the rattlesnake's hiss!
One moment, then onward. What sounds far and near?
The howl of the wolf, yet she turned not in fear,

Nor bent from her course, till her eye caught a gleam
From the woods of a meadow through which flowed a stream,
Pure and sweet with the savour of leaf and of flower,
By the night-dew distilled and the soft forest shower;
Pure and cold as its spring in the rock crystalline,
Whence it gurgled and gushed 'twixt the roots of the pine.

And blest above bliss is the pleasure of thirst,
Where there's water to quench it; for pleasure is nursed
In the cradle of pain, and twin marvels are they
Whose interdependence is born with our clay.
Yes, blessed is water, and blessed is thirst,
Where there's water to quench it; but this is the worst
Of this life, that we reck not the blessings God sends,
Till denied them. But Laura, who felt she had friends
In Heaven, as well as on earth, knew to thank
The Giver of all things, and gratefully drank.

Once more on the pathway, through swamp and through mire,
Through covert and thicket, through bramble and brier,
She toiled to the highway, then over the hill,
And down the deep valley, and past the new mill,
And through the next woods, till, at sunset, she came
To the first British picket and murmured her name;
Thence, guarded by Indians, footsore and pale,
She was led to Fitzgibbon, and told him her tale.

For a moment her reason forsook her; she raved,
She laughed, and she cried, "They are saved, they are saved!"
Then her senses returned, and, with thanks loud and deep
Sounding sweetly around her, she sank into sleep.

And Bœrstler came up, but his movements were known,
His force was surrounded, his scheme was o'erthrown.
By a woman's devotion—on stone be't engraved—
The foeman was beaten, and Burlington saved.

Ah! faithful to death were our women of yore!
Have they fled with the past, to be heard of no more?
No, no! Though this laurelled one sleeps in the grave,
We have maidens as true, we have matrons as brave;
And should Canada ever be forced to the test—
To spend for our country the blood of her best—
When her sons lift the linstock and brandish the sword,
Her daughters will think of brave Laura Secord.

IN THE NORTH-WEST.

WILLIAM WILFRED CAMPBELL.

"FORWARD!"
           The captain said,
Out of the morning's red
Brave and noble and dread,
With hero and martial tread,
Into the North and the Westward.

Over dim forest and lake,
Over lone prairie and brake,
The clamor of battle to wake,
For kindred and country's sake,
Into the North and the Westward.

"Forward!"
          'Neath northern sky,
Ready to fight and die :
Where the shadowy marshbirds fly
With their weird and lonely cry,
Far to the North and the Westward.

Only the rifle's crack,
And answer of rifle back ;
Heavy each haversack,
Dreary the prairie's track
Far to the North and the Westward.

"Forward!"
        Seeking the foe,
Starving and bleeding they go,
Into the sleet and the snow,
Over bleak rivers that flow
Far to the North and the Westward.

Falling on frozen strands;
Falling, devoted bands,
Sleeping with folded hands!
Dead, for home and for lands—
Dead in the North and the Westward!

THE VETERAN.

J. A. Fraser.

The call "To arms!" resounded through the city broad and fair,
And volunteers in masses came, prepared to do and dare;
Young lads, whose cheeks scarce showed the down, men bearded, stout and strong,
Assembled at the first alarm, in bold undaunted throng.
"I'll volunteer!" an old man cried, "I've served the Queen before;
I fought the Russ at Inkerman, the Sepoy at Cawnpore;"
And as he stood erect and tall, with proud and flashing eye,
What though his hair were white as snow,—he could but do or die!
"You are too old," the answer was; "too old to serve her now."
Then o'er his face a wonder flashed, a scowl came on his brow,
And then a tear stole down his cheek, a sob his strong voice shook,—
"Sir, put me in a uniform, and see how old I'll look!"

IN HOSPITAL.

Annie Rothwell.

Across the glittering snow stretches the long blue shadows fall,
And the golden flash of the sunset creeps up on the whitewashed wall;
If I ever reach Heaven, I wonder shall I see the sun set on the snows?
And if there are shadows in Heaven, will they be as blue as those?
Sick fancies? Maybe. Perhaps, if you'd lain here as long as I,
If your life was one long patience, and you knew that to change was to die,
You'd be thankful for even a fancy to take you out of your pain,
And lift you one minute,—what, crying?—there—hush, I won't say it again.

Too young? Ay, I 'm not very old, lady; but when death stares you hard in the face,
There's a wonderful change comes on you: and a hospital ward's not the place
To grow younger, exactly. What brought me? Sit nearer, and bend your ear,
For this plaguy breath comes short; 't would be hard for me now to join in a cheer.

We were comrades, me and Joe Linton; we shared one
  bench at school,
Together we worked in the harvest, and bathed in the shady
  pool;
He was little, and bright-eyed, and shapely, as straight as a
  balsam tree;
I'd strength, but I'd never no beauty,—folks never thought
  much of me.
To manhood we grew like brothers; then he took a strange
  fancy to roam,
And went away for a sailor, while I stayed with the old folks
  at home.
I missed him,—but 't wasn't so hard, somehow, as it might
  be to let him go;
I had learned to fear him a little—for I'd learned to love
  Mary Snow.

And I tried through the short bright summer to teach her
  to care for me;
My gentle darling, my rosebud, the sweetest girl that
  could be!
And sometimes I thought she had learned it, sometimes my
  hope was low;
But I never dared ask—an old story—but you bade me tell
  you, you know.
Well, Joe came back with the winter, and he asked me the
  question straight,—
" Have you made it out with Mary, Will? I'd as lief know it
  now as to wait."
I shook my head, for I couldn't speak, but my heart beat
  thick and fast,
As his dark eyes flashed, and—God help us both!—I saw
  the truth at last.

He was true to me, Joe. All winter he spoke to her never
  a word;
And her cheek grew pale, and the voice grew still that had
  warbled as gay as a bird;
My chance was gone, and I knew it, but a loyal heart had
  Joe,—
While I stayed he was dumb; so in spring-time 't would be
  my turn to go.

Well, the spring-time came, and the summons; you
  remember, it lady? the call
That rang out so sharp and sudden, and struck the fire in
  us all?
I was glad, for I wanted no better than a lawful chance to
  die;
But when Joe—I thought of Mary, and I wondered, and
  asked him, why?
Then he took my hand in the old-time grip, and smiled,
  as he softly said,—
"There's One we can seek without strife, lad, and both
  win,—living or dead.
I can't let you win her alone, lad; we'll look for her side by
  side;
And whichever comes back——." I knew what he meant.
  Oh, if only I had died!

Through the hard grand times that followed, we lived like
  brothers again;
Shared frost and fatigue and hunger, and duties of pleasure
  and pain;
Together through march and bivouac, we fared to the tenth
  of May,
And together, that Sunday morning, on the skirmish line
  we lay.

Ah! 'twas no home echo of church bells that Sabbath silence broke;
Command and obedience were priest and psalm, and our incense was rifle smoke.
But "obedience is better than sacrifice," I think I have heard it said;
Maybe ours will be reckoned for worship when the last great orders are read.

Need I tell the rest? You can guess it,—the shot, and the swift sharp word,
Half oath and half prayer, hurled towards me, as the grass where he lay was stirred:
And how I, on my knees beside him, in the waste and desolate place,
With his blood on my useless fingers, and his fainting eyes on my face,
In appeal for the help I had not, saw the desperate choice that must lie
Betwixt one mad effort to save him, or waiting to watch him die.
My arms were strong, and I clasped him,—the wide plain, as I raised him and ran,
Heaved to and fro around me. In that struggle of man for man,
My own heart choked me. . . . The distant lines seemed to mock my failing speed,
And no breath in the burden I carried gave me hope or strength in my need . . .
—— The end? Well, a crack in the distance, and something struck my wrist,
And I shifted the weight to my shoulder that I thanked God the bullet had missed.

A second,—my foot slipped,—I stumbled: was it only over
   a stone?
Ah! this time the lead gave its message,—took tribute of
   flesh and of bone.

That's all——   I had tried and failed. When they found us
   they scarce could tell
The dead from the living. Oh, had I but died when I
   fainted and fell!
But I've lingered these long months over ('tis a weary time
   since May!)
With pain my companion in darkness, and sorrow my
   comrade by day.
They gave Joe a soldier's burial,—he has earned a soldier's
   fame;
In the day so swiftly coming do you think I shall have the
   same?

Had I saved him, lady, I'd have given twenty lives, nor
   counted the cost;
But it's somewhat hard to fight one's best, yet know that the
   day is lost.
We shall know why it happens, maybe, some day, and
   perhaps we shall get our reward,
When the last retreat has been sounded, and the angels
   relieve the guard.

IN MEMORIAM.

Those Killed in the North-West, 1885.

FREDERICK GEORGE SCOTT.

GROWING to full manhood now,
With the care-lines on our brow,
We, the youngest of the nations,
With no childish lamentations,
Weep, as only strong men weep,
For the noble hearts that sleep,
Pillowed where they fought and bled,
The loved and lost, our glorious dead!

Toil and sorrow come with age,
Manhood's rightful heritage;
Toil our arms more strong shall render,
Sorrow make our heart more tender,
In the heartlessness of time;
Honour lays a wreath sublime—
Deathless glory—where they bled,
Our loved and lost, our glorious dead!

Wild the prairie grasses wave
O'er each hero's new-made grave;
Time shall write such wrinkles o'er us.
But the future spreads before us
Glorious in that sunset land—
Nerving every heart and hand,
Comes a brightness none can shed,
But the dead, the glorious dead!

Lay them where they fought and fell;
Every heart shall ring their knell,
For the lessons they have taught us,
For the glory they have brought us.
Tho' our hearts are sad and bowed,
Nobleness still makes us proud—
Proud of light their names shall shed
In the roll-call of our dead!

Growing to full manhood now,
With the care-lines on our brow,
We, the youngest of the nations,
With no childish lamentations,
Weep, as only strong men weep,
For the noble hearts that sleep
Where the call of duty led,
Where the lonely prairies spread,
Where for us they fought and bled,
Our ever loved and glorious dead.

VIII.—PLACES.

VIII.—PLACES.

THE TANTRAMAR REVISITED.

Charles G. D. Roberts.

Summers and summers have come, and gone with the flight of the swallow;
Sunshine and thunder have been, storm and winter and frost;
Many and many a sorrow has all but died from remembrance,
Many a dream of joy fall'n in the shadow of pain.
Hands of chance and change have marred, or moulded, or broken,
Busy with spirit or flesh, all I most have adored;
Even the bosom of Earth is strewn with heavier shadows,—
Only in these green hills, aslant to the sea, no change!
Here, where the road that has climbed from the inland valleys and woodlands
Dips from the hill-tops down, straight to the base of the hills,—
Here, from my vantage-ground, I can see the scattering houses,
Stained with time, set warm in orchards and meadows and wheat,
Dotting the broad bright slopes outspread to southward and eastward,
Wind-swept all day long, blown by the south-east wind.
Skirting the sun-bright uplands stretches a riband of meadow,
Shorn of the labouring grass, bulwarked well from the sea,

Fenced on its seaward border with long clay dikes from the
 turbid
Surge and flow of the tides vexing the Westmoreland shores.
Yonder, towards the left, lie broad the Westmoreland
 marshes,—
Miles on miles they extend, level and grassy, and dim,
Clear from the long red sweep of flats to the sky in the
 distance,
Save for the outlying heights, green-rampired Cumberland
 Point;
Miles on miles outrolled, and the river-channels divide
 them,—
Miles on miles of green, barred by the hurtling gusts.

Miles on miles beyond the tawny bay is Minudie.
There are the low blue hills; villages gleam at their feet.
Nearer a white sail shines across the water, and nearer
Still are the slim grey masts of fishing boats dry on the
 flats.
Ah! how well I remember those wide red flats, above tide-
 mark,
Pale with scurf of the salt, seamed and baked in the sun!
Well I remember the piles of blocks and ropes, and the net-
 reels
Wound with the beaded nets, dripping and dark from the
 sea!
Now at this season the nets are unwound; they hang from
 the rafters
Over the fresh-stowed hay in upland barns, and the wind
Blows all day through the chinks, with the streaks of sun-
 light, and sways them
Softly at will; or they lie heaped in the gloom of a loft.

Now at this season the reels are empty and idle; I see them
Over the lines of the dikes, over the gossiping grass.
Now at this season they swing in the long strong wind,
   thro' the lonesome
Golden afternoon, shunned by the foraging gulls.
Near about sunset the crane will journey homeward above
   them;
Round them, under the moon, all the calm night long,
Winnowing soft grey wings of marsh-owls wander and
   wander,
Now to the broad lit marsh, now to the dusk of the dike.
Soon, thro' their dew-wet frames, in the live keen freshness
   of morning,
Out of the teeth of the dawn blows back the awakening
   wind.
Then, as the blue day mounts, and the low-shot shafts of the
   sunlight
Glance from the tide to the shore, gossamers jewelled with
   dew
Sparkle and wave, where late sea-spoiling fathoms of drift-net,
Myriad-meshed, uploomed sombrely over the land.

Well I remember it all. The salt raw scent of the margin;
While, with men at the windlass, groaned each reel, and
   the net,
Surging in ponderous lengths, uprose and coiled in its
   station;
Then each man to his home,—well I remember it all!

Yet, as I sit and watch, this present peace of the land-
   scape,—
Stranded boats, these reels empty and idle, the hush,

One grey hawk slow-wheeling above yon cluster of hay-stacks,—
More than the old-time stir this stillness welcomes me home.

Ah, the old-time stir, how once it stung me with rapture!
Old-time sweetness, the winds freighted with honey and salt!
Yet will I stay my steps and not go down to the marsh-land,—
Muse and recall far off, rather remember than see,—
Lest, on too close sight, I miss the darling illusion,
Spy at their task even here the hands of chance and change.

LOW TIDE ON GRAND-PRÉ.

Bliss Carman.

The sun goes down, and over all
   These barren reaches by the tide
Such unelusive glories fall,
   I almost dream they yet will bide
   Until the coming of the tide.

And yet I know that not for us,
   By any ecstasy of dream,
He lingers to keep luminous
   A little while the grievous stream,
   Which frets, uncomforted of dream,—

A grievous stream, that to and fro
   Athrough the fields of Acadie
Goes wandering, as if to know
   Why one beloved face should be
   So long from home and Acadie!

Was it a year or lives ago
   We took the grasses in our hands,
And caught the summer flying low
   Over the waving meadow lands,
   And held it there between our hands?

The while the river at our feet—
  A drowsy inland meadow stream—
At set of sun the after-heat
  Made running gold, and in the gleam
  We freed our birch upon the stream.

There down along the elms at dusk
  We lifted dripping blade to drift,
Through twilight scented fine like musk,
  Where night and gloom awhile uplift,
  Nor sunder soul and soul adrift.

And that we took into our hands—
  Spirit of life or subtler thing—
Breathed on us there, and loosed the bands
  Of death, and taught us, whispering,
  The secret of some wonder-thing.

Then all your face grew light, and seemed
  To hold the shadow of the sun;
The evening faltered, and I deemed
  That time was ripe, and years had done
  Their wheeling underneath the sun.

So all desire and all regret,
  And fear and memory, were naught;
One to remember or forget
  The keen delight our hands had caught;
  Morrow and yesterday were naught!

The night has fallen, and the tide . .
  Now and again comes drifting home,
Across these aching barrens wide,
  A sigh like driven wind or foam:
  In grief the flood is bursting home!

THE INDIAN NAMES OF ACADIA.

ATTRIBUTED TO DE MILLE.

THE memory of the Red Man,
   How can it pass away,
While his names of music linger
   On each mount and stream and bay?
While *Musquodobit's* waters
   Roll sparkling to the main;
While falls the laughing sunbeam
   On *Chegogin's* fields of grain.

While floats our country's banner
   O'er *Chebucto's* glorious wave;
And the frowning cliffs of *Scaterie*
   The trembling surges brave;
While breezy *Aspotogon*
   Lifts high its summit blue,
And sparkles on its winding way
   The gentle *Sissibou*.

While *Escasoni's* fountains
   Pour down their crystal tide;
While *Inganish's* mountains
   Lift high their forms of pride;
Or while on *Mabou's* river
   The boatman plies his oar;
Or the billows burst in thunder
   On *Chickaben's* rock-girt shore.

The memory of the Red Man,
    It lingers like a spell
On many a storm-swept headland,
    On many a leafy dell;
Where *Tusket's* thousand islets,
    Like emeralds, stud the deep;
Where *Blomidon*, a sentry grim,
    His endless watch doth keep.

It dwells round *Catalon's* blue lake,
    'Mid leafy forests hid,—
Round fair *Discourse*, and the rushing tides
    Of the turbid *Pisiquid*.
And it lends, *Chebogue*, a touching grace
    To thy softly flowing river,
As we sadly think of the gentle race
    That has passed away for ever.

ON LEAVING THE COAST OF NOVA SCOTIA.

GEORGE FREDERICK CAMERON.

I STAND alone at midnight on the deck,
And watch with eager eye the sinking shore
Which I may view, it may be, nevermore ;
For there is tempest, battle, fire, and wreck,
And Ocean hath her share of each of these,—
Attest it, thousand rotting argosies,
Wealth-laden, sunken in the southern seas !
And who can say that evermore these feet
Shall tread thy soil, Acadia ? Who can say
That evermore this heart of mine shall greet
The loved to whom it sighs adieu to-day ?
Our sail is set for countries far away ;
Our sail is set, and now is no retreat,
  Though Ocean should but lure, like Beauty, to
     betray !

THE FAIRIES IN PRINCE EDWARD ISLAND.

(From " The Emigration of the Fairies.")

JOHN HUNTER-DUVAR.

FIRST halt.   They heard within a sugar patch
   The rhyming tic-a-tac of axes chopping,
So scouts were sent ahead to try to catch
   A glimpse of whom or what 'twas caused the lopping,
And bring back a description of the natives—
If they were cannibals or friends, or caitiffs.

The scouts returned and said where they had stole,
   They'd seen a score or so of stalwart creatures
In flannel shirts, not smock-frocks; on the whole
   They rather liked their friendly bearded features,
And that the first glance of these live Canadians
Impressed them favourably—(they were Acadians).

Then onward.   Sudden on the horizon came
   A burst of blaze like to a town on fire,
While smoke in columns and fierce tongues of flame
   Rose grandly heavenwards, high and ever higher—
They were so scared they went by with a rush,
And did not know 'twas choppers burning brush.

With feelings as on field of Waterloo,
   They came upon a space of blackened stumps;
"Alas!" cried they, "here greenwood temples grew,
   And columns, ruined now, have stood in clumps."
They thought that war had here wiped out a nation
And left this ghastly scene of desolation.

They reached a scaffold frame beside a weir
   With criss-cross beams, and rafters gaunt and slewed,
And in it agonising screams could hear,
   And saw a whirling fiend devouring wood—
It was a sawmill, and, too scared for speech,
They skirred away beyond the monster's reach.

It pleased them much to see the birds about,
   And one boy cried, "A robin ! big as thrush !
Ma, can that be Cock Robin grown so stout?"
   Whereon his mother, with her thoughts a-rush
With English memories, said (and checked a sob in),
" My dear, that is a fowl and not a robin."

They saw woodpeckers hanging by the toes,
   Bluejay they thought was a professional beauty ;
They looked for rooks but only lit on crows,
   Whose only link with crows, is both are sooty ;
And as to linnets, finches, and those others,
They looked on them in light of little brothers.

A number of strange other things they noted
   As quite unlike what they had seen at home,
To all of which they curiously devoted
   Attention, as a gentle hill they clomb,
Where on them burst a true colonial scene
Of wood and meadow land of living green.

THE VALE OF THE GASPEREAU.

(*From " Gaspareau."*)

ARTHUR JOHN LOCKHART.

WOE fell on you, ye genial race
   Ye exiled sons of lily France!
This is no more your dwelling-place,—
   Ye live in music and romance;
But oft as purple even-tide
   Bathes all these hills in fire and dew,
Some wanderer by the river side
   Shall drop a tear and dream of you.

The Vale still rings with childhood's song,
   Amid its yellowing sea of flowers,
While days of summer glide along
   On wings of light through all your bowers.
Here are the trees ye planted, here
   The remnants of your broken homes;
But to old graves from year to year,
   No ghostly mourner ever comes.

IN THE AFTERNOON.

Charles G. D. Roberts.

Wind of the summer afternoon,
Hush, for my heart is out of tune!

Hush, for thou movest restlessly
The too light sleeper, Memory!

Whate'er thou hast to tell me, yet
'Twere something sweeter to forget,—

Sweeter than all thy breath of balm
An hour of unremembering calm!

Blowing over the roofs, and down
The bright streets of this inland town,

These busy crowds, these rocking trees,—
What strange note hast thou caught from these?

A note of waves and rushing tides,
Where past the dikes the red flood glides,

To brim the shining channels far
Up the green plains of Tantramar.

Once more I snuff the salt, I stand
On the long dikes of Westmoreland;

I watch the narrowing flats, the strip
Of red clay at the water's lip;

Far off the net-reels, brown and high,
And boat-masts slim against the sky;

Along the ridges of the dikes
Wind-beaten scant sea-grass, and spikes

Of last year's mullein; down the slopes
To landward, in the sun, thick ropes

Of blue vetch, and convolvulus,
And matted roses glorious.

The liberal blooms o'erbrim my hands;
I walk the level wide marsh-lands;

Waist-deep in dusty-blossomed grass
I watch the swooping breezes pass

In sudden long pale lines, that flee
Up the deep breast of this green sea.

I listen to the bird that stirs
The purple tops, and grasshoppers

Whose summer din, before my feet
Subsiding, wakes on my retreat.

Again the droning bees hum by;
Still-winged, the grey hawk wheels on high;

I drink again the wild perfumes,
And roll, and crush the grassy blooms.

Blown back to olden days, I fain
Would quaff the olden joys again;

But all the olden sweetness not
The old unmindful peace hath brought.

Wind of this summer afternoon,
Thou hast recalled my childhood's June;

Wind of the summer afternoon,
Be still; my heart is not in tune.

Sweet is thy voice; but yet, but yet,—
Of all 'twere sweetest to forget!

A DREAM FULFILLED.

Barry Straton.

Thirsting for bounteous Nature's ease
I spread my white sail to the breeze,
And through the crystal balm of morn
My airy birch was softly borne.

A blue league to the verdant west
Sleep on the Saint John's placid breast,
Like second Edens kindly lent,
The bosky Islands of Content.

All day their beauty was my own;
And there, when deep-eyed night came down,
In rapturous dreams I viewed again
The glories of my bright domain.

I saw the dawn blow gold and red,
By fluted robins heralded;
While over meadows starred with dew
Inspiring airs of nature blew.

Like silver gleaming, white like snow,
Rose-tinted in that throbbing glow,
The blue its drifting clouds displayed,
Dappling the fields with light and shade.

The wafted mist-wreaths, melting, shed
The scent of flowers which they had fed;
And lakelets gleamed with lilies white,
And vales with buttercups grew bright.

The infinite secrets of the trees
Rustled unreadably in the breeze,
And through the brooding of my dream
Rang white-capped laughter of the stream.

I saw the grape-vine spreading o'er
The tangled thickets by the shore,
Where ferns and milk-weed, cherry spray,
And fronded sumachs cooled the day.

I heard the buzzing sea-like hush
Of wild bees in the willow bush,
And through the honeysuckle stirred
The sleep-song of the humming-bird.

The white gull soared with wings agleam,
The golden perch shone in the stream,
And on the weed-caught log the crane
Pecked at his captured shells again.

Through restful hours thus stole away
The perfect, consummated day;
And in the sky, and in the stream,
I saw the sunset's glory gleam.

And ere the golden glow passed by,
The silvery moonlight filled the sky;
Like sister angels kissing, they,
The waxing night and waning day!

Then with the setting of the sun
The circle of my dream was run,
And, half awake, the vision flown,
I felt the bondage of the town.

But recollection swiftly came:
I roused, and saw the east aflame,
And lo, before my raptured eyes
My dreams became realities!

THE ISLE OF DEMONS.

(*From "Marguerite."*)

GEORGE MARTIN.

TOGETHER o'er the mystic Isle
We wandered many a sinuous mile.
'Twas midway in the month of June,
And rivulets with lisping rune,
And bowering trees of tender green,
And flowering shrubs their trunks between,
Enticed our steps till gloaming grey,
Upon the pathless forest lay.
Think not I journeyed void of fear;
   Sir Roberval's hot malediction,
Like hurtling thunder, sounded near;
Our steps the envious demons haunted,
    And peeped, or seemed to peep and leer,
    From rocky clefts and caverns drear.
But still, defiantly, undaunted,
Eugene averred it had been held
By wise philosophers of eld,
That all such sights and sounds are mere
Fantastic tricks of eye and ear,
   And only meet for tales of fiction.
"Heed not," he said, "the vicious threat,
   'Twas but a ruffian's empty talk,
The which I pray thou may'st forget
   And half his evil purpose baulk."

A silent doubt and grateful kiss
Was all I could oppose to this.
But firmer grew my steps.   The air
    Was laden with delicious balm ;
Rich exhalations everywhere,
    From pine and spruce and cedar grove,
And over all a dreamy calm,
    An affluence of brooding love,
A palpable, beneficent
Sufficiency of blest content.

Amid the hours, in restful pause
    We loitered on the moss-clad rocks,
And listened to the sober caws
    Of lonely rooks, and watched thick flocks
Of pigeons passing overhead ;
Or where the scarlet grosbeak sped,
    A wingéd fire, through clumps of pine
Sent chasing looks of joy and wonder.
    Blue violets and celandine,
And modest ferns that glanced from under
Gray-hooded boulders, seemed to say,—
" O, tarry, gentle folk ; O, stay,
    For we are lonely in this wood,
And sigh for human sympathy
    To cheer our days of solitude."

The great rude world was far away,
And like a troubled vision lay
Outside our thoughts ; its cold deceits,
The babble of its noisy streets,

And all the selfish rivalry
That courts and castles propagate,
Were alien to our new estate.—
A fragment of propitious sky,
Whereon a puff of cloud might lie,
Through verdured boughs o'er-arching seen,
And glimpses of the sea between
Far stretches of majestic trees,
Such peaceful sanctities as these
Were our abiding joyance now.

Cheerily, and with lifted brow,
Eugene led on, where tamaracs grew,
And where tall elms their shadows threw
Athwart a little glen, wherein
A virgin brook seemed glad to win
The pressure of our thirsty lips.
   Pleasant it was to linger there
And cool our fevered finger-tips
   In that pellucid stream, and share
The solace of the ocean breeze.
   For summer heats were now aglow;
The fox sat down and took his ease,
   The hare moved purposeless and slow;
But louder rang the bluejay's scream,
   The woodpeck tapped the naked tree,
   Nor ceased the simple chicadee
To twitter in the noonday beam.—
My lover, wheresoe'er we strayed,
   Made search in every charmed nook,
   And angled in the winding brook
For all sweet flowers that love the shade,
To twine for me a bridal braid.

Pale yellow lilies, nursed by rocks
Rifted and scarred by lightning shocks,
Or earthquake; river buds and pinks,
   And modest snow-drops, pearly white,
   And lilies of the vale, unite
Their beauty in close-loving links
Around a scented woodbine fair
To coronate my dark brown hair.
The fragile fern and clover sweet
On that enchanted circlet meet;
Young roses lent their blushing hues;
Nor could the cedar leaf refuse
With helmet flowers to intertwine
Its glossy amplitude divine.—
Emerging from that solemn wood,
High on a rocky cliff we stood
At set of sun; far, far away
The splendours of departing day
Upon the barren ocean lay.—
There, on that lone sea-beaten height,
Investured in a golden light,
Eugene, with looks half sad, whole sweet,
Upon my brow the garland set,
At once a chaplet and aigrette,
And said, " Be crowned, my Marguerite! "

Was it sick fancy, sore misled,
That to my shuddering spirit said?—
" Those sounds that shake the midnight air,
Are threats of Shapes that will not spare
Your trespass on their fief accurst."
   " Hush, hush, my love," Eugene would say,
" That cry which o'er our cabin burst
   Came from the owls, perched royally

Among the pine-tops; you but heard
The language of some beast or bird;
The mooing of a mother bear
An hungered in her frozen lair;
The laugh and mooing of the loon
That welcometh the rising moon;
The howling of the wolves you hear,
In chase of some unhappy deer,
Impeded in its desperate flight
   By deep and thickly crusted snows,
    O'er which its lighter-footed foes
Pursue like shadows of the night.
That lengthened groan, that fearful shriek,
Was but the grinding stress and creak
Of aged trees; they seem to feel
The wrench of storms, and make appeal
For mercy; in their ducts and cells
The sap, which is their life-blood, swells
When frosts prevail, and bursts asunder
With sharp report its prison walls."

The double darkness walled us in,
   The blackness of the storm and night,
And still he came not! O, what sin,
   What blasphemy against the light
Of Heaven had my soul committed?
   Never before had eventide
   Once found him absent from my side.
Eugene came not! deceived, outwitted,
   Sore tempest-tossed and lured astray
By demons, when the night-owl flitted
   Across his face at close of day,

Groping for home, exhausted, faint,
No angel near, no pitying saint
   To aid his steps and point the way!

From ebb of day till noon of night,
And onward till return of light,
The signal horn, Nanette and I,
Alternate blew; but for reply
The wind's unprecedented roar,
And ocean thundering round the shore
Our labour mocked; and other sounds,
Nor of the land, nor sea, nor sky,
Our ears profaned; the unleashed hounds
Of spleenful hell were all abroad,
And round our snow-bound cabin trod,
And stormed on clashing wings aloof,
And stamped upon the yielding roof,
And all our lamentation jeered.
Down the wide chimney-gorge they peered
   With great green eye-balls fringed with flame;—
The holy cross I kissed and reared,
   And in sweet Mary's blessed name,
Who erst had buoyed my sinking heart,
Conjured the foul-faced fiends depart.
Their shriekings made a storm more loud
Than that before whose fury bowed
The hundred-ringéd oaken trees;
More fearful, more appalling these
Than thunder from the thunder-cloud.

THE SECRET OF THE SAGUENAY.

Arthur Weir.

Like a fragment of torn sea-kale,
Or a wraith of mist in the gale,
There comes a mysterious tale
　　Out of the stormy past ;
How a fleet, with a living freight,
Once sailed through the rocky gate
Of this river so desolate,
　　This chasm so black and vast.

'Twas Cartier, the sailor bold,
Whose credulous lips had told
How glittering gems and gold
　　Were found in that lonely land :
How out of the priceless hoard
Within their rough bosoms stored,
These towering mountains poured
　　Their treasures upon the strand.

Allured by the greed of gain
Sieur Roberval turned again,
And, sailing across the main,
　　Passed up the St Lawrence tide ;
He sailed by the frowning shape
Of Jacques Cartier's Devil's Cape,
Till the Saguenay stood agape,
　　With hills upon either side.

Around him the sunbeams fell
On the gentle St Lawrence swell,
As though by some mystic spell
   The water was turned to gold;
But as he pursued, they fled,
Till his vessels at last were led
Where, cold and sullen and dead,
   The Saguenay River rolled.

Chill blew the wind in his face,
As, still on his treasure chase,
He entered that gloomy place
   Whose mountains in stony pride,
Still, soulless, merciless, sheer,
Their adamant sides uprear,
Naked and brown and drear,
   High over the murky tide.

No longer the sun shone bright
On the sails that, full and white,
Like sea-gulls winging their flight,
   Dipped in the silent wave;
But shadows fell thick around,
Till feeling and sight and sound
In their awful gloom were drowned,
   And sank in a depthless grave.

Far over the topmost height
Great eagles had wheeled in flight,
But, wrapped in the gloom of night,
   They ceased to circle and soar;

Grim silence reigned over all,
Save that from a rocky wall
A murmuring waterfall
   Leapt down to the river shore.

O! merciless walls of stone,
What happened that night is known
By you, and by you alone :
   Though the eagles unceasing scream
How once through that midnight air,
For an instant a trumpet's blare,
And the voices of men in prayer,
   Arose from the murky stream.

SAGUENAY.

(From the French of Fréchette.)

J. D. EDGAR.

The forest has spells to enchant me,
    The mountain has power to enthrall;
Yet the grace of a wayside blossom
    Can stir my heart deeper than all.

O towering steeps, that are mirrored
    On Saguenay's darkening breast!
O grim rocky heights, sternly frowning,
    The thunders have smitten your crest!

O sentinels, piercing the cloudland,
    Stand forth in stupendous array!
My brow, by your shadows enshrouded,
    Is humbled before you to-day.

But, peaks that are gilded by Heaven,
    Defiant you stand in your pride!
From glories too distant, above me,
    I turn to the friend by my side.

QUEBEC.

Charles Sangster.

Quebec! how regally it crowns the height,
Like a tanned giant on a solid throne!
Unmindful of the sanguinary fight,
The roar of cannon mingling with the moan
Of mutilated soldiers years agone,
That gave the place a glory and a name
Among the nations.   France was heard to groan;
England rejoiced, but checked the proud acclaim,—
A brave young chief had fall'n to vindicate her fame.

Wolfe and Montcalm! two nobler names ne'er graced
The page of history, or the hostile plain;
No braver souls the storm of battle faced,
Regardless of the danger or the pain.
They passed unto their rest without a stain
Upon their nature or their generous hearts.
One graceful column to the noble twain
Speaks of a nation's gratitude, and starts
The tear that Valour claims and Feeling's self imparts.

MONTREAL.

William M'Lennan.

Sprung from the hope of noble hearts,
    Brought into being through sacrifice
Of men and women who played their parts,
    And counted not their lives as the price.
She has grown in her strength like a Northern Queen,
    'Neath her crown of light and her robe of snow,
And stands in her beauty fair, between
    The Royal Mount and the River below.

Changing its hue with the changing skies,
    The river flows in its beauty rare;
While across the plain eternal, rise
    Boucherville, Rougemont, and St Hilaire.
Far to the westward lies Lachine,
    Gate of the Orient long ago,
When the virgin forest swept between
    The Royal Mount and the River below.

With its convent buildings low and white
    Nun's Island lies, half wood, half plain;
While abreast of the city, green and bright
    Springs the wooded crest of Ste. Helène.
In the east the shimmer of waves is seen,
    Where the River spreads in its onward flow
From the Royal City that lies between
    The Royal Mount and the River below.

MONTREAL.

W. D. LIGHTHALL.

REIGN on, majestic Ville-Marie!
   Spread wide thy ample robes of state;
   The heralds cry that thou art great,
And proud are thy young sons of thee.
Mistress of half a continent,
   Thou risest from thy girlhood's rest;
   We see thee conscious heave thy breast
And feel thy rank and thy descent.
Sprung of the saint and chevalier!
   And with the Scarlet Tunic wed!
   Mount Royal's crown upon thy head;
And past thy footstool, broad and clear,
St Lawrence sweeping to the sea:
Reign *on*, majestic Ville-Marie!

THE ST LAWRENCE.

K. L. Jones.

Swift from Ontario's side,
    Hating the lake's cold embraces,
Laughing, the blue waters glide
    Into far pleasanter places;
Threading the maze of the isles,
    Shimmering, shivering ever,
Wearing a wreathlet of smiles,
    Rolls the great river;

Trending through darkness and day,
    Fondling the dawning and gloaming;
Tossing huge billows and spray
    High, when the Storm King is roaming;
Mirroring chalet-crowned rocks,
    Fern leaves, long grasses, and clover,
Wild fowls in myriad flocks
    As they fly over;

Sleeping in lily-starred bays;
    Rushing through factory races,
Where o'er the looms ever gaze
    Hundreds of bloom-bereft faces;
Wid'ning to lakelets and meres,
    Wildly o'er cascades careering,
Sweeping by bridges and piers,
    Ocean-ward bearing;

Chafing the Laurentide shore,—
   Cliffs frowning over, and under
Hurtling the dark waters roar
   As if they would tear them asunder,—
Past the grim fortress and plain
   Linked with brave Wolfe and his story,
Pealing in pœan's refrain
   Canada's glory;

Stretching her arms to the world,
   Wide, as a maid to her lover;
Coyly, with banners unfurled,
   Welcoming argosies over;
Wearied, her life's journey done,
   Grateful to God, the life-giver,
Her goal on the ocean's breast won,
   Rests the great river.

NIGHT IN THE THOUSAND ISLES.

Charles Sangster.

And now 'tis night. A myriad stars have come
To cheer the earth and sentinel the skies.
The full-orbed moon irradiates the gloom,
And fills the air with light. Each islet lies
Immersed in shadow, soft as thy dark eyes;
Swift through the sinuous path our vessel glides,
Now hidden by the massive promontories,
Anon the bubbling silver from its sides
Spurning, like a wild-bird whose home is on the tides.

Here Nature holds her Carnival of Isles.
Steeped in warm sunlight all the merry day,
Each nodding tree and floating greenwood smiles,
And moss-crowned monsters move in grim array;
All night the Fisher spears his finny prey;
The piney flambeaux reddening the deep,
Past the dim shores, or up some mimic bay;
Like grotesque banditti they boldly sweep
Upon the startled prey, and stab them while they sleep.

Many a tale of legendary lore
Is told of these romantic Isles. The feet
Of the Red Man have pressed each wave-zoned shore,
And many an eye of beauty oft did greet
The painted warriors and their birchen fleet,

As they returned with trophies of the slain.
That race has passed away; their fair retreat
In its primeval loneness smiles again,
Save where some vessel snaps the isle-enwoven chain;

Save where the echo of the huntsman's gun
Startles the wild duck from some shallow nook,
Or the swift hounds' deep baying, as they run,
Rouses the lounging student from his book;
Or where, assembled by some sedgy brook,
A pic-nic party, resting in the shade,
Spring pleasedly to their feet, to catch a look
At the strong steamer, through the watery glade
Ploughing, like a huge serpent from its ambuscade.

OTTAWA.

Before Dawn.

DUNCAN CAMPBELL SCOTT.

THE stars are stars of morn; a keen wind wakes
The birches on the slope; the distant hills
Rise in the vacant North; the Chaudière fills
The calm with its hushed roar; the river takes
An unquiet rest, and a bird stirs, and shakes
The morn with music; a snatch of singing thrills
From the river; and the air clings and chills.
Fair, in the South, fair as a shrine that makes
The wonder of a dream, imperious towers
Pierce and possess the sky, guarding the halls
Where our young strength is welded strenuously;
While in the East, the star of morning dowers
The land with a large tremulous light, that falls
A pledge and presage of our destiny.

AT THE FERRY.

E. Pauline Johnson.

We are waiting in the nightfall by the river's placid rim,
Summer silence all about us, save where swallows' pinions skim
The still grey waters sharply, and the widening circles reach,
With faintest, stillest music, the white gravel on the beach.
The sun has set long, long ago. Against the pearly sky
Elm branches lift their etching up in arches slight and high.
Behind us stands the forest, with its black and lonely pines;
Before us, like a silver thread, the old Grand River winds.
Far down its banks the village lights are creeping one by one;
Far up above, with holy torch, the evening star looks down.

Amid the listening stillness, you and I have silent grown,
Waiting for the river ferry,—waiting in the dusk alone.
At last we hear a velvet step, sweet silence reigns no more;
'Tis a barefoot, sun-burnt little boy upon the other shore.
Far thro' the waning twilight we can see him quickly kneel
To lift the heavy chain, then turn the rusty old cog-wheel;
And the water-logged old ferry-boat moves slowly from the brink,
Breaking all the star's reflections with the waves that rise and sink;

While the water dripping gently from the rising, falling chains,
Is the only interruption to the quiet that remains
To lull us into golden dreams, to charm our cares away
With its Lethean waters flowing 'neath the bridge of yesterday.
Oh! the day was calm and tender, but the night is calmer still,
As we go aboard the ferry, where we stand and dream, until
We cross the sleeping river, with its restful whisperings,
And peace falls, like a feather from some passing angel's wings.

NIAGARA.

(From " The U. E.")

WILLIAM KIRBY.

Now sailed the cloudless moon through seas of light
And dimmed the sleepless stars that watch the night,
As swiftly turning from the sandy lane
The riders crossed a spacious rolling plain,
Hedged by the lofty screen of dusky woods
That hide Niagara's deep-embedded floods.
White clouds of mist rolled upward on the breeze,
Swept o'er the brink, and dripped among the trees;
While earth and air, in tremor all around,
Shook in dread cadence to the rumbling sound
That rises up from Nature's troubled womb,
With war unbroken till the day of doom.
They hurried on; the woody veil withdrew,
The wondrous vision swept full into view;
Niagara's twin-born cataracts descend,
And eye and ear with their contention rend.
A spot of chaos, from Creation's day
Left unsubdued, to show the world alway
What was the earth ere God's commandment ran
That light should be, and order first began.

The riders halt, and for a moment stay,
While Ranger John half chid the brief delay.

Though often seen before, with fresh desire
The glorious vision still they each admire.
Spread o'er the south, a furious tumbling sea
Rolls down the steep incline, as wild and free
As when with tossing heads and flowing manes
The desert steeds in herds sweep o'er the plains,—
As in th' Olympic Stadium's final round
The chariot wheels revolve with thundering sound,
While veiled in clouds of dust the champions fly,
And shouts and turmoil shake the earth and sky!

Thus down the rocky rapids, side by side,
A thousand foaming currents madly ride;
Now mingling, now dividing, each and all
Still swifter hurry to the final goal.
There, waves that washed Superior's rocky strand,
And rolled transparent o'er her silver sand,
So pure and limpid, that they seemed to bear
The bark canoe afloat in very air,
Now, lashed to madness, o'er the rapids ran,
Yoked to the darker waves of Michigan;
St Clair's shoal streams, and Huron's haunted floods
That tumbled round the Manitoulin woods,
And fretful Erie's waters, in dismay
Sweep white with terror down the shelvy way.

In vain, Goat Island, dank, and grim with scars
Of an eternity of watery wars,
With stony shoulder stems the rushing tides
That right and left his dripping shore divides.
They 'scape his grasp, and o'er the jutting brink
Sheer down on either hand impetuous sink;

The vail of waters rending, as they go
'Mid storms of mist into the gulf below,
Where, face to face, the sundered torrents pour
In rival cataracts, with deafening roar,
Mingle their sprays, and with their mighty war
Shake earth's deep centre with eternal jar.

That dread abyss! What mortal tongue may tell
The seething horrors of its watery hell!
Where, pent in craggy walls that gird the deep,
Imprisoned tempests howl, and madly sweep
The tortured floods, drifting from side to side
In furious vortices, that circling ride
Around the deep arena; or, set free
From depths unfathomed, bursts a boiling sea
In showers of mist and spray, that leap and bound
Against the dripping rocks; while loud resound
Ten thousand thunders, that as one conspire
To strike the deepest note of Nature's lyre.

LAKE COUCHICHING.

W. A. Sherwood.

Oft have I loitered listening, Couchiching,
    To the soft lull of distant waving trees
At evening, and the sweet murmuring
    Of waters waken'd with the evening breeze
To one, whilst wandering thy shores along
Unseen, sweet voices hymn their evening song.

Long since the Red Man named thee Couchiching,
    Or built his wigwam rude upon thy shore;
But longer after shall the minstrel sing
    Of him that named thee but knows thee no more.
Unlike with thee had I that minstrel power,
I'd sing thee long, I'd sing thee every hour!

Hallowed that morn when first we learn to know
    How near to Nature are the hearts we prove;
More hallowed still in even's after-glow,
    How dear to Nature is the one we love.
Thus thy bright waters, joyous Couchiching,
O'er one I love for ever seem to sing.

THE HEART OF THE LAKES.

William Wilfred Campbell.

There are crags that loom like spectres
   Half under the sun and the mist,
There are beaches that gleam and glisten,
There are ears that open to listen,
   And lips held up to be kissed.

There are miles and miles of waters
   That throb like a woman's breast,
With a glad harmonious motion,
   Like happiness caught at rest;
As if a heart beat under
   In love with its own glad rest,
Beating and beating for ever
   Outward to east and to west.

There are forests that kneel for ever,
   Robed in the dreamiest haze
That God sends down in the Summer
   To mantle the gold of its days;
Kneeling and leaning for ever
   In winding and sinuous bays.

There are birds that like smoke-drift hover
   With a strange and bodeful cry,
Into the dream and the distance
   Of the marshes that southward lie,
With their lonely lagoons and rivers,
   Far under the reeling sky.

VAPOUR AND BLUE.

William Wilfred Campbell.

Domed with the azure of heaven,
Floored with a pavement of pearl;
Clothed all about with a brightness,
Soft as the eyes of a girl.

Girt with a magical girdle,
Rimmed with a vapour of rest,—
These are the inland waters,
These are the lakes of the west.

Voices of slumberous music,
Spirits of mist and of flame;
Moonlight memories, left here
By gods who long ago came;

And, long flitting, left but an echo
In silence of moon-dim caves,
Where haze-wrapt the August night sleeps,
Or the wild heart of October raves.

Here, where the jewels of Nature
Are set in the light of God's smile,
Far from the world's wild throbbing and beat,
I will stay me and rest me a while;

And store in my heart old music,
Melodies gathered and sung
By the genies of love and of beauty,
When the heart of the world was young.

MEDWAYOSH.

William Wilfred Campbell.

A REALM of dreams, where sky and water merge
In far dim vapours, mingling blue in blue;
Where low-rimmed shores shimmer like gold shot
    through
Some misty fabric. Lost, in dreams I urge
With lazy oar my skiff through sunny surge,
That rings its music round the rocks and sands;
Passing to silence, where far-lying lands
Loom blue and purpling from the morning's verge.

I linger in dreams, and through my dreaming comes,
Like sound of suff'ring heard through battle drums,
An anguished call of sad heart-broken speech;
As if some wild lake-spirit, long ago,
Soul-wronged, through hundred years its wounded woe
Moans out in vain across each wasted beach.

MANITOU.

William Wilfred Campbell.

[The island of the Manitou, the largest island in Lake Huron, believed by the Indians to be sacred to Manitou when he makes his abode on earth.]

GIRDLED by Huron's throbbing and thunder,
   Out on the drift and rift of its blue;
Walled by mists from the world asunder,
Far from all hate and passion and wonder,
   Lieth the isle of the Manitou.

Here, where the surfs of the great Lake trample
   Thundering time-worn caverns through,
Beating on rock-coasts aged and ample,
Reareth the Manitou's mist-walled temple,
   Floored with forest and roofed with blue.

Grey crag-battlements, seared and broken,
   Keep these passes for ages to come;
Never a watchword here is spoken,
Never a single sign or token,
   From hands that are motionless, lips that are dumb.

Only the sun-god rideth over,
   Marking the seasons with track of flame ;
Only the wild-fowl float and hover,—
   Flocks of clouds, whose white wings cover
     Spaces on spaces without a name.

Stretches of marsh and wild lake-meadow,
   Beaches that bend to the edge of the world ;
Morn and even, suntime and shadow ;
Wild flame of sunset over far meadow,
   Fleets of white vapours sun-kissed and furled.

Year by year the ages onward
   Drift, but it lieth out here alone ;
Earthward the mists, and the earth-mists sunward ;
Starward the days, and the nights bloom dawnward ;
   Whisper the forests, the beaches make moan.

Far from the world, and its passions fleeting,
   'Neath quiet of noonday and stillness of star,
Shore unto shore each sendeth greeting,
Where the only woe is the surf's wild beating
   That throbs from the maddened lake afar.

TO THE LAKES.

WILLIAM WILFRED CAMPBELL.

BLUE, limpid, mighty, restless lakes,
   God's mirrors underneath the sky;
Low rimmed in woods and mists, where wakes,
   Through murk and moon, the marsh-bird's cry.

Where ever on, through drive and drift,
   'Neath blue and grey, through hush and moan,
Your ceaseless waters ebb and lift,
   Past shores of century-crumbling stone.

And under ever-changing skies,
   Swell, throb, and break on kindling beach;
Where fires of dawn responsive rise,
   In answer to your mystic speech.

Past lonely haunts of gull and loon,
   Past solitude of land-locked bays,
Whose bosoms rise to meet the moon
   Beneath their silvered film of haze.

Where mists and fogs—in ghostly bands,
   Vague, dim, moon-clothed in spectral white—
Drift in from far-off haunted lands,
   Across the silences of night.

THE LEGEND OF RESTLESS RIVER.

WILLIAM WILFRED CAMPBELL.

INTO the vague unrest
Of Huron's mighty breast,
Runneth the Restless River;
Into the north and west,
Out of the forest's vest,
Its face is set for ever.

Moons wane through spaces white,
As marsh-birds wheel their flight,
As dawns reel into night,
As souls from souls dissever;
But over the sands to the bay,
Past the forests that pray,
The river it runneth for ever.

It was a curse, and worse,
A curse on the Restless River;
Moons and moons ago,
Before the ages of snow
And ice and rains that shiver,
Came the curse of the Restless River.

What was this terrible curse?
Never in tale or verse
Did singer or chief rehearse;
Warrior sang it never;
But only the Manitou,
Who knoweth all things, knew
The secret of Restless River.

Where other streams might sleep
In eddies cool and deep,
Beneath where cascades leap
In sunny snowy surges;
With never a dreaming place,
With never a breathing space,
In one wild tortuous race,
Its maddened tide it urges.

Why this horrible dread?
This fear of the midnight dead,
When the stars peer overhead,
Out of lone spaces winging?
Men say that the stars and moon
At the silence of midnight noon,
Never mirrored themselves in its singing.

That its song was only a moan
For a sin it could never atone;
Of all earth's waters, alone
It runs in the darkness for ever;
And that never the song of bird,
Save only in sadness, is heard
On the shores of the Restless River.

Men say, at noon of day,
In thickets far away
Where skies are dim and grey,
And birches stir and shiver,
That out of the gloomy air
A voice goes up in prayer
From the shores of the Restless River.

Whatever its sin hath been,
Its shores are just as green,
And over it kindly lean
Great forests heavenward growing;
And its waters are just as sweet,
And its tides more strong and fleet
Than any river flowing.

But for all its outward mirth,
And the glow that spans its girth,
Its voices from air and earth,
Its walls of leaves that quiver;
Men say an awful curse,
As dread as death, and worse,
Hangs over the Restless River.

And the dreamy Indian girl,
When she sees its waters curl
In many a silver whirl,
Hath pity on Restless River;
For she knoweth that, long ago,
Its tides, that once were slow,
By reason of some dread woe
Went suddenly swift for ever;
That a dread and unknown curse,
For a sin, or something worse,
Was laid on the Restless River.

MORNING ON THE BEACH.

June.

WILLIAM WILFRED CAMPBELL.

SEE, the night is beginning to fail,
    The stars have lost half of their glow,
As though all the flowers in a garden did pale
    When a rose is beginning to blow.

And the breezes that herald the dawn,
    Blown round from the caverns of day,
Lift the film of dark from the heaven's bare lawn,
    Cool and sweet as they come up this way.

And this mighty green bough of the lake,
    Rocks cool where the morning hath smiled ;
While this dim misty dome of the world, scarce awake,
    Blushes rose like the cheek of a child.

DAWN IN THE ISLAND CAMP.

October.

WILLIAM WILFRED CAMPBELL.

RED in the mists of the morning, angry, coloured with fire,
Beats the great Lake in its beauty,
Rocks the wild lake in its ire.
Tossing from headland to headland, tipped with the glories of dawn,
With gleaming wide reaches of beaches
That stretch out, far, wind-swept, and wan.

Behind, the wild tangle of island swept and drenched by the gales of the night;
In front, lone stretches of water
Flame-bathed by the incoming light;
Dim the dark reels and dips under, night wavers and ceases to be,
As God sends the manifold mystery
Of the morning and lake round to me.

LAKE HURON.

In October.

WILLIAM WILFRED CAMPBELL.

MILES and miles of lake and forest,
Miles and miles of sky and mist;
Marsh and shoreland, where the rushes
Rustle, wind and water kissed;
Where the lake's great face is driving,
Driving, drifting into mist.

Miles and miles of crimson glories,
Autumn's wondrous fires ablaze;
Miles of shoreland, red and golden,
Drifting into dream and haze,—
Dreaming where the woods and vapours
Melt in myriad misty ways.

Miles and miles of lake and forest,
Miles and miles of sky and mist;
Wild birds calling, where the rushes
Rustle, wind and water kissed;
Where the lake's great face is driving,
Driving, drifting into mist.

INDIAN SUMMER.

WILLIAM WILFRED CAMPBELL.

ALONG the line of smoky hills
   The crimson forest stands,
And all the day the blue-jay calls
   Throughout the autumn lands.

Now by the brook the maple leans,
   With all his glory spread ;
And all the sumachs on the hills
   Have turned their green to red.

Now, by great marshes wrapt in mist,
   Or past some river's mouth,
Throughout the long still autumn day
   Wild birds are flying south.

SAULT STE. MARIE.

Pamelia Vining Yule.

Laughing and singing
  With rythmical flow,
Leaping and springing,
  O light-hearted Sault!
Tossing up snowy hands
  In thy glad play,
Shaking out dew locks
  Bright with the spray,—
Joyously ever
  The bright waters go,
Yet wearying never,
  O beautiful Sault!

Kingly Superior
  Leaps to thy arms,
And all his broad waters
  Are bright with thy charms;
They sparkle and glitter,
  And flash in their play,
Chasing ripple and rainbow
  Away and away!
Weary, I ween,
  Of his solemn repose,
Gaily the mighty flood
  Flashes and flows;

And, buoyantly, brightly,
    Fleet-footed or slow,
Doth dance with thee lightly,
    Unwearying Sault!

Yet the dance is thine own,
    And the song and the glee;
Thou dwellest alone,
    Untrammelled and free!
Our ships may not glide
    O'er thy bosom,—our feet
May not trace out one path,
    Or explore one retreat!
We may hollow our channels
    To left or to right,
And glide on our way
    With thy gambols in sight.
Yet this, and this only,
    Of thee we may know,
Thou lone, but not lonely,
    Free, fetterless Sault!

Farewell, ye bright waters,—
    We part, and for aye!
My pathway leads on
    O'er the billows away;
These feet will grow weary
    In life's busy mart,
These eyes be oft tear-dim,
    And heavy this heart;
But thou wilt sing on
    In thy joyous unrest,
Unchanging, unwearying,
    Buoyant and blest.

While the slow-footed centuries
  Glide on their way,
And nations grow hoary
  And sink in decay,
Thou, tireless and tameless,
  Unchecked in thy flow,
Shalt sing on as ever,
  O beautiful Sault !

LE LAC DES MORTS.

Bishop George J. Mountain.

" Res obscura quidem est ignobilitate virorum . . . vidi praesens stagnumque lacumque."—Ov. Met.

LAKE of the Dead! I find not why
   This name is thine, from tale or song:
Living are none who meet the eye,
   Morn after morn, these wilds along.

It may be, in an earlier day
   Some Indian strife disturb'd the scene;
And man's red blood, of man the prey,
   Mix'd with thine azure waves serene.

It may be, that with maddening yells
   These wood-clad shores and isles have rung,
And chiefs, whose name no legend tells,
   Dead, in thy rocky depths were flung.

Perchance more late, some hardy crew,
   Charged with the northern hunter's spoils,—
Freight to far cities yearly due,—
   Closed in thy breast their earthly toils.

Oft did their bell-toned chorus sound
   In strains received from Norman sires:
Oft did the forest glare around
   In witness of their nightly fires.

Through many a whirling flood they sent
  Fearless and prompt their bark-built boat;
Anon their single canvas bent
  Glad idly in free space to float.

Too venturous once—if thence thy name,
  Fair Lake—and have such chances been?
Ah! let each lowly cross proclaim
  Along this lengthening journey seen.

Lake of the Dead! thy shores beside,
  In evening gloom now gathering fast,
No shadowy forms or phantoms glide,
  No shrieks unearthly swell the blast.

Yet if beneath thy lonely waves
  The bones of sinful man be spread,
Thou, like old ocean's hidden caves,
  Shalt yield thy long-forgotten dead.

THE BUFFALO PLAINS.

(Tecumseh, Act IV., Scene 7.)

CHARLES MAIR.

LEFROY.   We left
The silent forest, and, day after day,
Great prairies swept beyond our aching sight
Into the measureless West; uncharted realms,
Voiceless and calm, save when tempestuous wind
Rolled the rank herbage into billows vast,
And rushing tides, which never found a shore.
And tender clouds, and veils of morning mist,
Cast flying shadows, chased by flying light
Into interminable wildernesses,
Flushed with fresh blooms, deep perfumed by the rose,
And murmurous with flower-fed bird and bee.
The deep-grooved bison-paths like furrows lay,
Turned by the cloven hoofs of thundering herds
Primeval, and still travelled as of yore.
And gloomy valleys opened at our feet,—
Shagged with dusk cypresses and hoary pine;
And sunless gorges, rummaged by the wolf,
Which through long reaches of the prairie wound,
Then melted slowly into upland vales,
Lingering, far-stretched amongst the spreading hills.

BROCK.—What charming solitudes! And life was there!

LEFROY.—Yes, life was there! inexplicable life,
Still wasted by inexorable death.
There had the stately stag his battle-field,—
Dying for mastery among his hinds.
There vainly sprung the affrighted antelope,
Beset by glittering eyes and hurrying feet.
The dancing grouse, at their insensate sport,
Heard not the stealthy footstep of the fox;
The gopher on his little earthwork stood,
With folded arms, unconscious of the fate
That wheeled in narrowing circles overhead;
And the poor mouse, on heedless nibbling bent,
Marked not the silent coiling of the snake.
At length we heard a deep and solemn sound,—
Erupted moanings of the troubled earth
Trembling beneath innumerable feet.
A growing uproar, blending in our ears
With noise tumultuous as ocean's surge,
Of bellowings, fierce breath, and battle shock,
And ardour of unconquerable herds.
A multitude whose trampling shook the plains,
With discord of harsh sound and rumblings deep,
As if the swift revolving earth had struck,
And from some adamantine peak recoiled,
Jarring. At length we topped a high-browed hill,—
The last and loftiest of a file of such,—
And, lo! before us lay the tameless stock,
Slow-wending to the northward like a cloud!
A multitude in motion, dark and dense,—
Far as the eye could reach, and farther still,
In countless myriads stretched for many a league.

BROCK.—You fire me with the picture! What a
  scene!
LEFROY.—Nation on nation was invillaged there,
Skirting the flanks of that imbanded host;
With chieftains of strange speech and port of war,
Who, battle-armed, in weather-brawny bulk,
Roamed fierce and free in huge and wild content.
These gave Tecumseh greetings fair and kind,
Knowing the purpose havened in his soul.

THE LAST BISON.

CHARLES MAIR.

EIGHT years have fled since, in the wilderness,
I drew the rein to rest my comrade there,—
My supple, clean-limbed pony of the plains.
He was a runner of pure Indian blood,
Yet in his eye still gleamed the desert's fire,
And form and action both bespoke the Barb.
A wondrous creature is the Indian's horse;
Degenerate now, but from the "Centaur" drawn,—
The furious Fifty which dissolved with fear
Montezuma's plumed Children of the Sun,
And shared rough Cortez in his realm of gold!

A gentle vale, with rippling aspens clad,
Yet open to the breeze, invited rest.
So there I lay, and watched the sun's fierce beams
Reverberate in wreathed ethereal flame;
Or gazed upon the leaves which buzzed o'erhead,
Like tiny wings in simulated flight.
Within the vale a lakelet, lashed with flowers,
Lay like a liquid eye among the hills,
Revealing in its depths the fulgent light
Of snowy cloudland and cerulean skies.
And rising, falling, fading far around,
The homeless and unfurrowed prairies spread
In solitude and idleness eterne.

And all was silence, save the rustling leaf,
The gadding insect, or the grebe's lone cry ;
Or where Saskatchewan, with turbid moan,
Deep-sunken in the plain, his torrent poured.
Here loneliness possessed her realm supreme—
Her prairies all about her, undeflowered,
Pulsing beneath the summer sun, and sweet
With virgin air and waters undefiled.
Inviolate still! Bright solitudes with power
To charm the spirit, bruised, where ways are foul,
Into forgetfulness of chuckling wrong,
And all the weary clangour of the world.

Yet Sorrow, too, had here its kindred place,
As o'er my spirit swept the sense of change.
Here sympathy could sigh o'er man's decay ;
For here, but yesterday, the warrior dwelt
Whose faded nation had for ages held,
In fealty to Nature, these domains.
Around me were the relics of his race,—
The grassy circlets where his village stood,
Well ruled by custom's immemorial law.
Along these slopes his happy offspring roved
In days gone by, and dusky mothers' plied
Their summer tasks, or loitered in the shade.
Here the magician howled his demons up ;
And here the lodge of council had its seat,
Once resonant with oratory wild.
All vanished! perished in the swelling sea
And stayless tide of an encroaching power,
Whose civil fiat, man-devouring still,
Will leave at last no wilding on the earth
To wonder at or love.

                    With them had fled
The bison,—breed which overflowed the plains,
And, undiminished, fed uncounted tribes.
Its vestiges were here,—its wallows, paths,
And skulls and shining ribs and vertebræ;
Grey bones of monarchs, from the herds perchance
Descended, by De Vaca first beheld,
Or Coronado, in mad quest of gold.
Here hosts had had their home; here had they
        roamed,
Endless and infinite,—vast herds which seemed
Exhaustless as the sea. All vanished now!
Of that wild tumult not a hoof remained
To scour the countless paths where myriads trod.

Long had I lain, 'twixt dreams and waking, thus:
Musing on change and mutability,
And endless evanescence, when a burst
Of sudden roaring filled the vale with sound.
Perplexed and startled, to my feet I sprang,
And in amazement from my covert gazed;
For presently into the valley came
A mighty bison, which with stately tread
And gleaming eyes descended to the shore!
Spell-bound I stood. Was this a living form,
Or but an image by the fancy drawn?
But no,—he breathed! and from a wound blood
        flowed
And trickled with the frothing from his lips.
Uneasily he gazed, yet saw me not,
Haply concealed; then, with a roar so loud
That all the echoes rent their valley-horns,
He stood and listened; but no voice replied!

Deeply he drank, then lashed his quivering flanks,
And roared again, and hearkened, but no sound,
No tongue congenial answered to his call,—
He was the last survivor of his clan !

Huge was his frame ! emasculate, so grown
To that enormous bulk whose presence filled
The very vale with awe. His shining horns
Gleamed black amidst his fell of floating hair ;
His neck and shoulders, of the lion's build,
Were framed to toss the world ! Now stood he there
And stared, with head uplifted, at the skies,
Slow-yielding to his deep and mortal wound.
He seemed to pour his mighty spirit out
As thus he gazed, till my own spirit burned,
And teeming fancy, charmed and overwrought
By all the wildering glamour of the scene,
Gave to that glorious altitude a voice,
And, rapt, endowed the noble beast with song.

The Song.

Hear me, ye smokeless skies and grass green earth,
  Since by your sufferance still I breathe and live !
Through you fond Nature gave me birth
  And food and freedom,—all she had to give.
Enough ! I grew, and with my kindred ranged
Their realm stupendous, changeless, and unchanged,
  Save by the toll of nations primitive,
Who throve on us, and loved our life-stream's roar,
And lived beside its wave, and camped upon its shore.

They loved us, but they wasted not.   They slew,
   With pious hand, but for their daily need ;
Not wantonly, but as the due
   Of stern necessity which Life doth breed.
Yea, even as earth gave us its herbage meet,
So yielded we, in turn, our substance sweet
   To quit the claims of hunger, not of greed.
So stood it with us, that what either did
Could not be on the earth foregone, nor Heaven forbid.

And so companioned in the blameless strife
   Enjoined upon all creatures, small and great,
Our ways were venial, and our life
   Ended in fair fulfilment of our fate.
No gold to them by sordid hands were passed ;
No greedy herdsman housed us from the blast.
   Ours was the liberty of regions rife
In winter's snow, in summer's fruits and flowers,—
Ours were the virgin prairies, and their rapture ours !

So fared it with us both ; yea, thus it stood
   In all our wanderings from place to place,
Until the red man mixed his blood
   With paler currents.   Then arose a race—
The reckless hunters of the plains—who vied
In wanton slaughter for the tongue and hide,
   To satisfy vain ends and longings base.
This grew ; and yet we flourished, and our name
Prospered upon the earth, until the pale-faced concourse
      came.

Then fell a double terror on the plains,
   The swift inspreading of destruction dire,—

Strange men, who ravaged our domains
   On every hand, and ringed us round with fire;
Pale enemies, who slew with equal mirth
The harmless or the hurtful things of earth,
   In dead fruition of their mad desire;
The ministers of mischief and of might,
Who yearn for havoc as the world's supreme delight.

So waned the myriads, which had waxed before
   When subject to the simple needs of men.
As yields to eating seas the shore,
   So yielded our vast multitude; and then—
It scattered! Meagre bands, in wild dismay,
Were parted, and for shelter fled away
   To barren wastes, to mountain gorge and glen;
A respite brief from stern pursuit and care,
For still the spoiler sought, and still he slew us there.

Hear me, thou grass-green earth, ye smokeless skies,
   Since by your sufferance still I breathe and live!
The charity which man denies
   Ye still would tender to the fugitive!
I feel your mercy in my veins; at length
My heart revives, and strengthens with your strength.
   Too late, too late, the courage ye would give!
Nought can avail these wounds, this failing breath,
This frame which feels, at last, the wily touch of death.

Here must the last of all his kindred fall;
   Yet, 'midst these gathering shadows, ere I die,—
Responsive to an inward call,—
   My spirit fain would rise and prophesy.

I see our spoilers build their cities great
Upon our plains,—I see their rich estate;
   The centuries in dim procession fly!
Long ages roll, and then at length is bared
The time when they who spared not are no longer spared.

Once more my vision sweeps the prairies wide:
   But now, no peopled cities greet the sight,—
All perished now, their pomp and pride;
   In solitude the wild wind takes delight.
Nought but the vacant wilderness is seen,
And grassy mounds where cities once had been:
   The earth smiles as of yore, the skies are bright,
Wild cattle graze and bellow on the plain,
And savage nations roam o'er native wilds again!

   The burden ceased: and now, with head bowed down
   The bison smelt, then grinned into the air.
   An awful anguish seized his giant frame,
   Cold shudderings and indrawn gaspings deep,—
   The spasms of illimitable pain.
   One stride he took, and sank upon his knees,
   Glared stern defiance where I stood revealed,
   Then swayed to earth, and, with convulsive groan,
   Turned heavily upon his side, and died.

A PRAIRIE YEAR.

From "Eos: A Prairie Dream.'

NICHOLAS FLOOD DAVIN.

THE depths of infinite shade,
    The soft green dusk of the glade,
With fiery fingers the frost had fret,
    And dyed a myriad hue,
Making of forests temples of golden aisles:
      The swooning rose forgot to bloom;
    In fragrant graves slept violets blue;
    And earlier shook her locks of jet
    Night, with her subtle shadowy wiles,—
      Night, with her starry gloom,—
Before, like suns which could not set,
    Your eyes shone clear on mine,
Flushing the heart with feelings high,
Touching all life, as thrills the sky
When over cloudy pavements thunders rumble and
      roll;
    Then flamed the faltering bloodlike wine,
    And overflowed the soul.

Through wintry weeks, the sun above
    Oceaned in blue, the frost below;
Through blustry hours, when fiercely drove
    Winds razor-armed the drifting snow,
And peeled the face and pinched the ear,
And hurled the avalanche of fear

From roof-tops on the mufflered crowd;
  The air one blinding cloud;—
Through many a brisk and bracing day,
  The sky wide summer as in June,
  The joyous sleigh-bells' ringing tune
More blithe than aught musicians play;
  The pure snow gleaming white;
  Men's eyes fulfilled of finer light,
Of finer tints the women's hair;
  Their cheeks aglow, and full and pink;
  The skaters sweeping through the rink,
Like swallows through the air:
We talked and walked, and laughed and dreamed,
  And now snow-wreaths, auroral rays,
  The winter moon, day's blinding blaze,
  The merry bells, the skaters' grace,
  Recall thy laugh, recall thy face
As dazzling as it earliest beamed!

Love stirred in the frozen branches,
  And straight the world was crown'd with green;
And as a shipwright his trim craft launches,
Each bud put forth in a night its might,
  And the trees stood proud in summer sheen,
  Their foliage dense a grateful screen
'Gainst the bold bright heat and the full fierce light.
Like cathedral windows the gardens glowed;
  Mirrors of light the broad lakes gleamed;
His cunning in song the robin showed,
  And the shore-lark swung on a branch and dreamed;
And boats were gliding, lover-laden,
  Over lakes and streams that will yet be known,—

The boy in flannel, the blooming maiden
   In muslin white with a ribbon zone.
The chestnuts fell. From their dull green sheaths
   With satin-white linings the nuts burst free;
And as sun-down came, bright hazy wreaths
   The spirit of eve hung from tree to tree.
The weeks rolled on, the lush green fields
   Became billowy breadths of golden grain,
And all roots and fruits the kind earth yields
   Were piled on the labouring wain.—
And you were by the cliff-barred white-crested sea,
   And I where the delicate pink of the prairie rose
     Amid rich coarse grasses hides;
Where the sunset's boisterous pageantry,
   And the mornings the tenderest tints disclose,
   Where far from the shade and shelter of wood
   The prairie hen rears her speckled brood,
     And the prairie wolf abides;
And lonely memory, searching through,
   Found no such stars in the orbèd past,
As the glad first greeting 'twixt me and you,
   And the sad, mad meeting which was our last.

THE LAURENTIDES.

H. R. A. Pocock.

Of old men dream'd, and dream'd, and still do dream
Of wonder lands, and strange and vast expanses
  Amid unbalanced splendours and void planes,
In awful heights of space and lonely silence;
  Who peopled with imaginary life
The wide horizons of their ghostly vision;
  Whose senses, open'd in huge solitude,
The human hearing, taste, and sight transcending,
  Became the lenses of angelic sense
Unlimited. Far mightier spectacles
  Than those of dreams has Nature; larger realms,
Had men the gift to see them in their fulness,—
  But lust is as a film upon their eyes,—
Were men not moles, whose habitudes of darkness
  Make dim the needless vision of the soul.

Behold the mighty Laurentides. Could Slumber,
  Within the proscenea of our dreams,
Build such a scene as this? Could even Blindness
  Sit unastounded? Mark these utmost bounds,—
  The barren wastes, that chill cold Labrador,
  The voiceless terrors of the Polar seas,
  The thunder-riven mountains of the West;
  And, to the South, transcontinental fields
  Of sunlit prairie, and the mighty lakes,
  Whose stormy capes and sad-hued battlements
Defy the ceaseless menace of the waves.

Laurentia! Superb Laurentia!
The rude Norse gods, or hoary Jove, or Vulcan,
   Could not have breathed thy native atmosphere.
Child of primeval violence gigantic—
   Life's very father—old at History's birth,
   Untutored by the wisdom of decline
Of these last bland creations—whom the sunlight
Found aged, and the swarming seas in wonder
Beheld unpeopled. Where the forest herbage
   Upon the savage rocks could find no home—
Laurentia! In thy rude leagues there dwelleth
   Great Desolation, throned upon the heights,
Whose guarded boundaries of massy ice-fields,
   And rivers turbulent and forest wilds,
   Forbid the access of our gentle age;
And, better fit for Scandinavian heroes,
   Cyclopian dwellings, and Titanic war,
Seem haunted by the ghosts of vanish'd ages,
   Whose warfares rent the silver-veined hills,
And in the rudest wastes wrought worse destruction.

Whence came this eldest of the Earth's formations?
   Of her fecund womb by eruption born,
Like molten glass from the red crucible,
   Shot prematurely to the clouded air
In weird pre-solar gloom? Nay, it was wasted
   From the primæval hills in glitt'ring sand,
And pour'd by long-forgotten rivers downward
   Into a steaming cyclone-stricken sea,
To lie for ages on the Ocean's bosom.
   Uplifted last from the abysmal deep,
And menacing the sultry firmament,
   The mountain sides were delicately 'graved

And fashion'd by the patient sculptor Water,
    Whose sensible and watchful fingers wrought,
    Arm'd with th' unyielding chisel of the ice,
With glacier, avalanche, and boist'rous torrent;
    Who, on the architecture of the world,
Carved deep the mountain's haughty lineaments,
    And made mosaics in the ample plains,
And bas-reliefs of sculptured history,
    To tell Mankind the story of the world.

    While other lands were plunged beneath the sea,
And isles submerged rose to the air of heaven,
    And restless Change inhabited the world,
    Kneading the clay that should be moulded Man
    In after ages; while broad waters swarm'd
    With life innum'rable both small and great,
    And rivers, lakes, and fields brought forth their kind;
    And Nature bore all to their destined graves,
    And stamped their forms as seals upon the rocks—
    Seals to the bond whereby all creatures die—
    Laurentia in dreamless slumber lay;
    And Change, before her uninvaded shores,
    Beat on the shingled precinct of her sleep,
    And, like a wave, recoiled. Vast Laurentides,
In all thy first barbaric state sequestrate
    From lesser, trivial, and more changeful times,
Rude, with uncultured, unembarass'd greatness—
No garden for a petty mind's contentment,
    With measured littleness in order ranged;
But, like the sombre half-voiced forest,
    Peopled with startled echo, awesome shapes;
    Where wand'ring shafts of sunlight gild the leaves,
    And wand'ring thoughts illuminate the mind;

Where every tree should teach Mankind of greatness,—
To rear life's graces on a broad-based column
Of virtuous years, to cast a wide protection
   And hospitality o'er gentler beings,
To live in goodly neighbourhood with all men,
   And lift a brave face to the changeful sky.

Yet has age softened these austere cold wilds,
That are not void of Earth's most gentle tenants,
   Whose breasts, in these inhospitable wilds,
Would else be childless; and no barren consort
Of Power is the All-Mother who has nurtured
   The furry peoples of the northern wastes,
Made all the crystal waters bring forth silver,
   And beat the cold air with unnumber'd wings.
Bright humming-birds flash in the southern sunlight
   Of that strange land whose snows surround the Pole;
   The Moose, the antler'd Deer, the genial Bear,
   Range unprovoked wilds unexplored by Man;
   The Beaver's architecture dams the streams,
   And great fish in innumerable lakes
   Flash their cold silver where the mirror'd sky
Is framed in high impending rock, where woodlands
   Unmask the boyish unrestrain'd cascades,
   Whose leaping lights flash back the laughing sun.

   Laurentia! Superb Laurentia!
Thy mountains in the garments of the cloud;
The rivers pouring down o'er crystal leagues
Their glassy waters to the solemn sea;
Thine isle-gemm'd lakes; thine old old solitudes;
Thy woodland courses, where impetuous fires
Race madly o'er the desolated plain;

Thy waterways, where dwarf'd voyageurs pursue
The tenor of their uncompanioned way;
Thy sad-hued silent woodlands, where the snow
Lurks all the summer long, and sheets the moss,
And weighs the tree boughs down for half the year;—
Oh! all thy mountains, plains, lakes, seas, and snows
Are fraught with mighty teachings unto Man!—
It is a land of solitude and toil,
Where Man with Nature and himself may dwell,
And learn the mystery of life and death,
And read the story of the distant past,
And mighty promise of great things to be;
It is a stately temple, where are said
By wind and flutt'ring leaf, and rippling stream,
And all the eloquence of utter silence,
By congregation of all living things
The ceaseless Creed: "I do indeed believe!"
It is a Shrine, where all the dread blind Laws
Wield the huge Forces that command the World;
It is a Book, o'er which Mankind may pore,
And read the symbols and the signs of God.

THE LEGEND OF THUNDER.

H. R. A. POCOCK.

Note by Walpole Roland, Esq., C.E., with which this ballad is headed in his recent work "Algoma West:"—"Among the most popular traditions touching the origin of this suggestive title, 'Thunder Cape,' is the following as related in the Otchipiway, by 'Weisaw,' and very freely translated by a friend of the writer's:—' Long years ago, while my great-great-grandfather, then a young brave, was returning with a war party from a bloody encounter with our foes (the Sioux) near Dog Mountain, a place twenty-five miles north-west of the Kaministiquia River, their attention was suddenly arrested by loud and prolonged reverberations, accompanied by vivid flashes of lightning. Ascending the heights overlooking the Kitchee Gamee (Lake Superior) an appalling sight met their gaze. Far out in the bay towards the east, where the 'Sleeping Giant' Nanibijou usually reclined on his fleecy couch, all appeared in flames, while at intervals great pinnacles or shafts of flame and black clouds were driven upwards with terrible fury. . . . . Arriving at the mouth of the Kaministiquia River, they were told of the fate of two hunters from a distant tribe who, regardless of repeated warnings, provoked the fiery spirit of the great "Thunder Eagle," by ascending its home in the cloud-capped cliff, and perished in the vain attempt to bring down a great medicine. Previous to the advent of the white man our storms were grander and more frequent, and only upon rare occasions indeed could a view from a distance be obtained of the Cape or Nanibijou.'"

BEHOLD the gentle waters lap against the Giant's side,
The playful whispers of the winds that by his slumber glide,
The warm sun bending o'er his sleep, the breathing of the sea,
The cool grey shadows nestled down beneath each fragrant tree.
The Monarch of this sombre land, he dwells in clouded state

Beside the portals of the East, where yonder mighty gate
At morning sunders his broad leaves to let the daylight in,
When Night must quit the Giant's throne, and conqu'ring Day begin.
'Tis then across the waters that the earliest sunlight laves
The myriad spirit forms that throng that pathway o'er the waves,
The beings that come to take the form and humble garb of man,
That come to labour and to love, to tread their destined span
Of sorrow, sickness, and despair, of evil years and few,
Before the Potter comes to make the broken vessels new.

We fathers, and our fathers saw, before ye White Men came,
Yon mighty Giant heave in sleep, and breathe the sulphurous flame;
Have seen him roused to anger, lash these seas in furious wrath,
And all the torrents of his ire in lightning pouring forth;
Have seen him ever wrapt in smoke, and his tremendous form
For ever shrouded in his robe—his night-robe of the storm;
But never saw his rugged sides bared to the day, till ye
Brake through the mighty Gates as gods, the Masters of the Sea.

Once from some nation far away two wand'ring hunters strayed,
Their birch canoe all patched and old, their dress of deerskin made;

They rested in our Chieftain's lodge beside the stormy bay
Ere towards the setting sun in peace they should pursue
    their way.
They came towards the setting sun to seek his resting-place,
Where all the spirits of our dead and all the human race
Dwell where the sky is ever bath'd in floods of sunset light,—
The everlasting eventide that knows not death, or night,
Or fire or flood, or drought or war, where winter never reigns,
To the far happy Hunting Grounds upon the Golden Plains.

But when men of the Giant spoke, and his deep shroud of
    gloom,
And when they saw across the bay the clouded mountain loom,
And heard of the dread Thunder Bird whose nest is in the
    height,
Who guards the unassailed cliffs all wrapt in endless night;
And heard their fate who dared to seek his nest, and bring
    us down
The wondrous sacred medicine hid upon the mountain
    crown ;—
They laughed our fears to scorn, and said, "Should brave
    men danger fear?
And what is danger, if it bring the Life Hereafter near?
He who hath sought through doubt and dread the Mystery
    of Life,
And won a blessing for Mankind by warring giant strife
With deathless gods, hath vanquish'd death, and in his
    body slain
Lust, wrath, and darkness, self, and shame; and from a
    beast's flesh free
Stands naked—man—"
                  So, o'er the breast of that still
    moonlit sea

Led by the stranger braves we sped; and all the night time
   long
The startled clouds fled past the moon, the sad wind's dirge-
   like song
Wail'd in vague echoes down the heights, and moaned
   across the bay,
And moaned in tremulous low sighs from great cliffs far
   away.

So on the strangers sped :—the spray that from their paddles
   gleam'd
Made in the wake a path, whereon our long procession
   stream'd
A cortége to the grave; it seemed that in that midnight
   gloom
Huge enemies stalked by and frown'd, and moments big
   with doom
Fled wailing lost into the night. Oh, why should brave men
   die,
While coward hearts of thousands fail, and, wing'd with
   terror, fly!

So, when the East was cold with dawn, and all the clouds
   were grey,
The shadow of the mountain loom'd against the wak'ning
   day.
'Twas then an earnest conclave pray'd that Manitou should
   save
The strangers who amid the clouds sought wisdom or a
   grave.
The agates rattled as their skiff touch'd light the sombre
   main,—

We heard the solemn thunders warn, but warn the braves in
    vain.
With red plumes waving as they strode, they passed along
    the shore
To where a clouded canyon loom'd through broken rocks
    and hoar;
And high the ancient cliffs soar'd up on every side around,
And at their base the fragments lay, and brushwood strew'd
    the ground.
They, clamb'ring o'er the boulders, leapt from rock to rock,
    and climb'd
Right up amid the canyon's gloom, till troubled sight and
    mind
Had lost the tiny spots that moved among the shadows vast,
And every vestige of their forms passed from our sight at
    last.

Then morning instant sank to gloom, and gloom was steep'd
    in night,
The waters all so late at rest had crests of foaming white;
Our prayers assail'd and storm'd the heaven for tender
    youth, and age,
And the Great Spirit saved our barks amid the cyclone's
    rage.
The hurricanes swept by—a lull—a blast—a loud wild cry—
From the rent altitudes, the towers, and battlements on high;
And ancient crags crash'd down the heights, and, lo, each
    breaking wave
Scream'd in his triumph round a crag, and bounded o'er
    its grave!
The Giant shook with wrath; the trees, uprooted, hurl'd in
    space;
A hail of monster spears were shot adown the mountain face;

Against the precipice on high the wildest breakers hurl'd,
And round a whirlpool's circling deeps the broken waters
  swirl'd ;
And who can tell the lightning's glare, recount the thunder's
  roar,
Or the fierce shrieks that through the gloom the vengeful
  cyclones bore !

How long the tempests swept the bay, how long we fought
  for life,
How long among the lodges mourn'd the aged, child, and
  wife ;
How long before we saw the smoke of camp fires far away,
Just where the Kaministiquia is emptied in the bay ;
How long we slept, and wearied lay, restored to home at
  last—
We could not tell, but heard the squaws relate four days
  were past
Since they had seen the tempest rage about the Giant's bed,
And saw the seas contend with heaven, and mourned their
  braves for dead.

Full many suns were set behind the darksome western
  height,
And still the tempest roar'd by day and lightning glared by
  night,
And still these dark cliffs answer'd loud the thunders from
  the bay ;
The forests dared not sleep by night, the beasts were dumb
  by day !
We prayed that Manitou should aid the strangers to
  escape,—
'Twas then we named this "Thunder Bay," the mountain
  "Thunder Cape."

At last the shades of evening crept across the mighty sea,
When all the waters slept at last, the cloud-chained sky was
    free ;
And all the great blue vault on high was echoed in the
    deep,
And floating in two azure skies the mountains lay asleep ;
Then, as the waning sunlight flushed the crested cliffs on
    high,
There came to us a lone canoe across the nether sky.
It came not urged by sail or blade, but as a mother's
    breast
The bearing waters nestled it and laid it in its rest.
The little ripples at the sides laughed in their heedless play,
And in that cradle of the sea a dying warrior lay.

We laid him down beside the tents, and death-shades, like
    the night,
Upon his face were chased away by the red sunset light.
His dim eyes opened, and he spoke, but in the voice was
    told
The fever spirit dwelt within ; in each stern feature's mould
We saw that youth was changed to age, since on the
    mountain side
We ceased to find him in the gloom, and hope grew sick
    and died.

"I see the thunder clouds stoop down, and with their lean
    hands grasp
And hurl abroad their lightning fires—the mad winds halt
    and gasp—
The hills are sweating in their fear—the weary Air is
    slain—

The very crags crouch down and hide upon the upper plain.
The storm is breaking—lo, the trees as hail are hurl'd in space—
And all the huge rocks glow with fire along the mountain face;
From all the mountain mighty flames in fell contortion soar,
And through a whirling rain of fire unearthly cyclones roar!
In this great storm unaided man a thousand deaths had died—
Break, Giant, all this world to nought—Avenge—Thou art defied!
And thou, inviolate Thunder, hail, for Man has raped thy hold,
Thy nest is desecrate at last—the mighty secret told—
He strikes! And death is near—is come! Erect thy pride, my friend—
Lay down the life, but not the man, for death is *not* the End!
And he is dead—and I shall live to tell to all mankind
The vulture Death is slain by death, and deathless reigns the Mind.
But oh, the price!—For he is gone—he who had won the fight—
He who alone had grasped the Truth from that abyss of night;
By fire, by fever, or in fight, by lightning, ice, or wave,
There never sank a braver man than to yon hero's grave."

A mightier hero still than he who on the mountain died
Lay by the Kaministiquia.

Now all the bars aside,
And mighty barriers of death, were melted in the light
That stream'd from out the courts of Heaven o'er all the realms of Night.
The kingdom of the Life to Come reigned once o'er earthly sin,
For sunset opens wide the gates to let the dead come in ;
The Land of the Hereafter lay before our straining eyes,
The amethystine glories flashed across the amber skies ;
And in that light the Hero lay, and closed his eyes and slept—
The silver mists upon his brow their tears of parting wept ;
So all the air was filled with light, and all the earth with rest
As that brave Spirit took the trail that leads towards the West.

IX.—SEASONS.

IX.—SEASONS.

HEAT.

ARCHIBALD LAMPMAN.

From plains that seek to southward dim,
    The road runs by me white and bare;
Up the steep hill it seems to swim
    Beyond, and melt into the glare.
Upward, half-way, or it may be
    Nearer the summit, slowly steals
A haycart, moving duskily,
       With idly clacking wheels.

By his cart's side the waggoner
    Is slouching slowly at his ease,
Half-hidden in the windless blur
    Of white dust puffing to his knees.
This waggon on the height above,
    From sky to sky on either hand,
Is the sole thing that seems to move
       In all the heat-held land.

Beyond me, in the fields, the sun
    Soaks in the grass, and hath his will;
I count the marguerites one by one;
    Even the buttercups are still.

On the brook yonder not a breath
    Disturbs the spider or the midge;
The water-bugs draw close beneath
    The cool gloom of the bridge.

Where the far elm-tree shadows flood
    Dark patches in the burning grass,
The cows, each with her peaceful cud,
    Lie waiting for the heat to pass.
From somewhere on the slope near by,
    Into the pale depth of the noon
A wandering thrush slides leisurely
    His thin revolving tune.

In intervals of dreams I hear
    The cricket from the droughty ground;
The grasshoppers spin into mine ear
    A small immeasurable sound.
I lift mine eyes sometimes to gaze,
    The burning sky-line blinds my sight;
The woods far off are blue with haze,
    The hills are drenched in light.

And yet to me, not this or that
    Is always sharp or always sweet;
In the sloped shadow of my hat
    I lean at rest and drain the heat.
Nay more, I think some blessed power
    Hath brought me wandering idly here;
In the full furnace of this hour
    My thoughts grow keen and clear,

TO A HUMMING-BIRD IN A GARDEN.

George Murray.

Blithe playmate of the Summer time,
    Admiringly I greet thee;
Born in old England's misty clime,
    I scarcely hoped to meet thee.

Com'st thou from forests of Peru,
    Or from Brazil's savannahs,
Where flowers of every dazzling hue
    Flaunt, gorgeous as Sultanas?

Thou scannest me with doubtful gaze,
    Suspicious little stranger!
Fear not, thy burnished wings may blaze
    Secure from harm or danger.

Now here, now there, thy flash is seen,
    Like some stray sunbeam darting,
With scarce a second's space between
    Its coming and departing.

Mate of the bird that lives sublime
    In Pat's immortal blunder,
Spied in two places at a time,
    Thou challengest our wonder.

Suspended by thy slender bill,
    Sweet blooms thou lov'st to rifle;
The subtle perfumes they distil
    Might well thy being stifle.

Surely the honey-dew of flowers
    Is slightly alcoholic,
Or why, through burning August hours,
    Dost thou pursue thy frolic?

What though thy throatlet never rings
    With music, soft or stirring;
Still, like a spinning-wheel, thy wings
    Incessantly are whirring.

How dearly I would love to see
    Thy tiny *cara sposa*,
As full of sensibility
    As any coy mimosa!

They say, when hunters track her nest,
    Where two warm pearls are lying,
She boldly fights, though sore distrest,
    And sends the brigands flying.

What dainty epithets thy tribes
    Have won from men of science!
Pedantic and poetic scribes
    For once are in alliance.

Crested Coquette, and Azure Crown,
  Sun Jewel, Ruby-Throated,
With Flaming Topaz, Crimson Down,
  Are names that may be quoted.

Such titles aim to paint the hues
  That on the darlings glitter,
And were we for a week to muse,
  We scarce could light on fitter.

Farewell, bright bird! I envy thee,
  Gay rainbow-tinted rover;
Would that my life, like thine, were free
  From care till all is over!

IN THE GOLDEN BIRCH.

Elizabeth Gostwycke Roberts.

How the leaves sing to the wind;
   And the wind, with its turbulent voices sweet,
   Gives back the praise of the leaves, as is meet,
To the soft blue sky, where the cumulous clouds are thinned,
   And driven away, like a flock of frightened sheep,
   By the wind that waketh and putteth to sleep.

Here, in the golden birch,
   Folded in rapture of golden light,
   I taste the joy of the birds in their flight;
And I watch the flickering shadows, that sway and lurch
   And flutter, like dancing brownies, over the green,
   And the birch is singing wherein I lean.

From over the purple hills
   Comes the wind with its strange sweet song to the land;
   And the earth looks bright, as it might when planned
By the Maker, and left unblemished of human ills;
   And the river runs, like a child to its mother's knee,
   To the heart of the great unresting sea.

How perfect the day, and sweet!
   Over me, limitless heavens of blue;
   Close to me, leaves that the wind sifts through;
And the one sweet song, that the wind and the leaves
     repeat,
   Till the mild, hushed meadows listen, crowned with
     light,
   And the hill-tops own its might!

THE FIR WOODS.

Charles G. D. Roberts.

The wash of endless waves is in their tops,
   Endlessly swaying, and the long winds stream
   Athwart them from the far-off shores of dream.
Thro' the stirred branches filtering, faintly drops
Mystic dream-dust of isle, and palm, and cave,
   Coral and sapphire, realms of rose, that seem
   More radiant than ever earthly gleam
Revealed of fairy mead or haunted wave.

A cloud of gold, a cleft of blue profound,—
   These are my gates of wonder, surged about
     By tumult of tossed bough and rocking crest.
The vision lures; the spirit spurns her bound,
   Spreads her imprisoned wing, and drifts from out
     This green and humming gloom that wraps my rest.

CLOUDS.

Archibald Lampman.

The dew is gleaming in the grass,
    The morning hours are seven;
And I am fain to watch you pass,
    Ye soft white clouds of heaven.

Ye stray and gather, part and fold;
    The wind alone can tame you;
I dream of what in time of old
    The poets loved to name you.

They called you sheep, the sky your sward;
    A field, without a reaper;
They called the shining sun your lord,
    The shepherd wind your keeper.

Your sweetest poets I will deem
    The men of old for moulding,
In simple beauty, such a dream,—
    And I could lie beholding,

Where daisies in the meadow toss,
    The wind from morn till even
For ever shepherd you across
    The shining field of heaven.

FROGS.

Charles G. D. Roberts.

Here, in the red heart of the sunset lying,
  My rest an islet of brown weeds blown dry,
  I watch the wide bright heavens hovering nigh,
My plain and pools in lucent splendours dyeing!
My view dreams over the rosy wastes, descrying
  The reed-tops fret the solitary sky;
  And all the air is tremulous to the cry
Of myriad frogs on mellow pipes replying.

For the unrest of passion, here is peace;
  And eve's cool drench for midday soil and taint!
To tirèd ears, how sweetly brings release
  This limpid babble from life's unstilled complaint;
  While under tirèd eye-lids, lapse and faint
The noon's derisive visions,—fade and cease!

TWILIGHT.

Charles Heavysege.

The day was lingering in the pale north-west,
   And night was hanging o'er my head,—
   Night where a myriad stars were spread;
While down in the east, where the light was least,
   Seemed the home of the quiet dead.
   And, as I gazed on the field sublime,
   To watch the bright pulsating stars,
   Adown the deep, where the angels sleep,
   Came drawn the golden chime
   Of those great spheres that sound the years
   For the horologe of time ;—
Millenniums numberless they told,
Millenniums a millionfold
   From the ancient hour of prime !

THE WHIP-POOR-WILL.

"Fidelis."

Oh, whip-poor-will! oh, whip-poor-will!
When all the joyous day is still,
When from the sky's fast deepening blue
Fades out the sunset's latest hue,
We ever hear thy measured trill,—
Oh, whip-poor-will! oh, whip-poor-will!

In the soft dusk of dewy May,
In pensive close of autumn day,
Though other birds may silent be
Or flood the air with minstrelsy,
Thou carest not; eve brings us still
Thy plaintive murmur,—whip-poor-will!

When moonlight fills the summer night
With a soft vision of delight,
We listen till we fain would ask
For thee some respite from thy task;
At dawn we wake, and hear it still,
Thy ceaseless song,—oh, whip-poor-will!

"FIDELIS."

We hear thy voice, but see not thee;
Thou seemest but a voice to be,—
A wandering spirit,—breathing yet
For parted joys a vain regret;
So plaintive thine untiring trill,—
Oh, whip-poor-will! oh, whip-poor-will!

Oh! faithful to thy strange refrain,
Is it the voice of joy or pain?
We cannot know; thou wilt not tell
The secret kept so long and well,
What moves thee thus to warble still,—
Oh, whip-poor-will! oh, whip-poor-will!

A CANADIAN SUMMER EVENING.

Mrs Leprohon.

The rose-tints have faded from out of the west,
From the mountain's high peak, from the river's broad breast,
And silently shadowing valley and rill
The twilight steals noiselessly over the hill.
Behold, in the blue depths of ether afar,
Now softly emerging each glittering star;
While later the moon, placid, solemn, and bright,
Floods earth with her tremulous silvery light.

Hush! list to the whip-poor-will's soft plaintive notes,
As up from the valley the lonely sound floats;
Inhale the sweet breath of yon shadowy wood,
And the wild flowers blooming in hushed solitude.
Start not at the whispering, 'tis but the breeze,
Low rustling 'mid maple and lonely pine trees,
Or willows and alders that fringe the dark tide
Where canoes of the red men oft silently glide.

See, rising from out of that copse, dark and damp,
The fire-flies, each bearing a flickering lamp!
Like meteors, gleaming and streaming, they pass
O'er hillside and meadow, and dew-laden grass;
Contrasting with ripple on river and stream,
Alternately playing in shadow and beam,
Till fulness of beauty fills hearing and sight
Throughout the still hours of a calm summer night.

EVENING ON THE MARSHES.

Barry Straton.

We have roamed the marshes, keen with expectation,
    Lain at eve in ambush, where the ducks are wont to fly;
Felt the feverish fervour, the thrilling, full pulsation,
    As the flocks came whirring from the rosy western sky.

All day long the sun with heat, and breeze with coolness,
    Smote or kissed the grasses, and it seemed another lake
Flooded o'er the land and up the hills in fulness,—
    Shadows for the billows, sunshine for the waves that break.

Now beneath the pine, whose branches voice the breezes,
    Past the toil of day, we lie like gods in utter peace;
This is life's full nectar, this from care releases,—
    Oh, to rest for ever here where toil and tumult cease!

Slowly down the west the weary day is dying;
    Slowly up the east ascends the mellow, mystic moon;
Swiftly swoop the hawks; the hooting owls are flying;
    Through the darksome splendour breaks the lonesome cry
        of loon.

Ghost-like move the sails along the lake's dim distance;
    Faintly wafts the sailors' weirdsome song the waters o'er;
Faint the wavelets' music, as with low insistence,
    Break they softly singing on the drowsy sandy shore.

Wooing us in whispers, water, earth, and heaven,—
    Mystic whispers, wafted o'er the darksome waving deep,—
Win us to themselves, our old creative leaven,
    And we, mingling with them, softly sink to dreamless sleep.

THE FIRE-FLIES.

Charles Mair.

I SEE them glimmer where the waters lag
By winding bays, and to the willows sing;
And, far away, where stands the forest dim,
Huge-built of old, their tremulous lights are seen.
High overhead they gleam like trailing stars,
Then sink adown, until their emerald sheen
Dies in the darkness like an evening hymn,—
Anon to float again in glorious bars
Of streaming rapture, such as man may hear
When the soul casts its slough of mortal fear.
And now they make rich spangles in the grass,
Gilding the night-dew on the tender blade;
Then hover o'er the meadow-pools, to gaze
At their bright forms shrined in the dreamy glass
Which earth, and air, and bounteous rain have made.
One moment, and the thicket is ablaze
With twinkling lamps, which swing from bough to bough;
Another, and like sylphids they descend
To cheer the brook-side where the bell-flowers grow.
Near, and more near, they softly come, until
Their little life is busy at my feet;
They glow around me, and my fancies blend
Capriciously with their delight, and fill
My wakeful bosom with unwonted heat.

One lights upon my hand, and there I clutch
With an alarming finger its quick wing;
Erstwhile so free, it pants, the tender thing!
And dreads its captor and his handsel touch.

Where is thy home? On what strange food dost feed,
   Thou fairy hunter of the moonless night?
From what far nectar'd fount, or flow'ry mead,
   Glean'st thou, by witching spells, thy sluicy light?

MIDSUMMER NIGHT.

Archibald Lampman.

Mother of balms and soothings manifold,
    Quiet-breathèd Night, whose brooding hours are seven,
    To whom the voices of all rest are given,
And those few stars whose scattered names are told.
Far off, beyond the westward hills outrolled,
    Darker than thou, more still, more dreamy even,
    The golden moon leans in the dusky heaven,
And under her, one star, a point of gold.

And all go slowly lingering toward the west,
As we go down forgetfully to our rest,
    Weary of daytime, tired of noise and light.
Ah, it was time that thou shouldst come, for we
Were sore athirst, and had great need of thee,
    Thou sweet physician, balmy-bosomed Night.

THE AUTUMN TREE.

Charles Heavysege.

Hark to the sighing of yon fading tree,—
   Yon tree that rocks, as if with sense distressed;
Its seems complaining that its destiny
   Should send the gale to desolate its breast.
Oh, heed it, wind! oh, listen to its sigh!
   Regard the pathos of its falling leaves;
Attend unto its oft-repeated cry,
   And slack the fury that the bough bereaves.
Lo, have they not rejoiced in summer days;
   And have they not felt peace in summer nights?
Warded from beast the scorching noontide blaze;
   Guided, for man, the fire-flies' evening flights?
Oh, sweep not, then, so rudely o'er each spray,
But let them gently slowly pass away!

IN APPLE TIME.

Bliss Carman.

The apple harvest days are here,
   The boding apple harvest days,
   And down the flaming valley ways
The foresters of time draw near.

Through leagues of bloom I went with Spring,
   To call you on the slopes of morn,
   Where in imperious song is born
The wild heart of the goldenwing.

I roved through alien summer lands,
   I sought your beauty near and far;
   To-day, where russet shadows are,
I hold your face between my hands.

On runnels dark, by slopes of fern,
   The hazy undern sleeps in sun;
   Remembrance and desire, undone,
From old regret to dreams return.

The apple harvest time is here,
   The tender apple harvest time;
   A sheltering calm, unknown at prime,
Settles upon the brooding year.

THE AURORA BOREALIS.

John E. Logan—"Barry Dane."

Through one long northern night I sat, O Love!
  Watching swift arrows silently speed forth
  From God's great silver bow bent in the north,
And wondering whither, as they soared above.
And then methought one ever fondly strove
  To reach a distant star of brighter worth
  Than all the rest that smiled upon the earth;
At last the messenger the midnight clove,—
    At last, O Love, it laid one long, sweet kiss
      Upon the brow of that awaiting star,
After vast struggles through the weary night;
  O Love, it is my omen, and such bliss
    Awaiteth still these lips that are afar,
That yet shall touch thee as their star of light!

THE MAPLE.

Charles G. D. Roberts.

Oh, tenderly deepen the woodland glooms,
    And merrily sway the beeches;
Breathe delicately the willow blooms,
    And the pines rehearse new speeches;
The elms toss high, till they brush the sky,
    Pale catkins the yellow birch launches,—
But the tree I love, all the greenwood above,
    Is the maple of sunny branches.

Let who will sing of the hawthorn in spring,
    Or the late-leaved linden in summer;
There's a word may be for the locust-tree,
    That delicate, strange new-comer;
But the maple, it glows with the tint of the rose
    When pale are the spring-time regions,
And its towers of flame from afar proclaim
    The advance of winter's legions.

And a greener shade there never was made
    Than its summer canopy sifted;
And many a day, as beneath it I lay,
    Has my memory backward drifted
To a pleasant lane I may walk not again,
    Leading over a fresh green hill,
Where a maple stood, just clear of the wood—
    And oh, to be near it still!

OCTOBER.

Alexander M'Lachlan.

See how the great old forest vies
With all the glory of the skies,
   In streaks without a name;
And leagues on leagues of scarlet spires,
And temples lit with crimson fires,
   And palaces of flame!
And domes on domes that gleam afar,
Through many a gold and crimson bar,
   With azure overhead;
While forts, with towers on towers arise,
As if they meant to scale the skies,
   With banner bloody red!

Here, orange groves that seem asleep;
There, stately avenues that sweep
   To where the land declines;
There, starting up in proud array,
With helmets flashing to the day,
   Troop upon troop of pines!
Here, evergreens that have withdrawn,
And hang around the open lawn,
   With shadows creeping back;
While yonder, girdled hemlocks run
Like fiery serpents to the sun,
   Upon their gleaming track!

And, in the distance far apart,
As if to shame man's proudest art,
   Cathedral arches spread ;
While yonder ancient elm has caught
A glory, 'yond the reach of thought,
   Upon his hoary head.
But every object, far and wide—
The very air is glorified—
   A perfect dream of bliss !
Earth's greatest painters never could,
Nor poet in inspirèd mood,
   Imagine aught like this.

O what are all ambition's gains !
What matters it who rules or reigns
   While I have standing here !
Gleams of unutterable things,
The work of the great King of kings !
   God of the full-crown'd year !
October ! thou'rt a marvellous sight,
And with a rapture of delight
   We hail thy gorgeous pinion ;
To elevate our hearts thou'rt here,
To bind us with a tie more dear
   To our beloved Dominion !

FIRST SNOW.

John Talon-Lespérance—"Laclède."

    The sun burns pale and low
Along the gloomy avenue of pines,
And the grey mist hangs heavily in lines
    Above the torrent's flow.

    I hear, on the violet hill,
The caw of blackbirds fleeing from the cold;
And buzz of insects, hiding in the mould;
    Under the ruined mill.

    The deep embrownèd wood
Is garlanded with wreaths of fleecy white;
And the stark poplar stands, a Northland sprite,
    Muffled in snowy hood.

    Afar, the cottage roof
Glistens with gems; the bridge that spans the drain
Is carpeted with down; the harvest plain
    Gleams 'neath a crystal woof.

    Heigh ho! The silver bells—
The gaudy sleighs that glide so merrily along—
The crunch of skipping hoofs—the woodman's song
    Loud echoing in the dells!

The pine-knots cheerily blaze,
And shed a genial heat in wealthy homes;
The lords of earth, immured in cosy rooms,
    Heed not the wintry haze.

But, in the dark damp lanes,
Where shrinks the pauper girl in filth and rags,
How dismally falls the snow upon the flags,
    Athwart the broken panes!

With quick convulsive breath,
And hollow cough, the hopeless sufferers greet
In cruel winter's snow and ice and sleet
    The harbingers of death.

Ay! But chief, on thy headstone,
Who slept 'neath summer roses, cold flakes rest,
And filter icy drops upon thy breast,—
    Thy tender breast,—my own!

While on my drooping head—
Yea, on my sunken heart—distils the snow,
Chilling the warmth and life that in it glow,
    In pity for my dead!

Not till the crocus bloom,
And April rays have thawed the frost-bound slope,
O Rita, shall this heart to light re-ope,
    With the flowers on thy tomb!

INDIAN SUMMER.

Susanna Strickland Moodie.

By the purple haze that lies
   On the distant rocky height,
By the deep blue of the skies,
   By the smoky amber light
Through the forest arches streaming
Where Nature on her throne sits dreaming,
And the sun is scarcely gleaming
   Through the cloudlets, snowy white,—
Winter's lovely herald greets us
Ere the ice-crowned tyrant meets us!

This dreamy Indian summer day
   Attunes the soul to tender sadness;
We love—but joy not in the ray;
   It is not summer's fervid gladness,
But a melancholy glory
   Hovering softly round decay,—
Like swan that sings her own sad story
   Ere she floats in death away.

INDIAN SUMMER.

Isidore G. Ascher—"Isidore."

With dying splendour on her face,
Her robes of beauty laid aside,
The hectic Summer sighs to glide
    From the flushed earth, to yield a place

To the dry foliage sere and gold,
And trees whose rugged arms are bare,
And the shrill moanings of the air,
    And the dim glories of the wold.

Unnatural silence, like a pall,
Inwraps the world, and the sun streams,
In mellow waves of glinting gleams,
    A saintly splendour over all.

Hushed is the wind—disconsolate
That summer glories all should die,
While the calm azure of the sky
    Looks down in thronèd, regal state.

And grand old maples upward gaze
Like sentinels upon the road,
As if they mused of Nature's God,
    Who crowns them with a myriad rays

No summer sun shall pour his beams
Like those that flood my path to-day;
Pallid and beautiful each ray,
   Like shapings of our sweetest dreams.

O youthful prime! O golden hours!
Ephemeral glories that have flown;
O future yearnings mellowed down,
   Yet tinted with the hue of flowers!

O tempered sunlight! happy calms,
When nature sleeps, or wakes to see
The hours gliding silently,
   O'erloaded with a myriad balms.

Around our hearts the sunshine waves,
A calmèd splendour, like the morn;
While summer airs anew are born
   To sigh amid the flowerets' graves.

O golden moments toucht with balm!
Temper Fate's hostile storms abroad,
Instil a tranquil hope in God,
   And in our lives infuse your calm.

AN INDIAN SUMMER CAROL.

"Fidelis."

All day the dreamy sunshine steeps
   In gold the yellowing beeches,
In softest blue the river sleeps
   Among the island reaches.

Against the distant purple hills
   Rich autumn tints are glowing;
Its blood-red wine the sumach spills,
   Deep hues of carmine showing.

Upon the glassy stream the boat
   Glides softly, like a vision;
And, with its shadow, seems to float
   Among the isles Elysian.

About the plumy golden rod
   The tireless bee is humming,
While crimson blossoms star the sod
   And wait the rover's coming.

The birch and maple glow with dyes
   Of scarlet, rose, and amber;
And like a flame from sunset skies
   The tangled creepers clamber.

The oaks a royal purple wear,
    Gold-crowned where sunlight presses;
The birch stands like a Dryad fair
    Beneath her golden tresses.

So still the air—so like a dream—
    We hear the acorn falling;
And, o'er the scarcely rippled stream,
    The loon's long-quavered calling.

The robin softly, o'er the lea,
    A farewell song is trilling;
The squirrel flits from tree to tree
    Its winter storehouse filling.

Like him, we too may gather store
    From all this glorious Nature;
Then leave, my friend, your bookish lore
    And dreary nomenclature.

Leave the old thinkers to their dreams,
    The treasures of the ages;
Leave dusty scientific reams,
    And study Nature's pages.

Her poetry is better far
    Than all men write about her;
Old Homer's song of love and war
    Had scarce been sung without her.

Haste to the wood,—put books away,
    They'll wait the tardy comer;
For *them* there's many a winter day,
    But brief's our Indian summer!

TO WINTER.

Charles G. D. Roberts.

Ruling with an iron hand
O'er the intermediate land
'Twixt the plains of rich completeness,
And the realms of budding sweetness,
Winter! from thy crystal throne,
With a keenness all thy own
Dartest thou, through gleaming air,
O'er the glorious barren glare
Of thy sunlit wildernesses.
Thine undazzled level glances,
Where thy minions' silver tresses
Stream among their icy lances;
While thy universal breathing,
Frozen to a radiant swathing
For the trees, their bareness hides,
And upon their sunward sides
Shines and flushes rosily
To the chill pink morning sky.
Skilful artists thou employest,
And in chastest beauty joyest,—
Forms most delicate, pure, and clear,
Frost-caught starbeams fallen sheer
In the night, and woven here
In jewel-fretted tapestries.
But what tragic melodies,

As in the bord'ring realms are throbbing,
Hast thou, Winter?—Liquid sobbing
Brooks, and brawling waterfalls,
Whose responsive-voicèd calls
Clothe with harmony the hills;
Gurgling meadow-threading rills,
Lakelets' lisping wavelets lapping
Round a flock of wild ducks napping;
And the rapturous-noted wooings,
And the molten-throated cooings,
Of the amorous multitudes
Flashing through the dusky woods,
When a veering wind hath blown
A glare of sudden daylight down?—
Nought of these!—And fewer notes
Hath the wind alone that floats
Over naked trees and snows;
Half its minstrelsy it owes
To its orchestra of leaves.
Ay! weak the meshes music weaves
For thy snarèd soul's delight,
'Less, when thou dost lie at night
'Neath the star-sown heavens bright,
To thy sin-unchokèd ears
Some dim harmonies may pierce
From the high-consulting spheres;
'Less the silent sunrise sing
Like a vibrant silver string
When its prison'd splendours first
O'er the crusted snow-fields burst.
But thy days the silence keep,
Save for grosbeaks' feeble cheep,
Or for snow-birds' busy twitter
When thy breath is very bitter.

So my spirit often acheth
For the melodies it lacketh
'Neath thy sway, or cannot hear
For its mortal-cloakèd ear.
And full thirstily it longeth
For the beauty that belongeth
To the Autumn's ripe fulfilling ;—
Heapèd orchard-baskets spilling
'Neath the laughter shaken trees ;
Fields of buckwheat full of bees,
Girt with ancient groves of fir
Shod with berried juniper ;
Beech-nuts 'mid their russet leaves ;
Heavy-headed nodding sheaves ;
Clumps of luscious blackberries ;
Purple-cluster'd traceries
Of the cottage climbing-vines ;
Scarlet-fruited eglantines ;
Maple forest all aflame
When thy sharp-tongued legates came.

Ruler with an iron hand
O'er an intermediate land :
Glad am I thy realm is border'd
By the plains more richly order'd,—
Stock'd with sweeter-glowing forms,—
Where the prison'd brightness warms
In lush crimsons thro' the leaves,
And a gorgeous legend weaves.

A MID-WINTER NIGHT'S DREAM.

William Wilfred Campbell.

The snows outside are white and white;
The gusty flue shouts through the night;
And by the lonely chimney light
    I sit and dream of Summer.

The orchard bough creaks in the blast,
That like a ghost goes shrieking past,
And coals are dying fast and fast,
    But still I dream of Summer.

'Tis not the voice of falling rain,
Or dream wind-blown through latticed pane,
When earth will laugh in green again,
    That makes me dream of Summer.

But hopes will then have backward flown,
Like fleets of promise, long outblown,
And Love once more will greet his own;
    This is my dream of Summer.

WINTER NIGHT.

Charles Heavysege.

The stars are glittering in the frosty sky,
   Numerous as pebbles on a broad sea-coast;
While o'er the vault the cloud-like galaxy
   Has marshalled its innumerable host.
Alive all heaven seems; with wondrous glow,
   Tenfold refulgent every star appears;
As if some wide, celestial gale did blow,
   And thrice illume the ever-kindled spheres.

Orbs, with glad orbs rejoicing, burning, beam,
   Ray-crowned, with lambent lustre in their zones;
Till o'er the blue, bespangled spaces seem
   Angels and great archangels on their thrones;
A host divine, whose eyes are sparkling gems,
And forms more bright than diamond diadems.

CARNATIONS IN WINTER.

Bliss Carman.

Your carmine flakes of bloom to-night
   The fire of wintry sunsets hold;
Again in dreams you burn to light
   A far Canadian garden old.

The blue north summer over it
   Is bland with long ethereal days;
The gleaming martins wheel and flit
   Where breaks your sun down orient ways.

There, when the gradual twilight falls,
   Through quietudes of dusk afar,
Hermit antiphonal hermit calls
   From hills below the first pale star.

Then, in your passionate love's foredoom,
   Once more your spirits stir the air,
And you are lifted through the gloom
   To warm the coils of her dark hair!

ICICLE DROPS.

Arthur John Lockhart.

I.

Fast from yon icicle's inverted spire,
   Yon shining minims, glittering in the sun,
Fall brightly down, sheen drops of fluent fire,
   Momently hanging,—sinking, one by one,—
Sliding clear beads as down a silver wire;
   So archer-stars shoot thro' abysses dun;
So blood drips down from the knive's fierce desire;
   So fall our moments; so our tears do run.

With drop on drop, with everlasting flow,
   With changing atom, and revolving sphere,
Our never-resting lives must downward go;—
   Still hung in momentary brightness here,
Then sinking to that breast toward which incline
The drops that glow, and eke the beams that shine.

II.

The sun, at length, with a more fervent fire,
   Hath gained a subtle mastery of the dawn;
And, still more swiftly, from the less'ning spire
   The hastening gems descend, till all are gone.

But, lo! they come! The vanish'd ones surprise
   In golden mist, my wistful, musing sight;
Soul o' th' earth, its exhalations rise,
   And soon the drops return to air and light.

There shall they hang 'mid purple glooms aloof,
   With clouds noon-white, or tinct with crimson eve;
Or shine supreme in Iris' circling woof,
   Wherein his married hues the sun doth weave.
And so this falling life shall not remain
Sunk in the earth; 'twill rise to Heaven again.

THE SILVER FROST.

Barry Straton.

A breath from the tropics broke Winter's spell
With an alien rain which froze as it fell,
And ere the Orient blushed with morn
A beautiful crystal forest was born.

Blackthorn hedge and hawthorn bush
Dawned spectrally white in the first grey flush;
Drifted from night the circling trees
As icebergs drift from northern seas.

Branch above branch, an aerial maze
Of pendulous crystals and silvery sprays!
Tree behind tree impregnable,
Where beauty, and silence, and sweet thoughts dwell!

The elm boughs bend, like a searching thought,
With their silvery weight of beauty caught.
White limbs are asleep on the misty blue skies
Like lilies on lakelets in paradise.

Daylight refulgent floods over the hills,
And the forest, conscious of beauty, thrills;
Through the mazes of fragile mimicry
The dazzling sunrays flare and flee.

Pine, elm, and maple, in icy attire,
Burn with a myriad gems of fire;
The snow-billowed ground and the gossamer height
Are aflame with the scornful spirit of light.

Violet, orange, indigo, red,
Green, yellow, and blue from each diamond are shed;
More beautiful these than the jewels of a throne,
For the forest is nature's glory and crown.

The grape-vine over the lilacs laid
Gleams like a rainbowed, tossed cascade,
And he who beholds might pause to hear
The enlivened voices of waters there.

In the Balm of Gilead and poplar's spire
Are incarnate the spirits of water and fire;
In cedar and linden, and everywhere,
The flames of the passionless fires flare.

But wandering winds the frail boughs shake,
And rustling ripples of ruin awake,
And a myriad scintillant gems fall down,
Like thoughts transfigured of beauties flown.

THE JEWELLED TREES.

George Martin.

I.

On the verge of the month of the white new year,
When friend to friend gives heartiest cheer,
The rain and the frost for a night and a day
Have cunningly worked alternately.
They have thickened the crust of the dazzling snow
Over whose surface the cold winds blow;
They have fringed the eaves with their old device,
Enormous daggers of glittering ice;
And the nails in the walls, where in summer time
The scarlet-runners were wont to climb,
They have crowned with gems more bright, more fair,
Than eastern queens on their bosoms wear.
But scarcely a glance do we waste on these,
For our wonder is fixed on the jewelled trees;
Never before, in all their days,
Have they borne such beauty for mortal gaze;
On them the frost and the rain have wrought
A splendour that could not be sold or bought,
Heavily laden from foot to crown,
Like fairest of brides with heads bowed down,
In park and square, demurely they stand,—
Stand by the wayside all over the land.
Thick-crusted with pearls of marvellous size,
Whose lustre rebukes our aching eyes.

II.

Thus for a night and a day have they stood,
Modest and chaste in their virginhood;
But are they as happy, as joyful at heart,
As when, in green vesture, they gladly took part
In all the fresh bliss that to spring-time they owed,—
In all the hot pleasure that summer bestowed?
" Nay, verily, nay!" I hear them repeat;
The blood in our veins, even down to our feet,
Is gelid and still,—we are sick unto death;
Oh send us, ye heavens! oh send us a breath
Of warmth that will bear all these jewels away!
These fetters that we for a night and day
Have borne in silence with infinite pain!
Oh give us our freedom! our bare arms again!"

III.

A wind that had slept all this time in the south,
In an orange grove that was faint from drouth,
Heard the soft plaint of the jewelled trees,
And came in the guise of a gentle breeze,—
Came, and with kisses tenderly
Unbound the captives, and set them free.
Their crystalline chains were broken asunder,
Filling all earth with a blinding wonder;—
With a crash and a flash and a musical sound,
Like a shower of stars they fell to the ground;
And, freed from their bondage, the grateful trees
In their bare brown arms caressed the breeze,
Caressed the wind that came from the south,
From the orange grove that was faint from drouth;
And they wept for joy, their thanks they wept,
While the wind lay still in their arms and slept.

MARCH.

ISABELLA VALANCEY CRAWFORD.

SHALL Thor with his hammer
   Beat on the mountain,
As on an anvil,
   A shackle and fetter?

Shall the lame Vulcan
   Shout as he swingeth
God-like his hammer,
   And forge thee a fetter?

Shall Jove, the Thunderer,
   Twine his swift lightnings
With his loud thunders,
   And forge thee a shackle?

"No," shouts the Titan,
   The young lion-throated;
"Thor, Vulcan, nor Jove
   Cannot shackle and bind me."

Tell what will bind thee,
   Thou young world-shaker,
Up vault our oceans,
   Down fall our forests.

Ship masts and pillars
    Stagger and tremble,
Like reeds by the margins
    Of swift running waters.

Men's hearts at thy roaring
    Quiver like harebells
Smitten by hailstones,
    Smitten and shaken.

"O sages and wise men!
    O bird-hearted tremblers!
Come, I will show ye
    A shackle to bind me.

I, the lion-throated,
    The shaker of mountains!
I, the invincible,
    Lasher of oceans!

Past the horizon,
    Its ring of pale azure
Past the horizon,
    Where scurry the white clouds,

There are buds and small flowers—
    Flowers like snowflakes,
Blossoms like rain-drops,
    So small and tremulous.

These in a fetter
 Shall shackle and bind me,
Shall weigh down my shouting
 With their delicate perfume!"

But who this frail fetter
 Shall forge on an anvil,
With hammer of feather
 And anvil of velvet?

" Past the horizon
 In the palm of a valley,
Her feet in the grasses,
 There is a maiden.

She smiles on the flowers,
 They widen and redden;
She weeps on the flowers,
 They grow up and kiss her.

She breathes in their bosoms,
 They breathe back in odours;
Inarticulate homage,
 Dumb adoration.

She shall wreathe them in shackles,
 Shall weave them in fetters;
In chains shall she braid them,
 And me shall she fetter.

I, the invincible ;
  March, the earth-shaker ;
March, the sea-lifter ;
  March, the sky-render ;

March, the lion-throated.
  April, the weaver
Of delicate blossoms,
  And moulder of red buds—

Shall, at the horizon,
  Its ring of pale azure,
Its scurry of white clouds,
  Meet in the sunlight."

THE WINDS.

JOHN E. LOGAN—" BARRY DANE."

I.

Bold, blustering Boreas from the heights
    Of icy hills, where Esquimaux
Live through the weary winter nights
Lit by the weird Auroral lights
        As pallid as the snow.

Your frosty breath is sharp and clear,
    It pierces garments thick or thin;
I love you, though I also fear,
You nip my nose and pinch my ear,
        And whiten round my chin.

And yet you are a friendly wind,
    Although your voice be rude and loud;
For often in a mood more kind,
You sadly moan a dirge, and wind
        Some lonely wanderer's shroud.

And weep and wail from gorge and bluff,
    O'er victims of your own stern hand;
You meant it not, your touch is rough,
You deem the man should be as tough,
        Who ventures to your land.

II.

Soft Notus from the glowing south,
Thy breath is warm, thy touch is soft;
I love thee little, for full oft
    Thou bring'st the fatal drouth.

Thine odorous breath in whispered sighs
Woos through the languid summer day,
And comes again at night to lay
    Kisses on drowsy eyes.

Ah, yes, thou art an idle breeze,
And only fit for southern lands,
Where maidens sit with listless hands
    And loll about in ease.

And lovers sigh 'neath casements high,
And deftly touch the light guitar,
And sing their burning loves that are
    Changeful as southern sky.

III.

Ah, Zephyr! of the golden West,
  From mountain tops you hurry down,
    Across the plain
    You rush amain,
You touch the lakes and leave a crest
Where'er your wanton lips have pressed;
    Then raise a dust in town.

Ah, sure, you are a madcap air,
  In this land lying west by north;
    No classic breeze,
    For oft you freeze
Of hands and feet full many a pair,
Upon the prairie bleak and bare,
    When thus you frolic forth.

And yet, wild wind, I love you well,
  And to your wayward lips I trust
    A whispered word,
    Fly as a bird,
O, take the message that I tell,
And waft it over hill and dell,
    Far east, with many a gust.

IV.

But Eurus, from the eastern main,
    Thou hast my heart,
    Howe'er thou art,
I care not whether cold or warm,
With gentle breath, or howling storm,
  Thou sweep'st the boundless plain.

Thou bringest sounds from far away,
    Upon my ear
    I faintly hear
Sweet messages of faith and hope
Borne over lake and mountain slope,
    Blow ever, night and day.

And gaily glides my bark canoe
    O'er foaming crest
    By thee caressed ;
With lighter heart and stronger arm
I dip the cedar, when thy charm
    Comes wafted o'er the blue.

APRIL.

Archibald Lampman.

Pale season, watcher in unvexed suspense,
    Still priestess of the patient middle day,
Betwixt wild March's humoured pestilence
    And the warm wooing of green-kirtled May,
    Maid month of sunny peace and sober grey,
Weaver of flowers in sunward glades that ring
With murmur of libation to the spring.

As memory of pain all past is peace,
    And joy, dream-tasted, hath the deeper cheer.
So art thou sweetest of all months that lease
    The twelve short spaces of the flying year.
    The bloomless days are dead, and frozen fear
No more for many moons shall vex the earth,
Dreaming of summer and fruit-laden mirth.

The grey song-sparrows, full of spring, have sung
    Their clear thin silvery tunes in leafless trees.
The robin hops and whistles, and among
    The silver tasselled poplars, the brown bees
    Murmur faint dreams of summer harvestries.
The creamy sun at even scatters down
A gold green mist across the murmuring town.

By the slow streams the frogs all day and night
　　Dream without thought of pain or heed of ill,
Watching the warm long silent hours take flight,
　　And ever with soft throats that pulse and thrill
　　From the pale weeded shallow trill and trill,
Tremulous sweet-voices, flute-like, answering
One to another glorying in the spring.

All day across the ever-cloven soil
　　Strong horses labour, steaming in the sun,
Down the long furrows with slow straining toil,
　　Turning the brown clean layers ; and one by one
　　The crows gloom over them, till daylight done
Sends them asleep somewhere in duskèd lines
Beyond the wheat-lands in the northern pines.

The old year's cloaking of brown leaves that bind
　　The forest floorways, plated close and true,
The last love's labour of the wearing wind,
　　Is broken with curled flower buds, white and blue,
　　In all the matted hollows, and speared through
With thousand serpent-spotted blades upsprung,
Yet bloomless, of the slender adder-tongue.

In the warm noon the south wind creeps and cools,
　　Where the red-budded stems of maples throw
Still tangled etchings on the amber pools,
　　Quite silent now, forgetful of the slow
　　Drip of the taps, the troughs, and trampled snow,
The keen March mornings and the silvering rime,
And mirthful labour of the sugar prime.

Ah, I have wandered with unwearied feet
   All the long sweetness of an April day,
Lulled with cool murmurs and the drowsy beat
   Of partridge wings in secret thickets grey,
   The marriage hymns of all the birds at play.
The faces of sweet flowers, and easeful dreams
Beside slow reaches of frog-haunted streams;

Wandered with happy feet, and quite forgot
   The shallow toil, the strife against the grain,
Near souls that hear us call, but answer not,—
   The weariness, perplexity, and pain,
   And high thoughts cautered with an earthly stain;
And now the long draught emptied to the lees,
I turn me homeward in slow-pacing ease.

Cleaving the cedar shadows and the thin
   Mist of grey gnats, that cloud the river shore,
Sweet even choruses, that dance and spin
   Soft tangles in the sunset, and once more
   The city smites me with its dissonant roar;
To its hot heart I pass, untroubled yet,
Fed with calm hope without desire or fret.

So to the year's first altar step I bring
   Gifts of meek song, and make my spirit free
With the blind working of unanxious spring,
   Careless with her whether the days that flee
   Pale drouth or golden-fruited plenty see,
So that we toil, brothers, without distress
In calm-eyed peace and god-like blamelessness.

IN LYRIC SEASON.

Bliss Carman.

The lyric April time is forth
   With lyric mornings, frost and sun ;
   From leaguers vast of night undone
Auroral mild new stars are born.

And ever at the year's return,
   Along the valleys grey with rime,
   Thou leadest as of old, where time
Can nought but follow to thy sway.

The trail is far through leagues of Spring
   And long the quest to the white core
   Of harvest quiet, yet once more
I gird me to the old unrest.

I know I shall not ever meet
   Thy calm regard across the year,
   And yet I know thou wilt draw near,
Nor stir the hour asleep on guard

Beside the orchard, when athwart
   The dusk, a meteor's gleam unbars
   God's lyric of the April stars
Above the autumn hills of dream.

AN OLD LESSON FROM THE FIELDS.

Archibald Lampman.

Even as I watched the daylight how it sped
    From noon till eve, and saw the light wind pass
    In long pale waves across the flashing grass,
And heard through all my dreams, wherever led,
The thin cicada singing overhead.
    I felt what joyance all this nature has,
    And saw myself made clear as in a glass,
How that my soul was for the most part dead.

O light, I cried, and heaven with all your blue ;
    O earth, with all your sunny fruitfulness,
        And ye tall lilies of the wind-vexed field,
        What power and beauty life indeed might yield,
    Could we but cast away its conscious stress,
Simple of heart, becoming even as you !

THE FROGS.*

Archibald Lampman.

Breathers of wisdom won without a quest,
    Quaint, uncouth dreamers, voices high and strange,
    Flutist of lands where beauty hath no change,
And wintery grief is a forgotten guest ;
Sweet murmurers of everlasting rest,
    For whom glad days have ever yet to run,
    And moments are as æons, and the sun
But ever half-way sunken toward the west.

Often to me who heard you in your day,
    With close-wrapped ears, it could not choose but seem
That earth, our mother, searching in what way
    Men's hearts might know her spirit's inmost dream,
Ever at rest beneath life's change and stir,
Made you her soul, and bade you pipe for her.

In those mute days, when spring was in her glee,
    And hope was strong, we know not why or how,
    And earth, the mother, dreamed with brooding brow,
Musing on life, and what the hours might be,
    When love should ripen to maternity,
Then, like high flutes in silvery interchange,
Ye piped with voices still and sweet and strange,
    And ever as ye piped, on every tree

---

* The orchestras of frogs are a notable feature of settlement life. Their singing, in the distances of forest rivers, is really very musical.

The great buds swelled; among the pensive woods
　The spirits of first flowers awoke, and flung
From buried faces the close-fitting hoods,
　And listened to your piping till they fell,
　The frail spring beauty, with her perfumed bell,
The wind flower, and the spotted adder tongue.

All the day long, wherever pools might be
　Among the golden meadows, where the air
　Stood in a dream, as it were moorèd there
For ever in a noontide reverie;
Or where the birds made riot of their glee
　In the still woods, and the hot sun shone down,
　Crossed with warm shadows, on the brown
Leaf-paven pools, that bubbled dreamily;

Or far away in whispering river meads
　And watery marshes, where the brooding noon,
　Full with the wonder of its own sweet boon,
Nestled and slept among the noiseless reeds,—
　Ye sat and murmured motionless as they
　With eyes that dreamed beyond the night and day.

And when day passed, and over heaven's height,
　Thin with the many stars, and cool with dew,
　The fingers of the deep hours slowly drew
The wonder of the ever-heating night,
No grief or loneliness, or wrapped delight,
　Or weight of silence, ever brought to you
　Slumber or rest; only your voices grew
More high and solemn. Slowly with hushed flight

Ye saw the echoing hours go by, long drawn,
   Nor ever stirred, watching with fathomless eyes,
   And with your countless clear antiphonies
Filling the earth and heaven, even till dawn,
   Last risen, found you with its first pale gleam,
   Still with soft throats unaltered in your dream.

And slowly, as we heard you day by day,
   The stillness of enchanted reveries
   Bound brain and spirit and half-closed eyes
In some divine sweet wonder-dream astray;
To us no sorrow or upreared dismay,
   Nor any discord came; but evermore
   The voices of mankind, the outer roar,
Grew strange and murmurous, faint and far away;

Morning and noon and midnight exquisitely
   Wrapped with your voices, this alone we knew;
Cities might change and fall, and men might die,
   Secure were we, content to dream with you,
That change and pain are shadows faint and fleet,
And dreams are real, and life is only sweet.

BOBOLINK.

Alexander M'Lachlan.

MERRY mad-cap on the tree,
Who so happy are as thee;
Is there aught so full of fun,
Half so happy 'neath the sun,
With thy merry whiskodink?
    Bobolink! Bobolink!

With thy mates, such merry meetings,
Such queer jokes and funny greetings;
Oh such running and such chasing!
Oh such banter and grimacing!
Thou'rt the wag of wags the pink,—
    Bobolink! Bobolink!

How you tumble 'mong the hay,
Romping all the summer's day;
Now upon the wing all over,
In and out among the clover,
Far too happy e'er to think,—
    Bobolink! Bobolink!

Now thou'rt on the apple tree,
Crying, "Listen unto me!"
Now upon the mossy banks,
Where thou cuttest up such pranks,—
One would swear thou wert in drink,—
  Bobolink! Bobolink!

Nothing can'st thou know of sorrow,
As to-day shall be to-morrow;
Never dost thou dream of sadness,—
All thy life a merry madness;
Never may thy spirits sink,—
  Bobolink! Bobolink!

THE CANADIAN SONG-SPARROW.

J. D. Edgar.

From the leafy maple ridges,
From the thickets of the cedar,
From the alders by the river,
From the bending willow branches,
From the hollows and the hillsides,
Through the lone Canadian forest,
Comes the melancholy music,
Oft repeated,—never changing,—
    "All—is—vanity—vanity—vanity."

Where the farmer ploughs his furrow,
Sowing seed with hope of harvest
In the orchard white with blossom,
In the early field of clover,
Comes the little brown-clad singer,
Flitting in and out of bushes,
Hiding well behind the fences,
Piping forth his song of sadness,—
    "Poor—hux—manity—manity—manity."

IN JUNE.

The Canadian Rossignol on Mount Royal.

E. W. THOMSON.

> PRONE where maples widely spread
> I watch the far blue overhead,
> Where little fine-spun clouds arise
> From naught to naught before my eyes;
> Within the shade a pleasant rout
> Of dallying zephyrs steal about;
> Lazily as moves the day
> Odours float and faint away
> From roses yellow, red, and white,
> That prank yon garden with delight;
> Round which the locust blossoms swing,
> And some late lilacs droop for spring.

Anon swells up a dubious breeze
Stirring the half reluctant trees,
Then, rising to a mimic gale,
Ruffles the massy oak to pale
Till, spent its sudden force, once more
The zephyrs come that went before;
Now silvery poplars shivering stand,
And languid lindens waver bland,
Hemlock traceries scarcely stir,
All the pines of summer purr;
Hovering butterflies I see,
Full of business shoots the bee,

Straight to yon valley is his flight
Where solemn marbles crowd so white.
Half hid in the grasses there
Red-breast thrushes jump and stare,
Sparrows flutter up like leaves
Tossed upon the wind in sheaves.
Curve-winged swallows slant and slide
O'er the graves that stretch so wide,
Steady crows go labouring by—
Ha ! the Rossignol is nigh !

Rossignol, why will you sing
Though lost the lovely world of spring?
'Twas well that then your roulades rang
Of joy, despite of every pang,
But now the sweet, the bliss is gone—
   Nay, now the summer joy is on,
   And lo, the foliage and the bloom,
   The fuller life the bluer room,
   'Twas this the sweet spring promised me.
O bird, and can you sing so free?
And will you sing when summer goes
And leaves turn brown and dies the rose?
   Oh, then how brave shall autumn dress
   The maple out with gorgeousness !
   And red-cheeked apples deck the green,
   And corn wave tall its yellow sheen.
But, bird, bethink you well, I pray,
Then marches winter on his way.
   Ah, winter—yes, ah, yes—but still,
   Hark ! sweetly chimes the summer rill,
   And joy is here and life is strong,
   And love still calls upon my song.

No, Rossignol, sing not that strain,
Triumphant 'spite of all the pain,—
She cannot hear you, Rossignol,
She does not pause and flush, your thrall.
She does not raise that slender hand
And, poised, lips parted, understand
What you are telling of the years,
Her brown eyes soft with happy tears,
She does not hear a note of all.
Ah, Rossignol, ah, Rossignol!
But skies are blue, and flowers bloom,
And roses breathe the old perfume,
And here the murmuring of the trees
In all of lovelier mysteries ;—
And maybe now she hears my song
Pouring the summer hills along,
Listens with joy that still to thee
Remain the summer time and me.

HIS HONOR, McCARTHY'S MEETING IN NEW GLASGOW,
September 1st, 1894.

The Orangemen presented gifts of sweet flowers,
Culled from the gardens or the rarest bowers !
The speaker rose and in his majestic style
Addressed the people for just a long while.

I believe he has no love for a pervert :
Whateve he is—he is rather a convert ;
Throughout his great speech he had the clear ring,
And the past matters before us did plainly bring.

He is greatly in favor of public schools,
Even tho' that should act against Papal Bulls,
I believe his motto is, "Do what is right !"
And act in such way as not to fear the light.

We're glad he came—our Provinces he's never sold
Nor usurped our right to be by him controlled ;
Therefore let us thank him and wish him success,
And prove ourselves his friends, such as we profess.

When election day will come see that you act as one
And keep out all those who are foes, tho' they run.
May grace your votes decide, and never fear
For you shall never fail, if you in truth appear.

APPENDIX.

I.

THE OLD CHANSONS OF THE FRENCH PROVINCE.

ERNEST GAGNON'S "Chansons Populaires du Canada" are the store-house to which resort is generally had in any account of these floating lays. The number of these, he says, is incalculable—from the little nonsense-verses sung to the child in his cradle, up to the numberless songs which ring about his parish; "and when, in the evening, after a hot summer's day, he comes back to rest from his toil, balanced by the movement of his high-framed cart, and couched on a soft and sweet-smelling load of hay, he will be heard crooning in a tone monotonous but sweet some of those dear syllables and names which recall the *ancienne mère-patrie;* or, on the rafts or in the canoe, he will sing *La Bellë Françoisë*, or the complaint of a hapless *voyageur* engulfed in the rapids; or yet again, the beautiful Kyrie which those chant at church who are dear to him, and who have remained in the natal parish on the ancestral acres." A goodly number of these songs are still sung, in more or less similar forms, throughout the provinces of France; but no small number are embalmed in Canada alone, and lost in, though thus not to, the *mère-patrie*.

The most universal is *A la Claire Fontaine*. "From the little child of seven years up to the man of silver hair, all the people in Canada know and sing the *Claire Fontaine*. One is not French-Canadian without that." In Normandy they sing a similar *Chanson*, but the air, which here is monotonous but attractive, is different there. One of the translations we have given renders the lay into English. The original commences thus :—

>"A la clairë fontainë
>M'en allant proméner,
>J'ai trouvé l'eau si bellë
>Que je m'y suis baigné."

This chanson is typical in its airy mixture of rambling and poetry. The first stanza, it will be seen, is practically meaningless; but then there comes that beautiful little chorus, far more lovely in the quiet way in which the air tempts you to hum it :—

>"Lui ya longtemps que je t'aimë
>Jamais je ne t'oublierai.
>Ma mi-e!
>'Ya longtemps que je t'aimë
>Jamais je ne t'oublierai."

Sweet is the little address to the nightingale :—

>"*Chantë, rossignol, chantë,*
>*Toi qui as le cœur gai,*
>*Tu as le cœur à rirë*
>*Moi, je l'ai-t-à pleurer.*
>Lui ya longtemps que je t'aimë;
>Jamais je ne t'oublierai."

"*C'est la Belle Françoise*" is one more careless, and therefore still more defiant of deliberate rational sequence :—

>"C'est la belle Françoisë, bon gai,
>C'est la belle Françoisë,
>Qui veut s'y marier, ma luron, lurette,
>Qui veut s'y marier, ma luron, luré.
>
>Son amant va la voirë, &c.,
>Bien tard, après souper, &c.
>
>Il la trouva seulettë,
>Sur son lit, qui pleurait.
>
>Ah! qu'a' vous donc, la belle,
>Qu'a' vous à tant pleurer?

> On m'a dit, hier au soirë
> Qu'à la guerre vous alliez."

The lover goes on to comfort her with a promise to marry her on his return from the war, "Si j'y suis respecté," ending, of course, with the flippant "ma luron, lurette ; ma luron, luré !"

One of the best known is the *En Roulant*, of which William M'Lennan's translation is found in these pages. Several belong particularly to the raftsmen and lumberers of the St Lawrence and Ottawa rivers. Such is :—

> " V'là l' bon vent, v'là l'joli vent,
> V'là l' bon vent, ma mië m'appellë,
> V'là l' bon vent, v'là l'joli vent,
> V'là l' bon vent, ma mië m'attend."

Which, as sung on a huge raft, with shanties on it, descending one of these broad open rivers, by the rough and jolly crew, has a genuine inspiration of free life about it. Of a wild character, too, is *Alouette*, whose very beautiful air has made it a favourite college song. The words are nonsense. "Alouette" means a snipe in Canada, though a lark in France, and the burden goes :—

> " Alouettë, gentille allouettë
> Alouettë, je te plumerai."

The gaiety of France marks almost all of them, and most have some sudden touch of quaint humour :—

> " Ma mignonnette, embrassez-moi.
> Nenni, Monsieur, je n'oserais
> Car si mon papa le savait."

But who would tell her papa? "The birds of the woods" :—

> " Les oiseaux parlent-ils?
> Ils parlent français, latin aussi.
>
> Ils parlent français, latin aussi
> ' Hélas, que le monde est malin
> D'apprendre aux oiseaux le latin.' "

Others have the weird mediæval charm, which is perhaps best instanced in *Marianson, Dame Jolie*, and the sorcery-lay

Entre Paris et St Denis, both of which are presented in English form in this volume. Marlborough figures in a variety of forms as *Malbrouck*, so widely sung also in France. It is said that during the last North-West Rebellion, when one of the French-Canadian regiments, having endured much long and difficult marching, was overheard to say "When shall we return home?" the commander, Colonel Strange, instantly replied by quoting :—

" Malbrouck s'en va-t-en guerrë
Mais quand reviendra-t-il ?"

And the whole regiment, taking up the well-known refrain, pushed forward cheerfully with refreshed spirit.

Ballad-making still continues, but without quite the same interesting incentives as formerly, and therefore without the whole of the same charm. That charm has passed for the present into the poetry of the modern men of culture of French Canada.

II.

LEADING MODERN FRENCH-CANADIAN POETS.

FOUR names may be chosen as the present leading French singers. Octave Crémazie, of whom good judges frequently speak as the most powerful of all, has been long dead. The four I choose are :—Louis Honoré Fréchette, the Honourable Pierre J. O. Chauveau, Benjamin Sulte, and Pamphile Le May. Fréchette is fairly represented by the following, which expresses the sentiment of a loyalty to France still strong in many a heart among his countrymen, while allowing the justice of British government :—

LE DRAPEAU ANGLAIS.

REGARDE, me disait mon père,
Ce drapeau vaillamment porté ;
Il a fait ton pays prospère,
Et respecte la liberté.

C'est le drapeau de l'Angleterre ;
Sans tache, sur le firmament,
Presque à tous les points de la terre
Ill flotte glorieusement.

Oui, sur un huitième du globe
C'est l'étendard officiel ;
Mais le coin d'azur qu'il dérobe
Nulle part n'obscurcit le ciel.

Il brille sur tous les rivages ;
Il a semé tous les progrès
Au bout des mers les plus sauvages
Comme aux plus lointaines forêts.

Laissant partout sa fierè empreinté,
Aux plus féroces nations.
Il a porté la flamme sainté
De nos civilisations.

Devant l'esprit humain en marche
Mainte fois son pli rayonna,
Comme la colombe de l'arche,
Ou comme l'éclair du Sina.

Longtemps ce glorieux insigne
De notre gloire fut jaloux,
Comme s'il le fût cru seul digne
De marcher de pair avec nous.

Avec lui, dans bien des batailles,
Sur tous les points de l'univers,
Nous avous mesuré nos tailles
Avec des resultats divers.

Un jour, notre bannière auguste
Devant lui dut se replier ;
Mais alors, s'il nous fut injuste,
Il a su le faire oublier.

Et si maintenant son pli vibre
A nos remparts jadis gaulois,
C'est au moins sur un peuple libre
Qui n'a rien perdu de ses droits.

Oublions les jours de tempêtes ;
Et, mon enfant, puisqu' aujourdhui
Ce drapeau flotte sur nos têtes,
Il faut s'incliner devant lui.

Mais, père, pardonnez, si j'ose.
N'en est-il pas un autre, à nous?
Ah ! celui-là, c'est autre chose :
Il faut le baiser à genoux !

Benjamin Sulte is sufficiently illustrated in a little paraphrase of our English ballad, "Nobody axed you, Sir, she said," which he has succeeded in idealising exquisitely.

LA BELLE MEUNIÈRE.

CHANSON POPULAIRE ANGLAISE.

"Par les chemins, qui donc, ma belle,
Vous attire si bon matin?"
Et, rougissant, la jouvencelle,
Dit : Seigneur, je vais au moulin.

"Le cristal bleu de la rivière,
A bien moins de limpidité
Que ton joyeux regard, ma chère."
—Monseigneur est plein de bonté !

"Quel frais minois, quel port de reine !
Approche, enfant : vrai tu me plais !
A tant de grâce souveraine
Il faut pour logis un palais,

Monte en croupe et sois ma maîtresse,
Viens ! je suis chevalier—baron
Mais pourquoi cet air de tristesse
Et cet incarnat sur ton front ?

Ne fuyez pas, mademoiselle !
Vous aurez mon titre et mon cœur :
Je vous conduis à la chapelle."
—Merci, c'est beaucoup trop d'honneur.

" Qui donc êtes-vous, ma charmante,
Pour refuser un chevalier !
Quelque dame riche et puissante ? "
—Je suis la fille du meunier.

" Quoi ! du meunier ! Dieu me pardonne !
J'en suis marri pour ton bonheur :
Je ne puis t'épouser, ma bonne."
—Qui vous a demandé, seigneur ?

Pamphile Le May expresses chivalrous sentiments towards Queen Victoria in this

HOSANNA.

O REINE, comme au jour d'une splendeur suprême
Où ton front virginal ceignit le diadème,
Tu vois, dans leurs transports, tes sujets à genoux.
Dans mille accents divers et sous toutes les zones
L'hosanna retentit, des fers jusques aux trônes.
Arabes belliqueux drapés dans leurs burnous,
Noirs chasseurs du Birman aux brûlantes épaules,
Colons de l'Amérique et Rajahs de Nagpour,
Au levant, au ponant, au nord, jusques aux pôles,
Tous ceux que tu conquis t'acclament en ce jour.

Dans la tombe sacrée où toute aile se ploie,
Les vieux rois, tes aïeux, semblent frémir de joie
A cet hommage ardent qui vient de toutes parts.
A ton nom l'oiseau chante en nos forêts sauvages,
Notre fleuve géant roucoule à ses rivages,
Le vieux Québec ému fait tonner ses remparts.
Et nous, fils oubliés de l'immortelle France,
Nous les frères nouveaux de nos anciens vainqueurs,
Nous l'avons pour égide, il est notre espérance,
L'amour l'a buriné dans le fond de nos cœurs.

A ce nom l'Orient, la terre des aromes,
Agite de plaisir ses brillants cardamomes,
Les mhowas tout en fleurs et les santals si doux.
Allah, dit le croyant, c'est de toi qu'il émane.
Vichnou l'aime, répond l'ascétique Brahmane.
Et puis Delhi s'éveille aux cris des fiers Hindous,

Et sur la place accourt la foule admiratrice.
On dirait ce beau jour où, sonnant les clairons,
Joyeuse, elle acclamait l'illustre impératrice
Dont le sceptre puissant fait courber tant de fronts.

Béni soit le Seigneur des longs jours qu'il t'accorde !
Depuis un demi-siècle, au vent de la discorde
Plus d'un trône superbe a croulé : mais le tien
Ferme comme le roc où resplendit le phare,
Pendant qu'ailleurs, hélas ! la royauté s'effare,
Dans l'amour de ton peuple a trouvé son soutien.
Ton sceptre est un rameau qui refleurit sans cesse.
Tous les peuples l'ont vu s'avancer triomphant.
On l'acclame avec joie, on le craint sans bassesse :
La lyre le célèbre et le fer le défend.

Depuis un demi-siècle ô superbe Angleterre,
Ton vol glorieux plane au-dessus de la terre
Comme plane un vol d'aigle au-dessus du vallon.
Qu'il monte encore plus haut et craigne de s'abattre !
Que ton glaive vengeur ne cesse de combattre
Pour protéger le faible et briser le talon
Qui l'écrase ! Depuis un demi-siècle encore
Ta puissance a dompté les vastes océans,
Et ton drapeau que suit la victoire décore
Les temples, les palais de cent peuples géants.

Sous ce noble drapeau la terre s'est couverte
Et de fleurs et de fruits. Devant lui la mer verte
A fait jaillir soudain de ses replis épais
Des continents nouveaux. Il se déploie, il passe,
Et comme le soleil, ce drapeau de l'espace,
Il ne saurait tomber. Dans une douce paix
Les penseurs, à son ombre, exaltent la science,
Les lettres et les arts prennent un vif essor,
L'usine est un coursier qui bout d'impatience,
Et le comptoir actif s'emplit de louis d'or.

Hosanna ! que le ciel prolonge encor ton règne !
Tu veux que l'on t'estime et non que l'on te craigne.
Reine, tu resplendis parmi les souverains
Comme Véga la blanche au milieu des étoiles.
L'avenir à mes yeux a déchiré ses voiles ;

Il raconte ta gloire en d'immortels refrains.
Mère heureuse, tes fils, comme une autre couronne,
Font rayonner ton front d'une sainte fierté.
De son nimbe éternel la gloire t'environne,
Car où ton pied descend germe la liberté.

The Honourable Pierre J. O. Chauveau, Sheriff of Montreal, once Premier of his Province, is universally recognised as the *Doyen* of the literature of his people, a title which the following poem will show he merits :—

DONNACONA.

STADACONÉ dormait sur son fier promontaire ;
Ormes et pins, forêt silencieuse et noire,
    Protégeaient son sommeil.
Le roi Donnacona dans son palais d'écorce
Attendait, méditant sur sa gloire et sa force,
    Le retour du soleil.

La guerre avait cessé d'affliger ses domaines ;
Il venait de soumettre à ses lois souveraines
    Douze errantes tribus.
Ses sujets poursuivaient en paix dans les savanes,
Le lièvre ou la perdrix ; autour de leurs cabanes
    Les ours ne rôdaient plus.

Cependant il avait la menace à la bouche,
Il se tournait fiévreux sur sa brûlante couche,
    Le roi Donnacona !
Dans un demi-sommeil péniblement écloses,
Voici, toute la nuit, les fastidiques choses
    Que la vieux roi parla :

" Que veut-il, l'étranger à la barbe touffue ?
Quels esprits ont guidé cette race velue
    En deçà du grand lac ?
Pour le savoir, hélas ! dans leurs fureurs divines,
Nos jongleurs ont brûlé toutes les médecines
    Que renfermait leur sac !

" Cudoagny se tait : les âmes des ancêtres
Ne parlent plus la nuit ; car nos bois ont pour maîtres
      Les dieux de l'étranger ;
Chaque jour verra-t-il s'augmenter leur puissance ?
J'aurais pu cependant, avec plus de vaillance,
      Conjurer ce danger.

" J'aurais pu repousser, loin, bien loin du rivage
Le chef et son escorte, et châtier l'outrage
      Par leur audace offert ;
Mais de Cahir-coubat ils ont toute la grève
Et déjà l'on y voit un poteau qui s'élève,
      D'étranges fleurs couvert.

" Ils ont du tressaillir dans la forêt sacrée.
Les os de nos aïeux ! Ma poussière exécrée
      N'y reposera pas,
Les fils de nos enfants, bien loin d'ici peut-être,
Dispersés, malheureux, maudiront un roi traître,
      Qu' on nommera tout bas.

" Taiguraguy l'a dit : l'étranger est perfide,
Ses présents sont trompeurs, et la main est avide
      Qui nous donne aujourd'hui ;
Elle prendra demain mille fois davantage,
Mon peuple n'aura plus, bientôt sur ce rivage,
      Une forêt à lui.

" Taiguraguy l'a dit : de ses riches demeures,
Où, dans les voluptés, il voit couler ses heures,
      Leur roi n'est pas content.
Il lui faudrait encore et mes bosquets d'érables,
Et l'or qu'il veut trouver caché parmi les sables
      De mon fleuve géant.

" Jeunes gens, levez-vous et déterrez la hache,
La hache des combats ! que nulle peur n'arrache
      A vos cœurs un soupir !
Comme un troupeau d'élans ou de chevreuils timides,
Tous ces fiers étrangers, sous vos flèches rapides,
      Vous les verrez courir.

"Mais inutile espoir ! Leur magie est plus forte,
Et son pouvoir partout sur le nôtre l'emporte ;
    Leur Dieu c'est un Dieu fort !
Quand il fut homme, un jour, dans un bien long supplice,
De ceux dont il venait expier la malice.
    Ce Dieu reçut la mort."

*   *   *   *   *   *   *

Vieille Stadaconé ! sur ton fier promontaire
Il n'est plus de forêt silencieuse et noire ;
    Le fer a tout détruit.
Mais sur les hauts clochers, sur les blanches murailles,
Sur le roc escarpé, témoin de cent batailles
    Plane une ombre la nuit.

*   *   *   *   *   *   *

Donnacona ramène au pays des ancêtres
Domagaya lassé de servir autres maîtres,
    Aussi Taiguragui.
Les vieux chefs, tout parés, laissent leur sépulture,
On entend cliqueter partout comme une armure,
    Les colliers d'ésurgui.

Puis ce sont dans les airs mille clameurs joyeuses,
Des voix chantent en chœur sur nos rives heureuses,
    Comme un long hosanna.
Et l'on voit voltiger des spectres diaphanes,
Et l'écho sur les monts, dans les bois, les savanes,
    Répète : Agouhanna !

We have been obliged to shorten this a trifle, for which we apologise to Mr Chauveau, especially as his stanzas are all like gold. The perfection of the poem will strike every French-verse lover. It should be read slowly to get the richness of the music. Donnacona was the chief or "King" (Agouhanna) whom Cartier found at Stadacona, an Indian town on the site of Quebec. Cudoagny was one of their deities ; Calir-coubat, the river St Charles near by, where Cartier landed and set up a cross in the name of Francis I. Taiguragny and Domagaya were natives whom Cartier had taken to France the year previous. Cartier now carries off the Agouhanna himself, whose complaint forms the chief burden of the poem. He died there, and thus was never brought back. "Colliers d'ésurgui" are wampum belts.

EPICEDIUM.

JOHN TALON-LESPÉRANCE—"LACLÈDE."

Like a wail on the desolate sea-shore, that cold wild gust of December
    Makes moan round the gable at midnight, the last of the year ;
And, like the grin of a ghost, the light of a smouldering ember
    Flits in my empty face, and mocks me with visions of cheer.

O where are the dreams that we dreamed? and where the delirious follies
    We loved when the butterflies flittered in the warmth and fragrance of May?
And where are the vows that we made—those clusters of fiery hollies,
    Brightest and fairest to see on the very eve of decay?

The young man croons at his work, the maiden sings in the bower,
    And the air pulsates with the throbs of a cosmic, infinite love ;
But the feet are cold that have met in the sunset's sensuous hour,
    And the red leaves cover the trysting seat in the grove.

The old man crosses his hands, and droops his head in the shadows ;
    The goodwife stops at her wheel, for her eyes are heavy and dim ;
But O, on the fringe of the wood, and out on the billowy meadows,
    The great gold light is floating in a celestial dream.

The odour of lilacs still clings to the leaves of the family missal,
    And the date of our bridal is there—I remember 'twas writ in my blood ;
Ah me ! yet 'tis only this morning that I heard the cardinal's whistle,
    Up in the sumach that sheltered her grave, and where the hydrangea stood.

Yes, and the rains of the autumn fall chill on the purple slope, where together
    The bones of my babes are enlaced in the roots of that funeral tree ;
But still when I look out for them, in the buoyant crystalline weather,
    Their sweet white faces are radiant and smile upon me.

Such is the life of man—a shifting of scenes—with the ranges
  From one extreme to the next—the rise and ebb of the soul ;
And what is our bliss mid it all? Why, always to change with the
    changes,
  Though our single purpose is fixed on the one immutable goal.

Then, to-night, I will chase my sorrow, with that last wild gust of
    December ;
  The gloom where I sit is gone, and the gleams of the morning
    appear ;
The past shall be buried anew in the dust of the smouldering ember,
  For the future rises before me in the flush of the dawning year.

NOTES

BIOGRAPHICAL AND BIBLIOGRAPHICAL.

ISIDORE G. ASCHER.—Formerly an advocate of Montreal, now of London, England. Published "Voices of the Hearth," 1863. (Page 397.)

"BARRY DANE."—*See* John E. Logan.

CHARLES LEE BARNES (1857——).—A young physician in Georgetown, Prince Edward Island. (Page 175.)

BLISS CARMAN (1861——), Fredericton, New Brunswick.—Perhaps the most original of Canadian lyrists. His verse has frequently appeared in the *Atlantic* and the *Century*. He is enthusiastically patriotic. "*P.S.*—Dear me, I have forgotten all about my life. Well, sir, I was born in Fredericton, N.B., on 15th April 1861. Here I was educated at the Collegiate School (under George R. Parkin, Edward Thring's friend and biographer), and at the University of New Brunswick ; B.A., 1881 ; M.A., 1884. Published works, none. Yes, you are right, I am a relative of Roberts. My mother and Barry Straton's mother were both sisters of Roberts' mother." (Pages 157, 283, 389, 406, 422.)

GEORGE FREDERICK CAMERON, who was cut off in 1887 at the early age of thirty-three, was an impassioned singer. (Page 287, and see Introduction.)

"Mr Cameron is another of the gifted sons of Nova Scotia, who have reflected honour on their native province and on the Dominion. The incidents of his life are few. He was born at New Glasgow, in 1854. He spent some years in Boston, and wrote much for the American press, as most Canadians have to do who wish to gain the ear of the world. He entered as a student at Queen's University, Kingston, in 1882. One is struck with his burning hate of oppression and wrong wherever it exists, and with his passionate sympathy with the struggle for freedom everywhere—in Cuba, in Russia, in France, in America, in Ireland."

The Honourable PIERRE J. O. CHAUVEAU (*see* Appendix II.).—Mr Chauveau, though full of years, is still full of literary and physical fire and vigour, and an indispensable figure in literary circles.

ISABELLA VALANCEY CRAWFORD (*see* Introduction and Appendix II.).—She died at Toronto on the 12th of February 1887, her work scarcely noticed in her native country. An acquaintance describes her as a tall, handsome, light-haired young lady, apparently about thirty years old, somewhat eccentric in manner, but not very noticeably so. (Pages 107, 117, 119, 129, 177, 180, 411.)

Rev. WILLIAM WILFRED CAMPBELL, rector of Trinity Church, St Stephen, N.B.—The brilliant studies of lake scenery which Mr Campbell has made, and calls collectively "Lake Lyrics," will attract admiration. He is a young man, but like many of his countrymen has already won success with the great American magazines. His winter poems are published under the title of "Snowflakes and Sunbeams," 1888. (*See* Introduction. Pages 133, 321, 322, 323, 324, 326, 327, 330, 331, 332, 333, 404.)

Mrs SARAH ANNE CURZON (1833——), Toronto.—She early contributed, in England, to the *Leisure Hour*, and afterwards coming to Canada (about 1863) to the *Canadian Monthly*, developing here a strong Canadian feeling. Her "Laura Secord" volume is instinct with courageous national spirit. (Page 253.)

NICHOLAS FLOOD DAVIN, barrister, M.P. for Assiniboia.—Also owns and edits the well-known *Leader* newspaper. Mr Davin's work is interesting as prairie transcript, North-West verse being rare. (Page 349.)

Rev. ARTHUR WENTWORTH HAMILTON EATON, Acadian clergyman, and writer of pleasing ballads. Presently in New York. (Pages 87, 216.)

"*The Settlement of Acadia.*

"After the expulsion of the Acadians in 1755, the lands they had for so long owned and tilled lay waste, until finally, by invitation of the Government, a large number of New England people, chiefly from Connecticut, emigrated to Acadia, and entered into possession of the fertile French farms. They were conveyed to the shores of Minas Basin in a fleet of twenty-two vessels, arriving on 4th of June 1760."

"FLEURANGE," Mrs L. A. LEFEVRE, of Brockville, Ontario.—Wields a well-known and graceful poetic pen. The "Spirit of the Carnival" is the best carnival poem yet written. (Page 203.)

JAMES D. EDGAR, M.P.—A leading barrister and well-known politician of Toronto, who is not afraid to cultivate the muse. He attaches the following note to his pretty lines on "The Canadian Song Sparrow":—

"Every resident in the northern and eastern counties of the Dominion has heard the note of the song-sparrow in all the woods and fields through the early days of spring. While his voice is familiar to the ear, very few can boast of having seen him, so carefully does he conceal himself from view. He dwells long upon his first and second notes, and, in metrical phrase, he forms a distinct 'spondee.' He then rattles off at least three 'dactyls' in quick succession. In different localities different words are supplied to his music. Early settlers heard him echoing their despair with 'Hard times in Canada,

Canada, Canada.' Others maintain that he is searching for traces of a dark crime, and unceasingly demands to know 'Who-killed-Kennedy, Kennedy, Kennedy?' The thrifty farmer detects the words of warning, 'Come-now-sow-the-wheat, sow-the-wheat, sow-the-wheat.' The writer has distinctly recognised in the little song the melancholy sentiments indicated in these lines."

Mr Edgar has just published "The White Stone Canoe," founded on an Ojibway legend. (Pages 173, 306, 431.)

J. A. FRASER.—Till lately of Toronto. (Page 269.)

HELEN FAIRBAIRN.—" Frit," Montreal. (Page 192.)

"FIDELIS."—*See* Agnes Maule Machar.

ERNEST GAGNON (1834——), Secretary of the Department of Public Works of the Province of Quebec, founder of the Académie de Musique at Quebec, literateur, organist of the Basilica, composer of several musical pieces.—The work by which he is best known is his collection of ancient ballads known as " Chansons Populaires du Canada." (*See* Appendix I.)

CHARLES HEAVYSEGE (*see* Introduction).—Born Liverpool, 1816. Published "Saul," 1857; "Count Filippo," 1860; "Jephthah's Daughter," 1865; "The Advocate," a very curious novel, originally a blank verse drama no doubt, 1865. (Pages 379, 388, 405.)

Lieutenant-Colonel JOHN HUNTER-DUVAR.—One of the principal poets of the country, resides at his home " Hernewood," in the province of Prince Edward Island, one of the maritime provinces. He is of Scottish-English parentage, was born 29th August 1830, educated in Scotland, and is in the fisheries department of the Canadian Civil Service. His tastes are little classical, but he has given much attention to the older French and Italian literatures. Many of his lyrics are afloat in the Canadian press. Has printed for private circulation "John a' Var, his Lays," being a number of lyrics strung on the thread of a troubadour's adventures ; and has published " The Enamorado," a fine light drama of the Spanish school ; and recently a purely Canadian drama, " De Roberval," together with " The Triumph of Constancy," a romaunt, and "The Emigration of the Fairies," a light fanciful poem. Among his accomplishments is a talent in etching, equal to his poetical skill, and which has added attraction to at least one of his poems illustrated by it. (Pages 104, 288.)

CHARLES EDWIN JAKEWAY, M.D., Stayner, Ontario.—Patriotic balladist.

Rev. K. L. JONES, Barriefield, Ontario.—Contributor to the *Week*, &c.

Miss E. PAULINE JOHNSON is interesting on account of her race as well as her strong and cultured verse. She is of the Mohawks of Brantford. This race, to-day thoroughly civilised, and occupying high positions all over Canada, have had a wonderfully faithful record of unswerving British alliance for over two hundred and twenty years, during which their devoted courage was the factor which decided the predominance of the Anglo-Saxon in North America. They produced Brant and Tecumseh, and the visit of their chiefs to Queen Anne is recorded in the *Spectator*. At the close of the American Revolution they retired with the other loyalists to their present reserves, where they have prospered. Miss Johnson was born at the Johnson estate "Chiefswood," on the Grand River, on 10th March 1862. She was the youngest child of chief G. H. M. Johnson, head-chief of the Mohawks, and of his wife Emily S., youngest daughter of Henry Howells, Bristol, England, thus being a cousin of W. D. Howells the novelist. She writes poetry only, and contributes to the leading Canadian weekly journals and to many American papers. She was educated in childhood at home by a resident governess, then sent to the Brantford Model School; and after leaving school resided at Chiefswood until her father's death in February 1884, when the family went to Brantford, where they now live. (Pages 184, 315.)

WILLIAM KIRBY, F.R.S.C., of Niagara (*see* Introduction).—He holds the position of Collector of Customs at Niagara, a place surrounded with battle-grounds and natural wonders, which have inspired most of his poetry. (Pages 240, 317.)

ARCHIBALD LAMPMAN, of the Civil Service, Ottawa.—Contributor of exquisite verse to the *Century*, &c. His "In the Millet" (1889) has already made him some reputation. (Pages 369, 387, 419, 423, 424.)

JOHN E. LOGAN ("*Barry Dane*"), Montreal.—His poetic gift is a resource of recreation with him from business. Loving an athletic life, he has been greatly attracted by things seen by him in the North-West. Hence his "Nor'-West Courier," "The Injun," the lament of the Indian maid ("A blood-red Ring hangs round the Moon"), &c. (Pages 35, 142, 148, 166, 390, 415.)

Mrs LEPROHON (1832-1879), Montreal, wife of Dr J. L. Leprohon.—This poetess of charming disposition, by birth Rosanna Eleanor Mullins, contributed to *The Literary Garland*, and other leading publications. Wrote several novels, of which "Antoinette de Mirecourt" and the "Manor-house of Villerai" are well known, and are of the rare romances which deal with French-Canadian subjects. (Page 382.)

Mrs M. J. KATZMANN LAWSON, daughter of a German officer in Her Majesty's 60th Rifles, wife of Mr William Lawson, merchant, Halifax.—She has written a well-known poem on "The Gaspereau." (Page 236.)

JOHN TALON-LESPÉRANCE (1838-——).—The genial, unique "*Laclède*"—"The Only"—of the Montreal *Gazette* and *Dominion Illustrated*. Known for his strongly individual style, his learning, and his kindliness, all over the Dominion. He was born in the Mississippi Valley, of an old Creole family descended from the founders and original settlers. His whole life has been devoted to study and letters. Among his published works is "The Bâstonnais," an historical novel relating to the American invasion of 1776. He intends to publish a volume of spiritual poems entitled "The Book of Honour." The song "Empire First" is a popular one. (Pages 10, 394, and Appendix.)

PAMPHILE LE MAY, F.R.S.C. (1837-——).—The long-worn hair, and thin poetical appearance of this born brother of Gautier and De Musset, and ornament of the French-Canadian school of literature, are familiar to the people of Quebec city. He is the French-Canadian who has written most, and whose talent seems the most universal. Advocate and journalist at first, he is at present librarian of the Quebec Legislature. Appendix II.

WILLIAM DOUW LIGHTHALL ("*Alchemist,*" "*Wilfrid Châteauclair*").—Born Hamilton, Ontario, 27th December 1857, lives in Montreal; advocate. Published "An Analysis of the Altruistic Act," 1885; "Sketch of a New Utilitarianism," 1887; "Thoughts, Moods, and Ideals," a small collection of verse, 1887; "The Young Seigneur, or, Nation-Making," a story dealing with Canadian nationality and French-Canadian life, 1888.

NOTES.—" The battle of Laprairie (August 1691) was one of the first collisions of the British and French races in America, and, according to all original accounts, a very brave affair. A colonial force of 266 men, composed about half each of 'Christians' and Iroquois, came down Lake Champlain and the Richelieu River in canoes to strike a blow at French Canada. The fort was held by De Callières and 800 men; but so brisk and sudden was the attack, that the colonials were soon in possession of the militia quarter adjoining, where they were attacked; and, after making great slaughter, on hearing the immense disparity of their numbers, they withdrew 'like victors,' says Charlevoix (who loved to record a 'belle action' on either side), and marched back to their canoes, which they had left guarded on the Richelieu. Valrennes, with about 300 men, coming from Chambly, intercepted them, and they were forced to cut through, which they did after a fiercely contested fight of a couple of hours."

"Kanawâké ('By the rapid') is the present native form of the name of Caughnawaga Indian village, which is situated in its reservation, at the head of the Sault St Louis Rapid, and opposite Lachine, about twelve miles from Montreal."

Rev. ARTHUR JOHN LOCKHART ("Pastor Felix")—Is a Nova Scotian by birth and feeling, though in United States. Published "The Masque of Minstrels," 1888, with his brother. His best poems are exceedingly melodious and tender, and his prose sketches graceful to the point of genius. (Pages xxxvii., 290, 407.)

The Hon. THOMAS D'ARCY M'GEE (1825-1868).—One of the greatest orators of the century, one of the first Canadian martyrs, and perhaps the noblest statesman the Irish race has produced, was assassinated at Ottawa on the 7th of April 1868 by an emissary of Fenianism, while returning home late from delivery of a stirring appeal in Parliament for goodwill to the new Confederation. "Jacques Cartier" is a favourite poem in Canada. (Pages 44, 213.)

ALEXANDER M'LACHLAN (1820———).—Is termed "the Burns of Canada." "It strikes me, however, as Artemus Ward used to say, that I would rather be 'the Alexander M'Lachlan of Canada' than the Burns of any place except Scotland. His spirited and courageous songs have won for him, among a large group of admirers, the title of 'the Grand Old Man,' and he was a short time ago presented by citizens of Toronto with a farm at Amaranth, Ontario. He is a sweeping but kindly Radical, whose social diatribes in verse are always interesting. Besides this he ranks well as a Scottish dialect poet." In 1840 he came to Canada, and worked on a farm; in 1845 published a small collection of his poems; in 1858, "Lyrics;" 1861, "The Emigrant, and other Poems;" 1874, "Poems and Songs." He has a vigorous way of describing rural things, and great sympathy with nature, as instance his "Hall of Shadows" and "October." In his sphere—a wide and national one—he has no like. (*See* Introduction. Pages 109, 115, 168, 392, 429.)

GEORGE MARTIN, Montreal.—For many years a photographer there. Published "Marguerite, and other Poems," in 1887. He was a friend of Charles Heavysege. When the latter's second Boston edition of "Saul" was proposed by the publishers, he was in considerable trouble on account of not having the money necessary, and confided himself to Martin. The latter, who had put aside a sum for publication of his own volume, generously lent it to Heavysege. "Saul" turned out a financial loss, however, much to the sorrow of the latter, who went to George Martin on the day his note fell due. Martin took the note in his hands and tore it into pieces. It was never mentioned again to poor Heavysege. (Pages 38, 297, 427.)

KATHARINE L. MACPHERSON ("*Kay Livingstone*"), Montreal.—Graceful verse-writer. "Aca Nada" is based on a current etymology of the name "Canada" from two words signifying "nothing here,"—an expression attributed to early Spanish seekers for gold.

WILLIAM M'LENNAN.—A young professional man of Montreal, widely known as the author of "Songs of Old Canada" (translations of chansons), and of other verse. (Pages 71, 76, 80, 83, 308.)

CHARLES MAIR (1840———).—The "North-West" poet is a manly figure. He was educated at Perth, Ontario, and at Queen's University, Kingston. While studying medicine, his love and knowledge of North-West and *voyageur* history attracted the attention of the Government, who engaged him in researches in the Parliamentary library, and in collecting and collating evidence bearing upon the Hudson Bay Territories for the Commissioner appointed to go to England to treat for their transfer to the Dominion. This also led to his being sent to Red River in the autumn of that year, and it was while engaged in Ottawa upon these researches that he published his first volume, "Dreamland, and other Poems." Meanwhile Mr Mair began in Red River a series of letters descriptive of the country, which had hitherto been a *terra incognita* to the eastern people. These letters went the round of the whole Canadian press, and induced the first Canadian immigration to the North-West Territories by their graphic truthfulness and force. Subsequently the machinations of the enemies of Canadian extension in the Territories came to a head. After a series of complications and incidents the Governor was compelled to leave the country, and Mr Mair and the other loyal Canadians, led by Dr Schultz, afterwards Lieutenant-Governor of Manitoba, whose niece Mr Mair married in 1869, surrendered to the large insurrectionary party led by Riel. Being informed by

Riel that he meant to execute him, Mr Mair laid instant plans for escape, in which he succeeded. Hatless and coatless, on a midwinter night, he made his way from Fort Garry to the then hamlet of Winnipeg, where he got means of transport to the loyal settlement of Portage La Prairie, sixty miles west of that place. There he assisted in forming a party to capture Fort Garry by surprise, whose purpose was only thwarted by a furious blizzard. By a fatiguing night-walk through the snow of fifty miles, he returned to Portage La Prairie. Thence he almost immediately left for Canada, and by a snow-shoe tramp of nearly five hundred miles through the wilds of Dacota at length reached St Paul. In this rebellion he lost all his MSS., abandoned literature, and, being now married, entered into the fur trade in 1870. Discerning new troubles, he wound up his business at Prince Albert, and removed with his family to Ontario, where he began the composition of his drama "Tecumseh." Whilst engaged in the work the second rebellion broke out, and Mr Mair was attached as Acting Quartermaster to the Governor-General's Bodyguard, a cavalry corps. After sharing in the adventures of this campaign he returned and completed his drama, which had a remarkable sale. Two years ago Mr Mair returned to his old home at Prince Albert on the Saskatchewan, where he has large landed and other interests, and where, having a distaste for politics, he means to turn his serious attention to literature. (Pages 42, 262, 339, 342, 385.)

AGNES MAULE MACHAR ("*Fidelis*"), of Kingston and "Ferncliff," Gananoque, Ontario.—One of those who well disputes the palm for the leadership among Canadian poetesses, spends her summers in her villa on one of the Thousand Islands, whence perhaps the *sheen* of some of her nature-poems. Contributor to the *Century*, &c. About her twelfth year she presented her father—the late Rev. John Machar, D.D., sometime Principal of Queen's University—with a rhymed translation from Ovid of the story of Cagy and Halcyone, enclosed in an illuminated and illustrated cover of her own execution. She has written a number of books and serials, of which the principal are— "For King and Country," a fine story of the war of 1812; "Lost and Won," a tale of Canadian life; and "Stories of New

France" (Lothrop & Co., Boston, 1888). (*See* Introduction. Pages 15, 380, 399.)

GEORGE J. MOUNTAIN (1789-1863).—Second Anglican Bishop of Quebec.—"Songs of the Wilderness," 1846. (Pages 51, 337.)

GEORGE MURRAY, B.A. Oxon., F.R.S.C., born in London. England, where his father was foreign editor of the *Times*, is the G. A. Sala of Canada. At Oxford he had a very brilliant university career, and was in his time there regarded as one of its cleverest graduates. At the university he published "The Oxford Ars Poetica," a poem which attracted much attention in literary circles. Coming to Montreal soon after, he became classical master of the High School, and has since remained in that position. Though his unsurpassed talents have been greatly hampered by the drudgery of his work, and have only been intelligently appreciated by circles of the best culture, he has been a sought ornament in every literary movement of Montreal for years. His work in verse is principally confined to translations of the lyrics of Gautier, Hugo, De Musset, and other such of the more exquisite French writers, and these translations, it can we think be affirmed, are the most delicate and precise in the English language. (Pages 222, 371.)

Major JOHN RICHARDSON (1797-1860), who wrote the stanzas narrating the death of Chief Tecumseh (page 260), was the earliest of Canadian novelists, author of "Wacousta," "The Canadian Brothers," &c., which were once not uncelebrated. His poem "Tecumseh," published in 1828, was written in 1823, only ten years after Tecumseh's tragic death. Major Richardson was with Tecumseh in the battle of the Thames, and his evidence in all matters pertaining to the chief's death must be accepted as conclusive.

"The note which pertains to the first two verses adds very little to the vivid description there given. The Christian is Colonel Johnston, the leader of the Kentucky Riflemen, who drew a pistol from his belt and killed Tecumseh just as the latter was about to tomahawk him. The next note, which is the last in the book, says :—'Scarcely had Tecumseh expired, when a band of lurking enemies sprung upon the warrior and scalped him. Not satisfied with this, they absolutely tore the skin from off his bleeding form, and converted it into razor straps!'"

JOHN READE, F.R.S.C., Montreal.—One of the chief figures in Canadian literature, and probably the sweetest poet. Literary editor of the able *Gazette*, a journal established in 1775. Mr Reade is the *doyen* of English poetic literature in the Province of Quebec as Chauveau is of French. He lives a very retired life, devoted to study, his constitution being fragile. (Pages 3, 199, 228.)

CHARLES GEORGE DOUGLAS ROBERTS, sprung of an intellectual ancestry, was born on the 10th of January 1860, in Douglas parish, New Brunswick. His father (to whom he dedicates his first work) is the Rev. George Goodridge Roberts, M.A., rector of the English Church at Fredericton (the Cathedral). His youth, which can scarcely be called over, was passed under his father's tutorship in the sea-shore scenery of the Westmoreland district—

> "Where past the dykes the red flood glides
> To brim the shining channels far,
> Up the green plains of Tantramar,
> Among the long dykes of Westmoreland."

(*See* "Tantramar Revisited," in this volume.) He graduated with honours at the University of New Brunswick in 1879, obtained head-mastership of Chatham Grammar School in same year, and married, in 1880, Mary Isabel Fenety, daughter of George E. Fenety, Esq., Queen's Printer, and ex-Mayor of Fredericton. In 1880 also he published his "Orion, and other Poems," through the well-known American publishers Lippincott & Co., of Philadelphia. This volume, largely imbued with the spirit of ancient Greek ideals, and full of the most luxuriant artistic dealing with colour, won for him the recognition of the best critics in the Anglo-Saxon literary world, and the friendship of Matthew Arnold, Edmund Clarence Stedman, and others. In 1881 he took his degree of M.A. in course, and soon became editor of the Toronto *Week*, the present representative journal of Canadian literary endeavour, but, refusing to be curbed in his editorial methods, he resigned within four months. He returned to his own Province, and in 1885 was called to the Professorship of Modern Literature in King's College, Windsor, Nova Scotia, which position he at present retains. In the meantime he published many striking contributions to leading magazines, especially his "Canada" in the *Century*, which at once took Canadian hearts by storm ; and in 1887 he published this and others, some of them of the Greek character so prominent in his "Orion," in a volume entitled "In Divers Tones." It is in point of freedom and variety superior to "Orion," but not so equally finished. (Pages 18, 30, 32, 36, 114, 163, 187, 291, 376, 378, 391, 401.)—"Clote Scarp" was the Hercules of the Micmacs.

ELIZABETH GOSTWYCKE ROBERTS is a sister of the foregoing, and writes verse with good "body," and of a tone curiously reflecting the family likeness. (Page 374.)

Mrs ANNIE ROTHWELL, Kingston, Ontario, is a daughter of the well-known Canadian artist Mr D. Fowler, R.C.A. (Canada, by-the-way, has a Royal Academy). Contributor of serial novels to *St James's Magazine, Chambers's Journal, Appleton's Journal, The Dominion Monthly*, &c., and authoress of a fine novel "Loved I not Honour More." (Page 270, and *see* Introduction.)

CHARLES SANGSTER was born near Kingston, on the 16th of July 1822, the youngest of the family. His father was a shipwright in the Royal Navy, his grandfather a brave Fifeshire sergeant in the 60th Foot, who had been offered a commission for courage and ability on the field. His mother was early left a widow with a large family of small children, whom she brought up honourably. Sangster's mind had to struggle with every disadvantage in the way of his education, except a little schooling on the first two R's. Hence such stanzas as

> "I long for diviner regions,—
>   The spirit would reach its goal ;
> Though this world hath surpassing beauty,
>   It warreth against the soul."

Making cartridges during the early time of the Canadian Rebellion of 1837-38, he was next made to do duty as an orderly clerk. Then he struck out in the new path of editor of the *Amherstburg Courier*. The publisher of the *Courier* died within a year, and he at once returned to Kingston and took a position on the daily press of that city, first with Dr Barker, the publisher of the first daily paper ever issued in what is now Ontario, and again on the rival daily, a period of over fifteen years in all. During this period of newspaper work Mr Sangster published his two volumes of poems,—" The St Lawrence and the Saguenay, and other Poems," in 1856; and " Hesperus, and other Poems and Lyrics," in 1860. In 1868 he was given a Civil Service position, with, later, the title of Private Secretary to the Deputy Postmaster-General,—solely on literary grounds,—in which position he remained until the breaking down of his health in March 1886, in September of which year he was placed on the superannuated list. Since then he has made Kingston his home. When he left for Ottawa he took with him the manuscript of a third volume of his poems, but failed to find time, or more properly opportunity, to publish the work. (Pages 25, 45, 190, 254, 307, 313.)

CHARLES DAWSON SHANLY.—Editor of *Punch in Canada* a generation ago. Became a noted art critic in New York. "The Walker on the Snow" appeared in the *Atlantic Monthly*, and is quoted nearly in full by John Burroughs in "Pepacton." (Page 181.)

DUNCAN CAMPBELL SCOTT (1862-   ).—A civil servant in the Indian Department, Ottawa, and contributor of sketches on French-Canadian life to *Scribner's Magazine*. "At the Cedars" is a sharply graphic picture of the excitement and danger of rafting. (Pages 91, 314.)

Rev. JOHN LOWRY STUART (1849-1881).—Wrote good verse, chiefly at the University of Toronto. "Skating" is the best brief bit on that sport the editor has seen. Another good poem of his was on "The St Lawrence." He died in Florida, of consumption, but by his own request was buried in Canadian soil at Toronto. (Page 197.)

BENJAMIN SULTE (1861-——).—French poet, and brilliant historian, journalist, and lecturer. His great "Histoire des Canadiens-Français" is an original and standard history of his people, and his verse and general superiority have obtained for him many recognitions in Canada and France. He has been president of the French literature section of the Royal Society of Canada. His best known volume of poetry is "Les Laurentiennes." He is now in the Dominion Civil Service at Ottawa. (Appendix I.)

W. A. SHERWOOD.—Toronto.

"SERANUS," Mrs J. F. W. HARRISON.—Has earned by bright-witted writing and active literary enterprise a prominent place in Dominion circles. She chose the curious *nom-de-plume* "Seranus" from an accidental error made concerning her signature "S. Frances." (*See* Introduction.) "Crowded Out," a collection of prose sketches, is her chief prose work. (Pages 67, 94.)

BARRY STRATON (1854-——), Fredericton, New Brunswick.—A very promising poet; journalist by profession; has published "Lays of Love," "The Building of the Bridge," and "The Hunter's Handbook." At present engaged on a forthcoming prose work, "Gallant Deeds of Canadian Soldiers." (Pages 24, 294, 383, 409.)

KATE B. SIMPSON, Regina, North-West Territory.—"Rough Ben" appeared in the *Leader* there. (Page 136.)

MARY BARRY SMITH.—Nova Scotian authoress.

Rev. WILLIAM WYE SMITH'S (1827-——) "Poems" are popular in Canada. They strike fresh, native notes. There is not much art about them, but the born qualities of a cheerful singer. "The Second Concession of Deer" strikes a Canadian as familiarly as roast beef would a Briton abroad. "Concession" is a term for a range of farms. The "first concession" is usually the row facing on a river; the "second concession" would mean the row just behind them, and so on. The term comes from the "conceding" of lands by the early

French *seigneurs* to their vassal tenants. "The Canadians on the Nile" is a reference to Lord Wolseley's employment of a corps of *voyageurs* there. (Pages 11, 27, 125.)

Rev. FREDERICK GEORGE SCOTT, B.A. (1861-——).— Has a style of Tennysonian ring. Author of "The Soul's Quest, and other Poems," (1888) Kegan Paul & Co. "Wahonomin" is an Indian cry of lamentation. (Pages 52, 275.)

E. W. THOMSON, Toronto. — Litterateur and journalist. (Page 432.)

ARTHUR WEIR, B.A. Sc. (1864-——), Montreal.—Journalist by choice ; author of "Fleurs-de-Lys, and other Poems" (1887). (Pages 195, 219, 303.) One of the young generation of Canadian poets.

Sir DANIEL WILSON, F.R.S.C. (18—-——).—President of Toronto University, and (1888) of the Royal Society of Canada. Sir Daniel is a man of the most varied abilities, and of the very highest reputation throughout the world as a scientist. (Page 127.)

Mrs PAMELIA VINING YULE, Woodstock, Ontario.—"Poems of the Heart and Home." (Page 334.)

NOTE OF THANKS.

ACKNOWLEDGMENTS are due to the authors and their representatives who have, where such were required, readily supplied MSS. and given copyright consents, as well as aided with suggestions of names, &c.

The assistance of the Rev. Arthur John Lockhart, who had collected a great quantity of material for an anthology of Maritime Province poetry, and of Mrs Sarah Anne Curzon, who had been gathering names and information for a general collection, has been invaluable. My indebtedness to Mr John Reade is equally great. His rare library and stores of information have been freely placed at my service. Mr George Murray has obliged with some critical advice.

Messrs A. Stevenson and G. Mercer Adam of Toronto, John Lovell of Montreal, and H. L. Spencer of St John, New Brunswick, have supplied facts of value; while Mr James Bain, public librarian of Toronto, among other assistance, provided facilities for examining the unique collection of Canadian poetry belonging to the institution under his care.

The "Selections" of the Rev. Dr E. H. Dewart have been indispensable as a survey of the verse of a generation ago. Henry James Morgan's "Celebrated Canadians," Dr Æneas Dawson's "Lecture on Canadian Poets," Mr Lespérance's Royal Society paper on "The Poets of Canada," the "Birthday Book" of Seranus, the *New Dominion* and *Canadian* monthlies, the *Literary Garland*, the old *Canadian Review*, the *Maple Leaf*, and various other periodicals, have been of use in particulars.

Other sources requiring acknowledgment are—Messrs J. R. Dougall, Dr W. G. Beers, Ernest Gagnon, Dawson Brothers (proprietors of certain of Heavysege's poems), the publishers of Toronto *Grip;* and Messrs Flint, Forest, Vandersmissen (University of Toronto Library), Sir Daniel Wilson, D. Urquhart, N. F. Davin, M.P., E. Crow Baker, M.P. (British Columbia), R. Starke, and Rev. Silas Rand, of Hantsport, Nova Scotia.

W. D. L.

Printed by WALTER SCOTT, *Felling, Newcastle-on-Tyne.*

THE YOUNG SEIGNEUR

OR

NATION-MAKING.

A ROMANCE OF FRENCH-CANADIAN LIFE,

BY

WILFRID CHÂTEAUCLAIR

(W. D. LIGHTHALL).

Published by Drysdale & Co., Montreal.

Well received by all the leading Dominion Journals and Critical Periodicals. The London *Academy* says of it:—

"*The Young Seigneur* is an ambitious book, for the author's aim is nothing less than 'to map out a future for the Canadian nation, which has hitherto been drifting without any plan.' At the same time it is not a political work, for which the muse of fiction be thanked. As for Mr Wilfrid Châteauclair's qualification for his task there can be no doubt. He is obviously an ardent patriot, and a careful and discriminate observer. His romance is, not less obviously, the production of a man of wide culture, refined taste, and exceptional literary faculty; and as a picture of the most vital and characteristic aspects of French-Canadian life it is without rival. While every one interested in Canada should read *The Young Seigneur*, it deserves attention on its own merits as a romance."

www.ingramcontent.com/pod-product-compliance
Lightning Source LLC
Chambersburg PA
CBHW051200300426
44116CB00006B/386